Ed Jocelyn and ... ...sity in England in 198... ...rch 1997 after a car... ...the USA and ... ...ober 1997 aft... ...their jobs as ... ...celyn at *China In...* ...'New Long Ma... ...as editor at China Featur... ...currently on the Long March II expeditio... ...of the alternative historic routes (ww... ...gmarch2.com).

THE LONG MARCH

The true story behind the legendary journey that made Mao's China

Ed Jocelyn & Andrew McEwen

Constable

Constable & Robinson Ltd
3 The Lanchesters
162 Fulham Palace Road
London W6 9ER
www.constablerobinson.com

First published in the UK by Constable,
an imprint of Constable & Robinson Ltd 2006

ISBN-10: 1-84529-255-3
ISBN-13: 978-1-84529-255-3

Printed and bound in the EU

Contents

Timeline: The Long March of the Red First Front Army

16 October 1934	Long March begins as first Red Army units cross Yudu River. Red Army numbers approx. 86,000 soldiers.
25 November–1 December	Battle of the Xiang River. Reds lose approx. 30,000 dead, wounded and deserted.
12 December	Tongdao Meeting. Military and political leaders discuss the crisis. Mao Zedong proposes Red Army change course of Long March. Proposal approved – Mao's first major success for two years.
15–17 January 1935	Zunyi Meeting. Politburo and military leaders debate recent setbacks. Mao attacks leadership of Bo Gu and Otto Braun. Meeting supports Mao, whose faction is now dominant. New plan directs Red Army to move north across Yangtze River. Army now numbers approx. 45,000.
28 January	Battle of Tucheng. Red Army defeated. Retreats west across Chishui River.
5 February	Zhaxi Meeting (1: Huafangzi). Mao supporter Zhang Wentian replaces Bo Gu as senior Communist Party leader. Nearby, Mao's wife gives birth to a daughter.
7 February	Zhaxi Meeting (2: Dahetan). Plan to cross Yangtze cancelled. 'Zunyi Resolution' passed, sealing approval for Mao's speech at Zunyi Meeting.
10 February	Zhaxi Meeting (3: Zhaxi). Red Army

Timeline

	directed to re-cross Chishui River and retake Zunyi.
27 February	Battle of Zunyi. Only major Red victory of Long March.
15 March	Battle of Luban Chang. Red Army defeated, forcing a retreat across Chishui River (third crossing of the Chishui).
21–22 March	Fourth crossing of the Chishui.
29 April	Reds feint against Kunming. Panic grips city.
8 May	Red Army completes crossing of River of Golden Sands. Approx. 30,000 soldiers remain. Begins trek north across Sichuan Province.
12 May	Huili Meeting. Mao criticized by First Army Group General Lin Biao. 'You're a baby,' answers Mao. 'What do you understand?'
22 May	Yihai Alliance. Reds seal oath of blood brotherhood with Yi minority leader.
29 May	Battle of Luding Bridge.
12 June	Mao's army begins crossing Jiajinshan, the first Snow Mountain. Meets advance party of Zhang Guotao's Red Fourth Front Army. Two armies unite, more than 100,000 soldiers in total. Reds now in Tibetan region.
27 July	Red leaders cross final Snow Mountain, Dagushan.
22 August	Crossing of Swamps begins.
25 August	First Red units exit Swamps.
10 September	Combined First-Fourth Front Army splits. Mao leads rump force north; Zhang Guotao turns south, re-crosses Swamps.
16 September	Battle of Lazikou. Mao's force breaks through, crosses Minshan range and leaves Tibetan region. Less than 10,000 men left.
19/20 September	Reds find newspapers in Hadapu confirming existence of Soviet Area in northwest Shaanxi Province.
19 October	Red Army reaches Shaanxi Soviet Area at Wuqi Zhen. Long March ends. Approx. 4,000 survivors.

A Note about Spellings and Transliteration

Most Chinese names in this book are rendered in English according to the *pinyin* standard for romanizing Chinese, which was adopted by the People's Republic of China in 1958 and updated in 1979. Thus we refer to Mao Zedong rather than Mao Tse-tung, as he is known under the old Wade-Giles system of transliteration. We have, however, persisted with the more familiar spellings for Sun Yat-sen (Sun Zhongshan in *pinyin*) and Chiang Kai-shek (Jiang Jieshi).

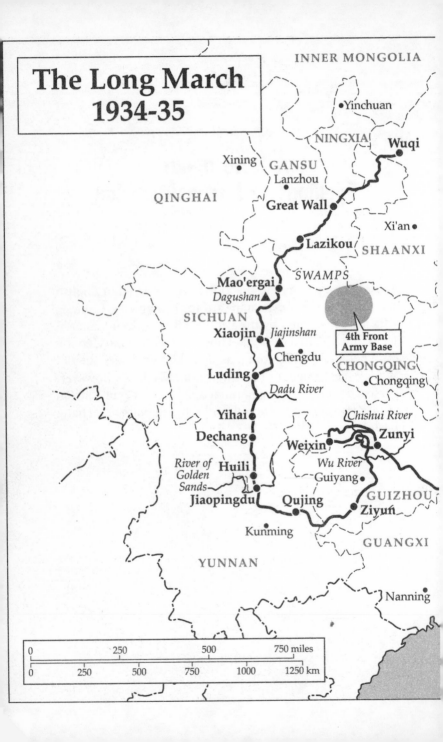

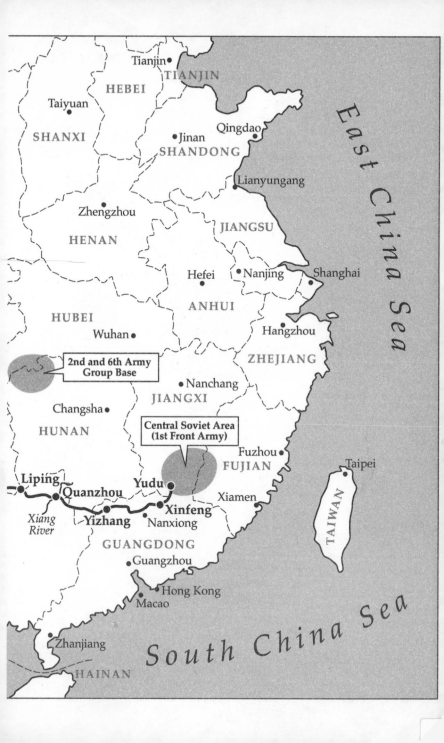

Introduction

*'Too few people now still have a hard-struggle
attitude. People now only know about money. They
only know about wealth and making money. Who
will listen if you talk about hard struggle?
Who wants to hear about hard-struggle attitude?
You won't listen to me either. You won't listen even
though you ask.'*

General Zeng Shaodong, Beijing,
12 November 2001

In my memory, it looks like this. A bustling network of
hutong alleys and *siheyuan* courtyard homes sprawls on
either side of Chang'an Dajie, the Avenue of Eternal
Peace. The narrow lanes are lined with trees, whose
branches arch and meet to form a summer canopy that
shades shoppers and strollers just a mile-or-so west
of Tian'anmen Square. Thriving communities crowd
the courtyards. Many families have lived here for
centuries.

That was the Beijing Xidan area the way I first saw it in
1997. Five years later, this ancient district had vanished.
Andy and I hustled across the windswept 'Xidan Culture
Square', over a traffic-choked six-lane boulevard, past
monstrous shopping centres and the concrete Bank of
China headquarters. We were looking for a piece of

history – hurrying to capture it before it disappeared along with the rest of old Xidan.

In an alley by the Times Square Shopping Mall, one two-storey courtyard defied the developers. The local authorities had offered the owner whatever he wanted, but he refused to move. An ordinary citizen could easily have been forced out, but this man had a certain status. The authorities could do nothing but wait for General Zeng Shaodong to die.

The general was just out of hospital, but still alert and eager to share his infectious, high-pitched laugh. He was delighted to play host. 'Have some tea,' he insisted. 'Have some fruit.'

General Zeng was dressed in a plain, olive-green outfit of military cut. His home was simply furnished. In the main room where we sat was a single armchair, a dining table with half a dozen straight-backed wooden chairs, and in the corner a desk covered in photographs of the general and his wife with old comrades. For Andy and me, this was a unique opportunity. We had spent months trying to meet someone like Zeng. You might imagine that a retired revolutionary hero would be free to make his own decisions, but almost everyone in Beijing must defer to a 'leader'. Zeng's leader, like all the others, had ordered him not to talk to foreigners. The eighty-three-year-old general was unimpressed. He told his leader if he wanted to talk to foreigners, then he'd talk to foreigners.

'I was a cowherd for a landlord before I joined the Red Army in May 1934,' recalled Zeng. 'At that time, thousands and thousands of local people joined, men and women, old and young. In some cases, whole families joined the army. I was very young, but in one way that was a good thing. Because I was too young to get promoted, I'm still alive today. If I were even a company commander, I would have died. They had to fight at the front and protect others. When they fought I hid behind the lines. I was just a little boy. Children were afraid of death.'

Zeng joined up at a time of crisis for the Red Army and its master, the Communist Party of China. The revolutionaries had established a base comprising a few poor counties of southern Jiangxi and western Fujian provinces, which they ambitiously declared the Chinese Soviet Republic (no relation, other than ideological, to the Soviet Union) on 7 November 1931. Mao Zedong was made Chairman of the Republic, thereby acquiring his most enduring title. But by the summer of 1934, the Red base was surrounded by up to 500,000 soldiers in the service of Generalissimo Chiang Kai-shek, leader of China's ruling Guomindang party. Chiang's men advanced slowly, building fortifications and improving communications to their rear. The economy of the Soviet Republic withered and its borders shrank as the enemy gradually moved in. By the summer of 1934, the Communist Party leadership realized they faced a stark choice: stand and die, or run for their lives.

They took the discreet option. In the third week of October 1934, fifteen-year-old Zeng Shaodong was one of 86,000 Red Army men, women and children who waved goodbye to their homes.

'My mother waited for me at the Yudu River,' said Zeng. 'Many families waited there. She gave me two silver dollars and a bag of salt. Two soldiers waited for me. They were afraid I might run away. They urged me to go, "Be quick. Otherwise we won't catch the army up".'

Zeng would not see his mother again for eighteen years.

Soldiers talked about a '*da ban jia*', a 'big house moving operation'. Not only the combat units were moving out; the Soviet Republic itself was packed into boxes and loaded onto thousands of bearers. Government records, medical equipment, revolutionary drama scripts, even a printing press weighed down the immense baggage train. Wives and sweethearts mostly had to be left at home. Only around thirty-five women began the Long March; among them was Mao's pregnant wife, He Zizhen, who was assigned to the convalescent unit. Children were also left behind. Mao's two-year-old son was given into the care of his brother, Zetan, who was married to He Zizhen's sister.

The Reds slipped through the Guomindang encirclement and marched west in search of a new home. Their route was plain to Chiang Kai-shek – two months earlier, a Red reconnaissance mission had blazed the trail after escaping the Jiangxi Soviet base – and he responded by marshalling even more troops to block their progress. During its first major engagement with the enemy, the Red Army was broken in two at the Xiang River and its supply train and rear units were decimated.

Fresh plans for the Reds to move north across the Yangtze River were frustrated at every turn. It took more than three months and 1,000 miles to find a route north, and by this time the Red Army had marched to the edge of the Tibetan Plateau. Conditions deteriorated the further they went. Not only did they have the Guomindang at their heels, but there were also hostile locals to deal with. As the 'army of the poor', the Reds traditionally depended on support from the peasantry – 'the sea in which the Red Army swims', as Mao put it.[1] But they were now marching through country inhabited by ethnic minorities who had little interest in Robin Hood reputations. All they saw was yet another army of foreign invaders, and so they hid their food, retreated to the hills and turned Mao's own guerrilla tactics against him.

The biggest killer, however, was the land itself. To continue north, the Red Army had to cross the Snow Mountains, a series of 13,000-foot passes that even in summer were deep in snow and ice. Exhausted soldiers staggered into drifts and could not get out. Others collapsed from altitude sickness. Those like Zeng Shaodong who survived this trial next faced something even worse – the Swamps of northern Sichuan, a vast, treeless expanse 12,000 feet above sea level and more than 60 miles across, where the bogs could suck a man down like quicksand. Zeng spent between five and ten days on this featureless plain, without food or shelter. Hundreds of people died around him, lost in the bogs or struck down by exhaustion and starvation.

Twelve months and three days after leaving home, the Red Army finally reached sanctuary – a distant corner of north-west China where local Communists already controlled a base area and the surrounding provincial forces were more concerned about Japanese invaders than the Red menace. Only Zeng and a few thousand of his comrades survived. Friends had died in battle and starved to death. They had fallen from mountainsides and drowned in rivers, been swallowed by bogs, murdered by wild tribes and poisoned by strange plants and stagnant waters. Zeng had watched many men die of sheer tiredness.

'Have a banana,' said the General. Sixty-six years earlier, he had been so hungry he ate undigested grain picked out of vanguard soldiers' faeces.

'When we walked through the Swamps, many soldiers died. Those who died were covered up by soldiers following behind. Some were too sick to walk on and about to die. Their hearts were still beating, but they were covered up too. We had to cover them, or at least their face, otherwise it was too ugly. If someone hadn't eaten for a long time, his face turned dark, thin and dry.'

Andy asked, 'But you were just a child. How could you have survived?'

'We took care of each other,' said Zeng. 'I can tell you

one story. I was carrying a few silver dollars, but when we were in the Swamps, I threw them into the water. They were too heavy, and there were no villages and nothing to buy. Some older soldiers went to pick them up. I said, "Why do you want those? You probably won't get across the Swamps. I'll probably get across, but not you."'

Zeng was wrong. Despite carrying the extra weight, the soldiers who took his money were also among the survivors when the Red Army reached the northern edge of the Swamps.

'After we finally got out of the Swamps, I had no silver dollars left and I couldn't buy any food. So I went to the older soldiers to ask for my money back. They said, "Why do you want it now?" I said, "I'm hungry." They gave me my money back.'

At the end of the road, Mao Zedong made a speech in which he announced that the Red Army's 'Long March' was an achievement without parallel in history. He told survivors that they had walked '25,000 *li*', which works out at 12,500 kilometres (7,800 miles). He told them they were an army of heroes, whose achievement would inspire millions to join them and overthrow the rotten old regime.

Our friend and interpreter for the day, Li Mingxia, asked one of those heroes a final question: 'These two foreigners are going to try to retrace your Long March. Do you think they'll make it?

'No,' said General Zeng Shaodong. 'It's too difficult. They can't walk the Long March.'

Zeng's odyssey is part of the founding myth of the modern Chinese state. The Long March is like Dunkirk, the Battle of Britain and the Great Escape all rolled into one. It's a patriotic epic drummed into every citizen of the People's Republic since the 1949 Revolution. It's heroic, thrilling and the cornerstone of the Chinese Communist Party's historical appeal and legitimacy. Our plan was to follow this myth to its source, all the way along a legendary trail of towns, villages and empty spaces that outsiders never visit. We hoped we might track down and interview veterans and witnesses. It would be an adventure in living history.

The idea first came to me in a whimsical holiday moment in south-east Guizhou. I was vaguely aware that the Red Army had passed through this region on the Long March, but it wasn't until I saw the land itself that my imagination set to work. From the window of a train, I watched mile after mile of tightly packed, thickly wooded hills roll by. Their rich greens reminded me of West Yorkshire. As we moved away from the railway line and through tiny, wooden villages, these hills became stepped, cut away into terraces for rice paddies – sometimes all the way around and right to the top, leaving just a tuft of trees on the crown.

I'd never seen a land so difficult to find a way through. By the urban middle-class standards I'd brought with me, it was also terribly poor. As well as no decent roads to foster development, there was simply no room in the valleys to build any industry. The people who lived here mostly belonged to the Miao or Dong ethnic minorities, apparently shunted off into the worst available land by population pressure. Even the vegetables in the markets looked stunted.

I began to wonder, if this place is still so remote in 2000, perhaps along the old paths there might still be a China closer to the 1930s than to the Olympic city of 'New Beijing'. It struck me that the Long March had taken place nearly seventy years ago, just close enough for there to be people who might still remember. To retrace the Long March would be to take a journey through both past and present, discovering not only what had happened in the 1930s, but also how the people and places along the Red Army's route had been affected by the Communists' eventual victory. Andy agreed: it would certainly beat going to the office.

As the idea grew into a plan, General Zeng wasn't the only one to have doubts. It wasn't that people didn't like the idea; it was that they thought it was impossible. China only began to open to the outside world in the 1980s. Most people, foreign and Chinese, assumed that because the Long March trail passed through such remote regions, many of these would still be closed to foreigners and, therefore, the only way we could retrace the Red Army would be to acquire 'government permission'. Because of the political significance of the Long March, few thought the authorities would be willing to grant this permission to two unknown foreigners. Besides, Andy and I were both very much city folk. We had almost no experience of trekking, zero knowledge of survival techniques and had never spent more than two consecutive days living in a Chinese village. To retrace the Long March according to the Red Army's schedule would take 369 days at a daily average of 21 miles. Even close friends doubted we'd last more than a month or two.

By the time we met General Zeng, our Long March was much more than a whim. While Andy and I looked for old soldiers, we delegated organization of the journey to Jia Ji, a twenty-four-year-old Beijing woman with an eclectic CV that ranged from tour guide to marketing assistant, but which did not include experience in historically motivated expeditions across darkest China. For safety and survival tips, we turned to our oldest friend in Beijing, Yang Xiao, otherwise known as 'Gear Guy'. Yang Xiao was raised until the age of eleven in the Tibetan province of Qinghai, where his father worked as a surveyor. As a child, he rode horses on the great Qinghai prairies. The love of the outdoors had never left him: he had trekked in lonely places all over China and made a living looking after foreign clients on hiking trips, mostly to the Great Wall north of Beijing. He wrote a column for a local outdoor magazine under the 'Gear Guy' nickname and always looked like he'd walked straight out of a camping catalogue – even after a wet weekend training the two of us in the mountains north of Beijing.

Yang Xiao loved the idea. He remembered revolutionary poetry from his schooldays and taught us Long March doggerel:

'Bitter or not
Think and think again
Of the Red Army's Long March
Of 25,000 *li*.'

At the time, Yang Xiao was an education and an inspiration. Much later, he would be my salvation.

To solve the permission problem we needed someone official to take responsibility for our activities. The search for this 'sponsor' was dispiriting. It seemed every other day brought another meeting, another interested party, another promise of 'co-operation'. And yet our Long March should have been an easy sell. It's hard to overstate the desire in China for greater engagement with the outside world, and for the outside world to pay greater attention and respect to China. For two foreigners to take on the founding myth of the modern Chinese state, well, everyone in Beijing could see the appeal. But when push came to shove, no one was willing to offer anything more than warm words. It always came back to the same thing – 'government permission'. Everyone wanted us to have it, but no one wanted to give it to us.

Finally, we opted for revolutionary tactics. Like Andy, I had by now worked with the Chinese media for the best part of five years. We knew local journalists would bite at our story and that there was no intrinsic reason it couldn't be run. As long as you don't say anything bad about the

Communist Party, mention the three Ts – Tian'anmen, Tibet or Taiwan – or use the word 'lesbian', the goalposts are fairly wide. We decided to get as much coverage as we could, on the principle that if it's in the papers and on TV, it must be true. Who could doubt we were going to retrace the Long March if they had seen us say so on television?

The first story ran on 11 August 2002, in *Beijing Youth Daily*. Just before it went to press, the editor called Andy and asked, 'Have you got government permission?'

'Of course,' Andy said.

And just a few days later, the 1.7 million readers thought so, too.

Andy and I made one final application for support to a department of the Beijing Municipal Government, where it was considered and rejected by the astounded deputy head of the Beijing Communist Party. 'I thought they already had government permission,' he told our representative. 'I saw them on the news.'

Despite this propaganda triumph, on the day of departure from Beijing a well-connected friend still called to counsel against boarding the train. 'You could get into big trouble,' she said.

Our friend didn't only have political problems in mind. 'Safety' is an important issue for foreigners in China. Even in relatively cosmopolitan cities like Beijing, Chinese hosts are often nervous and over-protective of foreign guests. There also seems to be a nebulous assumption that the Chinese countryside is full of something dangerous. Chinese authorities also like to stress safety, perhaps because they are genuinely concerned, but also because it allows them to intrude on other people's business and generally keep an eye on who's doing what. Police harassment is almost always preceded by an assurance that the officers are here 'for your safety'.

We felt safety was the least of our worries. We reckoned we could negotiate our way around local cops. We worried about the 25,000 *li* (12,500 kilometres). We worried our Chinese was inadequate, a worry made worse by people telling us the peasants would speak incomprehensible dialects we'd never understand. We worried that we'd never walked 20 miles in a day in our lives, that our bags weighed 44 pounds each and our maps had nothing but empty spaces where the Long March trail should be.

Four friends, including Andy's very supportive girlfriend Jiao Pei, joined us for the overnight train to Nanchang, followed by a bus 200 miles south to Ruijin, capital of the Chinese Soviet Republic from 1931 to 1934, and where most people think the Long March started.

Thanks to Jia Ji's propaganda work, we pulled in to find we were not the subjects of a police investigation, but of daily reports in the *Jiangnan City News*, the biggest newspaper in Jiangxi. My former colleague Sarah Bai studied the latest article.

'Do you like fish balls?' she asked me.

'What? Not particularly. Why?'

'It says here you like fish balls.'

'But they haven't even interviewed me yet. What else do I like?'

'It says Andy thinks Jiangxi is "like the face of a beautiful young woman".'

We couldn't really be annoyed at *Jiangnan City News*. Andy's imaginary poetic musings didn't do our public relations any harm, and I could put up with a plate of fish balls now and then.

Ruijin today is a small county town, which puts it around halfway down the Chinese administrative hierarchy. (China is basically divided into provinces, then cities, then counties. Below the counties are the larger *zhen* and the smaller *xiang*. Last come the villages, the cradle of China's peasant revolution and still home to more than half the Chinese population). Although Ruijin is dusty and dark at night, its historical importance has helped attract government money to keep up appearances. The central square is surrounded by clean, new buildings five or six storeys high, and the square itself is decorated by a fountain lit in garish colours and the same multi-coloured neon lights that have decorated public areas all over Beijing since the fiftieth anniversary of the People's Republic in 1999.

We were only there to see the revolutionary sights – our Long March was due to begin 40 miles to the south-west, from a town called Yudu, and the people of Ruijin weren't happy about this choice of departure point. From the head of the Foreign Affairs Bureau to the guide at the Museum of the Jiangxi Soviet Government, they patronized us for our ignorance and insisted our journey should start from their town.

For many Red soldiers, the Long March did indeed start from Ruijin. But Chinese history sees this as the starting point for one reason only – the *leaders* started from there. Andy and I wanted an alternative starting point if only to make a statement against the cult of the leaders, but we also had solid reasons to reject Ruijin. The Red forces had been scattered all over the soviet area, but during the first half of October 1934 they all gathered in and around Yudu County Town. We reckoned this was the most logical place to start.

The people of Yudu were delighted.

'Absolutely right,' said Mr Zhong of the local Foreign Affairs Bureau. 'Of course Yudu is where the Long March started. It's like if you were going on a group holiday, where would you say you started? You'd say, for example, Beijing Airport, not your house.'

A concrete obelisk today marks one of the eight points where the Red soldiers crossed the Yudu River. This 'First Ferry of the Long March' is about half a mile from the centre of town, and singled out because this is where Mao Zedong began his journey on 18 October 1934 – two days after the first units began to move out. At the time, however, Mao's pre-eminence lay in the future. Although he had been a leading member since the foundation of the Party, and one of only thirteen delegates to the First Congress of the Chinese Communist Party in Shanghai in 1921, he was at odds with many colleagues over his views on the primary role of the peasantry in any Chinese revolution. The years between 1931 and 1934 saw a concerted effort to sideline him from the Party and Red Army leadership. The Communist Party at this point was dominated by a group of Moscow-educated young men, who mistrusted Mao's unorthodox style and thinking. Very likely, they also looked down on him. Mao's education had gone no further than high school. He had made it to Peking University, but only as a librarian. He had never been out of China.

As the Long March began, the highest authority in the Red Army was the so-called 'three man group'. Theoretically, the last word was with Bo Gu, a twenty-six-year-old who had spent four years in Moscow and taken charge of the Chinese Communist Party with the blessing of the Comintern – the Communist International – which basically did Stalin's bidding to advance the interests of the Soviet Union. Number two was Zhou Enlai, thirty-six, Political Commissar of the Red Army and future Premier of the People's Republic of China. Third was a thirty-four-year-old German Communist named Otto Braun, a man with a colourful past in revolutionary politics. Braun had been charged with high treason in Berlin in 1926. Two years later, his girlfriend led the group of Communists that broke him out of prison, after which he fled to the Soviet Union. He was sent to China by Soviet military intelligence in 1932.

In photographs, Braun looks a cheerful fellow. While

the Chinese leaders preferred to contemplate the lens with Victorian seriousness, the best-known portrait of Braun, probably taken in Yan'an in 1937, shows him grinning broadly for the camera. It's hard to square this image with the Braun who appears in Chinese history books and films. The official Otto Braun is a kind of cartoon bad guy, a ranting buffoon almost single-handedly responsible for the failure to repel Chiang Kai-shek's advance and for the disasters that would soon overtake the Red Army on the Long March. In a 2001 Chinese television drama about the Long March, Braun spends at least 90 per cent of his screen time banging tables, yelling at his Chinese comrades and dismissing their sensible advice. He is most memorably seen chasing a Red Army girl with his trousers round his ankles. The girl is saved by Chairman Mao, who enfolds her in a fatherly embrace while denouncing Otto Braun's disrespect for Chinese womanhood – a superb ironic joke, given the Chairman's well-known enthusiasm for shagging peasant girls.[2]

As we stood on the north bank of the Yudu River sixty-eight years later, Otto Braun was still the only foreigner known to have walked the whole route of the Long March.

The river is about 70 yards wide at the First Ferry. A handful of dredgers coughed among piles of stone two-thirds of the way across. Little else disturbed the slow water. The sun was barely up when we arrived on 16 October. To see us off, we had a couple of Yudu officials, a cameraman from Yudu TV station, a photographer from *Jiangnan City News* and half a dozen curious early birds.

A few primary school pupils straggled past the Biggest Moment of Our Lives on their way to class. A few stopped to say 'hello' or just to stare at our unlikely gathering. Andy and I posed for pictures, then we followed the riverside path about half a mile to where a modern bridge stands at the point where the Third Army Group crossed on a pontoon.

A banner over the north end of the bridge announces it as the 'First Bridge of the Long March'.

I didn't want to think of the road ahead: the ice and altitude sickness of the Snow Mountains, the poisoned bogs and empty spaces of the Swamps, the wild animals, the 25,000 *li*. And those were just the highlights in the history books. I didn't know what to expect in between. I didn't know Andy was already chronically ill. I didn't know if foreigners were allowed to walk everywhere along the Long March trail. Aside from the famous landmarks, I wasn't even sure where we were supposed to be going.

I always rejected suggestions we were interested in 'recreating' the Long March. That's ridiculous, I said, we want to make it as easy and safe as possible. But we did have one thing in common with the Red Army as we crossed that bridge on 16 October 2002 – we were taking the biggest gamble of our lives.

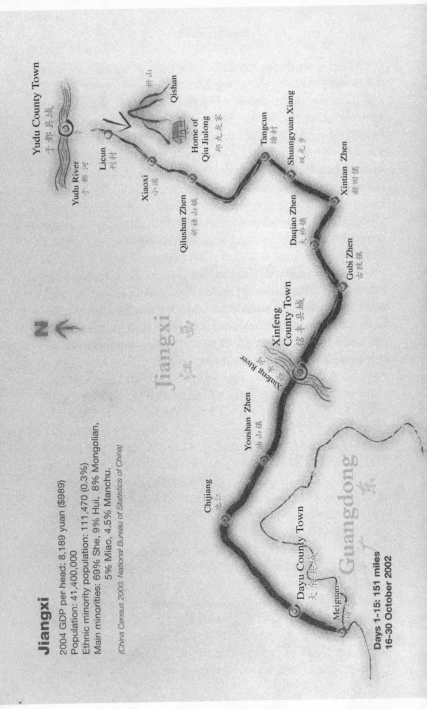

Jiangxi

2004 GDP per head: 8,189 yuan ($989)
Population: 41,400,000
Ethnic minority population: 111,470 (0.3%)
Main minorities: 69% She, 9% Hui, 8% Mongolian, 5% Miao, 4.5% Manchu.

(China Census 2000, National Bureau of Statistics of China)

N↑

Jiangxi 江西

Guangdong 广东

Yudu County Town
于都县城

Yudu River
于都河

祈山

Qishan

Home of
Qiu Jiulong
邱九龙家

Licun
利村

Xiaoxi
小溪

Qilushan Zhen
祁禄山镇

Tangcun
塘村

Shuangyuan Xiang
双元乡

Xintian Zhen
新田镇

Daqiao Zhen
大桥镇

Gubi Zhen
古陂镇

Xinfeng
County Town
信丰县城

Xinfeng River
信丰河

Youshan Zhen
油山镇

Chijiang
池江

Dayu County Town
大余县城

Mei'guan
梅关

Days 1-15: 151 miles
16-30 October 2002

Chapter 1

First Steps

The road to Licun leaves the highway about half a mile south of the bridge over the Yudu River. It is lined on both sides by stone posts about 18 inches high, inscribed with the Chinese characters for the Buddhist mantra '*Om mani padme hum*' (which the Dalai Lama translates as 'great and vast'). The fields are full of the sound of rice threshers – wooden-box contraptions driven by foot pedals, the pedals driven by women. The threshing never falters, not even when I pause to stare, nor when the women say, 'Please don't!' when I ask if I can take a photo. In other fields, sweet potatoes are almost ready for harvesting. Villagers gave them to the Red soldiers as they left sixty-eight years earlier, but no one offers us any. Instead, we suck on fresh mandarins while resting below a sign that announces, 'The army loves the people, the people support the army. The army and people are united in one family.'

I feel a nervous flutter as the first police car of the day approaches, but the driver gives a friendly honk and carries on without stopping. Nearing Licun, another police car slows. We smile and wave. A hand waves out the passenger window and the officers go on their way. As worries about imminent arrest subside, we ignore subsequent police vehicles and they ignore us.

In retrospect, Licun is a fine place with abundant mod

cons. The village is on a sealed road with regular buses to the county town. It has rudimentary corner shops known as *xiao mai bu* (literally 'small sell office'), mainly dedicated to cigarettes and alcohol, but also known to supply tolerable non-alcoholic drinks and even edible snacks. There are simple restaurants and a guesthouse. The guesthouse has electricity – occasionally – and a black-and-white TV in rooms that charge 5 yuan (around 60 US cents at the time) a bed. Guests who want a wash are given a red bucket full of hot water and directed to a badly tiled washroom on the second floor, where the toilet is the standard Chinese squat-over-a-hole inconvenience.

The problem on Day 1 of the Long March is that we have no frame of reference. For two fat city boys, Licun looks like a grim start to a grim new life. Our four friends have walked with us this far, a nice flat stroll of less than 10 miles, but now they are waving down the bus back to Yudu. They empty their pockets and hand us all their change – the 100-yuan bills (about US$12) in our Long March treasury will be hard to break out here. Andy finds a quiet corner and mutters awkward goodbyes to Jiao Pei.

It has been drizzling much of the day, but soon after our friends leave a thunderstorm appears to knock out the electricity all over Licun. We play magnetic chess by candlelight while a chicken jogs around the table, looking for scraps on the dirt floor. Our companion pecks at a cigarette butt while the boss of the guesthouse frets over dinner options.

Andy has not eaten meat since the age of seventeen. I'm fairly confident no vegetarian has walked the Long March trail, and so Andy, at least, is on course to record a unique achievement. Most Chinese people, however, do not view this fact in a positive light. The popular imagination sees meatless Andy as a weak, helpless being, prone to sickness, faint-heartedness and, surely, a chronic lack of muscle power.

In a place where road markers feature Buddhist incantations, you might think vegetarianism would be a respectable concept – especially since meat was a luxury for most peasants before the commune system was ended only twenty-five years ago.

The communes were large collective enterprises that ensured Party control over the agricultural production and distribution process. This was useful to Mao's government as it tried to screw surpluses out of the countryside to support centrally planned industrial development. But because they stifled individual initiative, the communes tended towards mediocrity and stagnation. Three years after Mao's death in 1976, the new leadership under Long March veteran Deng Xiaoping began to introduce the 'household responsibility system'. Under this system, individual families contracted land from the state and then took responsibility for how they farmed 'their' land. Apart from a small state quota, families owned whatever they produced. It was a kind of public-private fudge, but at a stroke it restored the profit motive and gave enough sense of long-term stability to encourage investment and improvement. Agriculture has flourished on this basis.

Perhaps rural memories are short.

'I don't eat meat,' says Andy.

'What?' says the boss's wife.

It doesn't really matter what you say the first time you speak Chinese to someone in the Chinese countryside. They almost always respond with a 'What?' or a 'Don't understand'. At first, we assume it's because we're foreigners, but as our journey progresses we see similar conversations develop between urban Chinese and peasants. (I don't mean to be rude by calling them 'peasants', by the way. The official *China Daily* English-language newspaper regards 'peasant' as offensive and translates '*nongmin*' as 'farmer'. But the lifestyles, social organiza-

tion and agricultural practices of most *nongmin* are
nothing like 'farmers' as we think of them in the West.)
Communication confusion happens all the time to friends
from Beijing who join us on the road – much to their
annoyance and to our equal and opposite satisfaction.
The peasants tend automatically to assume they can't
understand what this alien being is saying, and so at first
they don't bother to listen. It's like adjusting the dial on a
radio – usually, it just takes a couple of sentences for the
peasant to tune into the strange accent.

'I don't eat meat,' Andy repeats.

'You don't eat meat!' The landlady pauses to digest this
astounding statement. 'What do you eat?'

'What vegetables do you have?' asks Andy.

'*Bai cai.*'

Cabbage. Andy hates cabbage. He especially hates
Chinese cabbage, stir-fried and slopped on to a plate in
a pool of oil and water.

'What else do you have?'

There is a pause. Our hostess stares at Andy, then asks,
'Do you eat chicken?'

In Chinese schoolbooks, the real Long Marchers 'ate
bitterness', a common Chinese phrase to express suffering. Our Long March Menu, Day 1, reads 'Limp cabbage
and cold white rice'.

The next morning, I find Andy on the muddy street in the
middle of a crowd of about twenty villagers.

'Is there anyone here who remembers the Red Army?'
he says.

There is much head-scratching and general discussion
among the crowd. Andy fields the reciprocal questions
about who we are and what on earth we are doing in
Licun, while I entertain the locals by trying to mime a sore
throat. Finally, a seventy-year-old gentleman by the name
of Gao Jiuhua takes charge.

'There is one very old man who was here back then,' he says.

Some of the other village elders tell Gao to shut up and not waste our time.

I scribble on a notepad, 'Can we go and see him?'

'Certainly,' says Gao.

He leads us a couple of hundred metres into an old part of the village, where all the homes are ragged structures of mud brick and dark wood, and sits us in a dingy room at a square wooden table. We rise immediately as an ancient, shrunken man hobbles in on two sticks. He wears a blue Mao suit and a brown knitted hat with a bobble on top. His name, says Gao, is Chen Yingchun.

It's quickly apparent why the others told Gao not to bother.

'Euurayah,' says Chen, motioning for us to sit.

'Hello,' says Andy. 'We're studying the Long March, and Mr Gao told us you were here when the Red Army was in Licun.'

'Eugha,' says Chen.

Chen's granddaughter, Chen Quandi, hands us cups of hot boiled water and a plate of home-grown peanuts. 'My grandfather's very old,' she says. 'He's been completely deaf for ten years now, so he can't understand what you say.'

Chen might not understand why two foreigners are sat in his home, but he seems pleased anyway. He takes out his pension book and shows it to us. He was born in 1913 and receives 360 yuan (US$44) a month. This is rather remarkable, as peasants normally receive no money from the state. Grandson Chen Yanming explains:

'My grandfather joined the Red Army when it came here in 1934. He marched with them as far as Xinfeng, but his unit was in the rear and got cut off by the Guomindang before it could cross the river. He couldn't get through, so he came back home.'

As it left the Soviet Republic, the army marched in a three-column formation, with the Party leadership and military headquarters in the centre. Because the Chinese Red Army was organized quite differently to the British Army, it's not easy to translate its structure into English. The forces in the Jiangxi base area were grouped into the First Front Red Army (*hong yi fangmian jun*), with Zhu De as Commander-in-Chief and Zhou Enlai as Political Commissar. At the beginning of the Long March, the First Front Army was comprised of five *jun tuan*, or 'Army Groups', each headed by a military commander whose rank was roughly equivalent to a British Army general. Alongside each general was a political commissar, who in theory ranked above his military colleague. Below Army Group level, the designations corresponded more-or-less to British Army equivalents, e.g., regiment, battalion, company, each of which also had its own political commissar.

The 5th Army Group guarded the rear, where new recruit Chen Yingchun was assigned. He marched just seven days before his company lost touch with the main force during the Battle of Xinfeng. But even though he lasted only a week, here is a man who actually was on the Long March. If he had managed to get across the river at Xinfeng, he would almost certainly have died. On the other hand, like other survivors of the Long March, he might have risen to the very top of Chinese society. Like General Zeng, who grew up not far from here, he may have ended his days in a fine courtyard in central Beijing. Instead, he has worked the fields his whole life, with nothing to show but a pension book for his bold choice of seventy years ago.

Chen doesn't have any exciting revelations for us, no tales of heroic derring-do. No historians from Beijing have ever come to listen to his story or write his name in their books. Only his family cherish the memories of his life.

But I'm thrilled to eat his peanuts, even though they have lost their crunch. For me, this is exactly what the Long March is all about. Andy and I are walking through the blank spaces in between the highlights of the history books, looking for personal connections with the past.

Our map is also full of blank spaces, and we get lost in one on Day 3. In the Chinese countryside, there are basically two kinds of path: the '*xiao lu*' and the '*ma lu*' – literally 'small road' and 'horse road'. I know the latter is a general term for road, but the first time I hear *xiao lu* I assume it is what it sounds like, maybe a wide dirt track as opposed to the sealed highway. Actually, *xiao lu* means footpath.

There are only about 10 miles between the towns of Xiaoxi and Qilushan, and the proper path is completely flat. In the end, it takes us about two and a half days, and in the process we learn almost everything there is to know about asking directions and *not* following loggers' trails up mountains at sunset.

The path we take is actually a cul-de-sac – the end of a bamboo cutters' trail. By sunset, it is a water-soaked chute of bamboo cuttings, some the size of a pint beer glass, others the length of a soccer goal crossbar. There are no stable toeholds or handholds. We clutch at roots and branches while the bamboo rolls, slips and knocks together under our feet. It sounds like we're assaulting a xylophone. The hillsides are steep and thickly overgrown. There's not a flat space anywhere – except just above us, where the bamboo workers have cut one for camping. As we collapse onto it in the last of the fading daylight, I bless the loggers even as I curse them for making the path that has led us astray.

Andy slides back down the bamboo to get water. I call Jia Ji.

'What's your report?' she asks.

'We're at the guesthouse in Qilushan,' I lie. 'We're fine.'

At this stage, and after so much fuss about 'safety', we are worried what the authorities might think. We live in constant fear of being sent home, believing we have only come this far through a kind of confidence trick. And I'd rather the authorities didn't know I set out to retrace the Long March on foot without knowing the word for footpath.

The next morning we have not seen another human being for almost twenty-four hours when a pair of peasants heaves into view, each with a pole balanced across their shoulders, monstrous 30-pound baskets of grain swinging from either end. Qiu Jiulong and his wife Yang Jiangxiu are carrying rice from market in Qilushan. Qiu smiles and offers to take us there – it's very close, he says, but first, how about breakfast?

Qiu's farmhouse is typical of this part of Jiangxi – the walls made of mud bricks from the land's rich red soil, the buildings covered front and back with a layer of whitewash. From a distance, you might almost think you were in rural France. When the homes are as well built as Qiu's, they are a fine sight. We share a breakfast of crispy battered potatoes, sweet potatoes, garlic and hot chilli relishes, a variant of the runner bean and some wild pickled vegetables. It is washed down with honey water, courtesy of the beehives Qiu keeps under the roof.

'What are you doing here?' asks Qiu. 'There's nothing interesting here for tourists.'

'We're not tourists,' I say. 'We're retracing the Long March.'

'Ah, the Long March. Why didn't you get the bus to Qilushan?'

'We're not getting the bus. We're walking all the way.'

'You're walking!? You've got real spirit!'

'Did the Red Army come through this place?' asks Andy.

'Around here, yes. There's a memorial to the Long March on the mountain above here, where the army walked along the ridge from Pangushan to Qilushan. We go up there sometimes to pick mushrooms. I can take you there after breakfast. Why don't you stay here with us for the day? You could stay the night.'

'Thanks, but we're late already,' says Andy. 'We really must get to Qilushan.'

'How far is the memorial?' I ask.

'Not far.'

'How far is not far?' asks Andy.

'It's only two hours away,' says Qiu. 'We could go and see that, then I'll take you to Qilushan after.'

Creepers cling to our feet and the stone track turns into mud then turns into no track at all as Qiu and his ten-year-old son Lujun cut a trail up the mountain – the same mountain we camped on the night before. ('See, we weren't lost,' I say. 'We were on the Long March trail all the time.') Lujun stoops to decapitate a snake with his mini machete. Andy is perturbed.

'Are there any other wild animals here?' he asks.

'Oh, yes,' says Qiu. 'There's wild boar and wild oxen as well as snakes.'

During breaks, Qiu and Lujun dig around the bamboo looking for edible roots. I quench my thirst with the juice from one after another of the mandarins Lujun collected from the single tree that grows on the edge of their property. They are the best mandarins I've ever tasted, their sweetness tinged with just a hint of sour. Qiu grins and praises the soil – so good, he says, it needs no fertilizers.

'You know, I heard the old people say the Red Army had to wade through the rice paddies here on the Long March, because the paths were too narrow for all of them at once. When they came out covered in wet soil, they really were a red army."

'So Mr Qiu, do you reckon it's far?' asks Andy.

'Not far.'

'How far?'

'Not far.'

As a Beijing friend put it once when I complained about this kind of to-ing and fro-ing, 'Chinese is a vague language, like a poem sometimes.'

'Two hours' turns out to mean 'at least eight hours' in Qiu's poetic rural idiom. Halfway up the mountain, Qiu admits we can't make it to the top this afternoon. It rains all the way back home.

'Why don't you stay the night?' Qiu suggests. We are soaked through and the sun is about to set. Andy scowls. Qiu gets his way.

While we eat dinner, the volume is turned down on the family's 12-inch black-and-white television. Saddam Hussein silently brandishes a rifle in celebration of a referendum giving him another seven years in power. In the next item, pictures of George W. Bush and American aircraft carriers suggest Saddam's time is already running out.

But Qiu isn't interested in power politics on the TV. He wants to talk about the power politics *of* the TV.

'We can't always run the TV and the lights at the same time, you know,' he says. 'Our electricity's from a generator I put in the stream, so how much power we have depends on how much it rains.'

'How long have you had electricity?' asks Andy.

'A long time. Two or three years. But change here is too slow. The local government won't put electricity out here because there's too few people and they think it's too expensive.'

Qiu is dissatisfied. He returns several times to the same theme – change is too slow and no one cares about people like him. Perhaps he has kept us here just to have someone to talk to.

'Tell them in Beijing, tell them how life is here. They'll listen to you. Who listens to us?'

Qiu has four children. The eldest, a seventeen-year-old son and a fifteen-year-old daughter, are already away working in the south China boomtown of Shenzhen, the most famous of the new cities built on the 'Deng Xiaoping Theory'.

Deng Xiaoping began the Long March at the age of thirty, eleven years younger than Mao, who turned forty-one two months into the Red Army's odyssey. Two years after Mao's death in 1976, Deng established himself as the Chairman's long-term successor, the pragmatic core of what came to be known as the 'second generation' leadership. Deng revised Communist orthodoxy to propose that China follow the path of 'socialism with Chinese characteristics'. The practical result of this was a brand of state-sponsored capitalism, pioneered in Shenzhen and three other Special Economic Zones designated in 1980. Shenzhen at the time was a fishing area in the Pearl River Delta, just north of Hong Kong. Its resident population was around 300,000. Twenty years later, it was an industrial city of more than 7 million, nearly 85 per cent of whom were designated as 'temporary residents'.[1]

Shenzhen fairly bulges with peasants who have gone to *da gong*, a phrase we will hear hundreds of times on our path through rural China. If someone has gone to *da gong*, it means they have left the countryside to work in the city at jobs that range from factory labour to construction to serving as a masseuse or cleaner. We will also meet many young people who have returned home, unable to bear the strain of working in conditions that sound rather like Victorian England – the kind of factory conditions, indeed, that inspired the work of Marx and Engels.

Qiu Jiulong's youngest children, Lujun and Luhua,

attend school in Qilushan, 3 miles away. Qiu smiles at Lujun and says, 'This one cost me 1,000 yuan.'

In Qiu's area, peasants are restricted to two children by 'planned birth' regulations (*jihua shengyu* in Chinese, usually summed up as the One-Child Policy by Western media). Extra children cost Qiu 1,000-yuan fines (US$120), which he gladly paid to have the children properly registered – he shows us the government document that lists his children. The money came from the market in Qilushan, where Qiu sells the farm's produce and wild fruits and vegetables from our favourite mountain. On a good day at this time of year, Qiu says, he can dig up 5 kilos (11 pounds) of bamboo root. This sells for 6 yuan a kilo. His marvellous mandarin tree might produce 110 pounds that sell for 2 yuan each.

Nothing goes to waste in this household. Leftovers from breakfast are mixed in with fresh dishes. And despite the fact Chinese people traditionally put on a show for guests, not a scrap of meat is eaten – much to Andy's relief. They are charming and generous hosts and if all the peasants on the Long March trail turn out to be like this, our journey could take about ten years.

Andy spews up his egg-fried rice shortly out of Qilushan on Day 5. He's never been a great breakfast eater. He has tried to change his habits to build up strength for the Long March, but it hasn't worked. From here on, he quits breakfast, snacks mid-morning instead, and all seems well.

Our landlord in Qilushan has drawn us a map on the back of a cigarette box, and despite Andy's stomach troubles we manage the necessary 15 miles before nightfall. For the first time, we have entered what the Chinese call a *shan qu*, a 'mountain district', and the chill of winter is keen. Having installed ourselves in the only available accommodation in Tangcun, we steel ourselves for dinner.

After he thanks her for delivering a dish, our waitress stops and eyes Andy.

'You are too polite,' she says, and turns back to the kitchen before Andy can apologize. She returns with another dish of stir-fried something.

'Thank you,' says Andy.

'Stop that!' the waitress says. 'We don't do that here.'

I find Chinese etiquette equally disconcerting. People emerge from the kitchen, point to our food and say, 'It's not good, is it?'

Since it usually isn't good, I both fear and loathe this question. I thought I'd left this false modesty nonsense behind in England. Have I come halfway round the world, to a place where no foreigner has ever set foot, only to say, no, no, your house is very clean, your new hairstyle's great, your bum doesn't look big in those trousers?

The Tangcun chef approaches. I make a pre-emptive strike.

'That food was delicious,' I lie.

'Oh no, it wasn't,' says the chef.

'No, really, you're a great cook.'

'No, no, I'm no good at all.'

'Yes you are.'

'No, I'm not.'

It's infuriating, but really, just imagine if we all suddenly started speaking directly and truthfully. Our two great civilizations would collapse in a puff of embarrassment.

As we move south-west towards the border between Jiangxi and Guangdong Province, the daily march stretches out to 20 miles and beyond. Back in Beijing, we trained by packing rucksacks with a dozen 3-pint bottles of water and then walking around the city's Third Ring Road. An hour of this was worth between 2.5 to 3 miles. We managed 20 miles just once, by the end of which I had lost the nail on my left little toe and had so many blisters I couldn't wear my boots for a week. With ten-minute breaks every hour, plus an hour off for lunch, we are now on the road at least nine hours a day. But the footpaths and dirt tracks of the Long March trail are much gentler than the tarmac of the Chinese capital. My feet haven't blistered and every day I grow physically stronger. The mental challenge, however, is undiminished. I try never to think beyond the next break, splitting the day up into manageable stages, never more than an hour at a time. Andy and I often walk separately, at our own pace, so that neither has the chance to get irritated by the other's rush/slowness. We chop and change strategies for passing the time. For example, Andy asks, 'If you could choose any three women to accompany you on the Long March, who would they be?' After which we move on to naming every province in China.

In August 1934, two foreign missionaries were kidnapped by a unit of the 6th Army Group shortly before it united with He Long's 2nd Army Group in Guizhou Province. During more than 400 days in captivity, Rudolf Bosshardt and Arnolis Hayman came up with similar strategies for killing time. Bosshardt wrote: 'As a memory aid we would recall as many passages [of Scripture] as possible on certain subjects, such as sacrifice, holiness, love, long-suffering; first selecting those beginning with "A," then "B" and so on through the alphabet.'[2] Shortly after entering Xinfeng County, Andy adapts this pastime into a game that reveals fictitious sexual liaisons between alphabetically juxtaposed celebrities. Thus, Jim Rosenthal and Steve Strange form an unexpected union, while Quentin Tarantino, Abel Xavier (comedy-haired former Portugal international left-back) and Catherine Zeta-Jones perform increasingly colourful acts of debauchery.

The colour and shape of the land is changing. Xinfeng County is officially 'Orange County'. The local government has decided there is money in the orange business and everywhere we can see traditional agriculture being abandoned for the new craze. Fresh soil – also orange – is exposed on all sides where the land has been cleared and the hills terraced to receive row upon row of dark green trees, mostly less than 6 feet high. These new orange groves are three years from maturity, but already there are orchards bearing fruit the locals claim will rival imports from the USA. Red banners blaze from the hilltops, extolling the virtues of agricultural development. Red characters 3-foot high daubed on the walls of houses declare, 'Growing oranges is better than raising children.'

The largest town before Xinfeng County Town itself is Gubi, close to the battlefield where the Red Army broke the Guomindang's second of four blockade lines. Once again, they met little resistance. The blockade lines were designed as part of a strategy of encirclement to squeeze the life out of the Communist base area, cutting off communications and wrecking the local economy. They were not designed to confront the exodus of the entire Red Army. The Reds would not face a serious challenge until the fourth and last of the blockade lines, drawn at the Xiang River in Guangxi, two provinces away.

I trail into Gubi just after dark to find Andy waiting on the steps of a small grocery store, a bottle of fizzy pop in hand and a new friend in the store owner. He points upwards. Above looms the China Mobile mast. Mobile phones took off in China well before England. They were already commonplace when I arrived in 1997, and by mid-2005 the official number of users was over 350 million, around one in four of the population.[3] On the Long March, we're learning to recognize the mobile telephone mast as the number-one symbol of development – a mast means shops, places to

eat and paid accommodation. Beyond the grocery and
the mast, the road bends around into a broad street
about 20 yards wide, lined with charmless two-storey
buildings, many covered with the white tiles (think
English public toilet) that are Symbol No.2 of development. Nothing looks much more than twenty years
old. Most is probably a lot newer. In towns like Gubi,
we see construction proceeding at a frantic pace, without great regard for quality or longevity. Places that
look shiny from a distance are, on closer inspection,
falling apart even before they are finished. Windows
rarely shut, doors never lock – very handy for policemen keen to inspect our documents and stick their
noses into our business.

Our shopkeeper friend takes us to a guesthouse, then
leaves us to make arrangements with the boss. The
establishment doubles as a restaurant, and a crowd of
a dozen drunks around its largest table makes us feel like
we've come to the wrong place.

'Sit down, sit down, have a drink!' says the largest and
loudest of the drunks.

'Yes, thank you, but we're just going to put our bags
away and rest a little,' I say, making sure not to break
stride. If there's one thing we don't want to do at the end
of a long day, it's socialize. Every day is the same. We're
desperate to find a quiet space, close the door and switch
off for a few minutes. But this is the hardest thing of all to
achieve. Privacy, personal space, peace and quiet – these
are Western bourgeois luxuries.

We escape upstairs to our room. Almost immediately
there is a commotion at the door, which bursts open to
reveal No.1 Drunk and a crowd of hangers-on. The drunk
wrestles an arm around Andy's neck and drags him
towards the corridor.

'Come and drink with us. We're friends.'

I race to the door, uncouple Andy, grab No.1 Drunk's

hand and shake it enthusiastically – all the while pushing him firmly out the door.

'We'll be down in a minute, friend.'

We barricade ourselves in, wait for the noise to subside, and then, against Andy's wishes, tiptoe downstairs. 'We have to eat,' I say. This time I'm in luck – the drunks have already moved to a back room. We dash out the door and back to our grocer friend, who takes us to an empty restaurant. Andy describes the drunken scene in our bedroom.

'Ah, the town Party Secretary,' says the grocer.

'Is he always drunk by 6 o'clock?'

Our friend ignores the question. He says, 'If you want to do anything in this town, you have to go to the Party Secretary first.'

'Does that include the local government, as well?'

'Yes, even the mayor.'

It's a disturbing thought. Of course, I know the Communist Party has the last word on all major questions, but back in Beijing, the Party seems an impersonal or even an abstract entity. You know it's out there somewhere, but it doesn't bust through your door waving a bottle of booze. In the big city, you don't often see the Party's power embodied in a single person. You don't see how the Party rules, through a massive network of petty despotisms – some enlightened and benign, others boorish and oppressive.

Dawn doesn't improve Gubi's appearance. The rural districts we pass through are largely clean. Most villagers have limited access to modern goods and foodstuffs, and so there isn't much plastic waste around their homes. Human, animal and vegetable waste is recycled as efficiently as it has been for thousands of years. In the towns, however, trash is everywhere. My diary for Gubi wonders, 'What's the point of having a Communist dictatorship if you can't make people clear their litter up?' That morning, Andy has collected a day's worth of plastic wrappers and bottles and is looking for a home for them. He addresses the attendant at the petrol station at the west end of town.

'Can I use your rubbish basket?'

'No, just throw it there,' the attendant replies, pointing into the stream that runs under the road at that point. It is less a stream of water than a tide of trash. Andy does a double take, 'Are you serious?'

'Of course, it's no problem, just throw it in there. I don't want it.'

Finding a respectable place for our rubbish is a daily problem, and we rarely find a satisfactory solution. In winter, stoves and open fires rid us of paper waste; otherwise, we can do no better than find a person who says they will take care of it. We hand over our trash bags hoping 'taking care of it' doesn't mean throwing it into the river out back. On walls, houses and billboards across the nation, a hundred thousand slogans urge conscientious study of the latest political movements and stricter application of planned birth, but not a single sign says, 'Keep China tidy'.

Lü Sitao meets us in Xinfeng County Town. He dumps two bulging plastic bags on Andy's bed.

It would be nice to report we are delighted to see Sitao solely because he is our old friend, and not because . . .

'Pizza!' cries Andy.

Andy first met Sitao in Beijing in 1997. In those days, Sitao was a struggling insurance agent who had given up a cushy job in the Qingdao Port Authority to seek his fortune in Beijing. Since then he has moved on to become co-owner of a string of struggling clothes shops. He considered joining the Long March full time, but business trapped him in Guangzhou, searching the factories for the best deals. Sitao's Long March has been compressed into the two days he can spare in Xinfeng, one of the rare towns we pass through with a railway line, five hours from Guangzhou.

'What kind of a Long March is this?' Sitao asks, surveying the feast of pizza and snack foods now spread around Andy's room in the Meifanshi Hotel (as recommended by the local police, who stopped us for a chat on our way into town).

'It's a *New* Long March,' says Andy. 'It means eating as little bitterness and as much pizza as possible.'

As we tuck in, Sitao relaxes with a copy of *Jiangxi Daily* we picked up last week in Tangcun – featuring a third-page feature about us under the headline, 'England is Very Bold!' He makes a sound peculiar to Chinese people, a kind of rising 'uuuu-UH?' that indicates surprise and a measure of amused disbelief.

'It says here Ed is very good at singing revolutionary songs. You sang one when you were leaving Yudu. Is that true?'

'What? Of course not.'

'And it says Andy said he would like to quote former Premier Zhou Enlai to praise the people of Jiangxi.'

'But I don't even know what Zhou said about Jiangxi people,' says Andy.

'And you gave up smoking sixty a day to go on the Long March,' continues Sitao.

We are all laughing now. Andy quit smoking more than ten years ago. But Sitao is both shocked and amused. He shakes his head. 'I can't believe it, I can't believe it.'

It's the first time Sitao has read a story in the Chinese press about a subject he knows intimately, and while it had occurred to him journalists might get their facts wrong, he never realized they might just make things up. Having both worked in the Chinese media, Andy and I are less surprised. A particularly fond memory is of the *Beijing Evening News* report that said that the United

States Congress was threatening to move to either Miami, Florida or Charlotte, North Carolina unless it got a retractable roof on the Capitol Building. The source for the story was the satirical newspaper *The Onion*. The *Evening News* was eventually obliged to admit that 'some of [the article's] contents were identical to *The Onion*'s joke article,' but went on to explain that 'some small American newspapers frequently fabricate offbeat news to trick people into noticing them, with the aim of making money.'

All Sitao knows about country life, he admits, comes from the racier sections of the Chinese press, which are not afraid to print tales of neo-feudal corruption by village leaders. Now he wants first-hand confirmation.

'I heard a village head is like a king,' says Sitao. 'He can do whatever he wants, even sleep with whichever girls he likes. I really want to know if this is true.'

Sitao's thirst for knowledge is perturbing. I'm caught in two minds – I'd also love to know what the village head gets up to, but at this stage I'm afraid to ask. I don't want us to be mistaken for journalists, whose movements in China are carefully controlled and monitored. If word got around that two English journalists were walking through rural Jiangxi and interviewing peasants about their leaders' sex lives, the Long March might be brought to a premature climax.

The next day we leave Xinfeng for Youshan. Outside a village called Heqiu, Sitao accosts a peasant while we take a break.

'How much money does the village head here make?' he asks.

'Between 2,000 and 3,000 yuan a month,' says the peasant.

'That's not much,' says Sitao. 'Why would anyone want to be the village head for that much money?'

'Well, that's just the money we know about. There are

other ways for him to make money. For example, if a family has an extra child, they must pay a fine, and the village head will keep some of the money.'

'Wouldn't you like to be the village head?' asks Sitao.

'Yes, but it's impossible,' says the peasant, 'Even though we vote, no one knows really what is the true result.'

In most cases where we asked, villagers elected their village head (the exceptions were in certain ethnic minority areas). The village head's authority is theoretically subordinate to the Party Secretary, who is unelected. This is as far as popular democracy, in the Western sense, goes in China. By and large, village heads are exactly the kind of people you would expect to emerge as leaders in the kind of democratic system we're used to in the West – drawn from the wealthiest, best educated families in the village. The Heqiu peasant's cynicism was symptomatic of an attitude we encountered in Jiangxi and Guangdong, where people appeared more openly cynical about their leaders than anywhere else.

Sitao turns his attention to a passing family with three children, two more than stipulated by the local planned birth regulations.

'How much did you have to pay for the extra children?' he asks.

'Five thousand yuan each,' says the father.

Sitao is staggered. A peasant family in Jiangxi would do well to make 5,000 yuan in a year. 'Where do you find that kind of money?'

'We borrowed it from other members of the family, and we pay it back bit by bit as we earn.'

The family has also been taxed 100 yuan a year per family member to build the road on which we are walking, the 'Da A Section' of the Xinfeng-Chijiang highway. The town of Da A is the administrative centre of the area, and just before reaching it, we come across a marble memorial recording contributions to the building of the road. A donation of 500 yuan or more is enough to get your name inscribed on the stone.

Sitao is vexed again. 'Look, the primary school gave 26,000 yuan, but the local agricultural bank only gave 1,800. The middle school gave 15,000, but the tax office gave 1,100.'

To me, it's more surprising that such a low-level local government is responsible for a section of a major highway. The peasant who paid his taxes to support the road says he did so gladly, as a better road is in his interests as well as everybody else's. He got a poor return on his investment, though, because as soon as we reach the border of Da A with the next administrative district, the road stops being a sealed highway and becomes a semi-sealed strip of mud. We see this time and again – a well-maintained road in one district turning into a wretched track in the next. Locals put these anomalies down to 'corruption', which seems the standard excuse for anything not up to scratch.

The Long March draws curious crowds throughout Jiangxi, but Youshan is the first place we are chased down the street by a mob of screaming kids.

Sitao seems embarrassed.

'Is this how they normally behave when you arrive?' he asks.

'Haven't you seen foreigners before?' I ask one pre-teen girl.

'Oh yes,' she says.

'Where?'

'On TV.'

That's it! That's who we are to children. We aren't real; we're a TV show. Best of all, we are free and we are interactive. The English students lead the charge.

'Do you like Chinese food?'

'How do you like Youshan?'

'Do you like your country?'

'Do you like China?'

'I can't take this much longer,' says Andy. 'Where the hell is the guesthouse?'

'No guesthouse. No guesthouse,' says our young audience, loath to lose us.

I force a passage to the local government office, where I find a young man who leads me to an unmarked store doubling as accommodation. I explain why we are in Youshan.

'Really! The boss here is an old revolutionary,' says the young official.

'You're kidding!'

'No, I think he even did the Long March.'

You think? How strange that in such a small town anyone should be unsure of Chen Jie's remarkable life story. Chen greets me clad in a spotless, deep-blue Mao suit. He moves slowly but without frailty and seems nervous of me at first. But after I explain our journey he leads us to a restaurant across the street and sits with us while we eat, gradually sharing memories of his life as a revolutionary soldier.

'I was eleven years old when I joined the Red Army,' he says. 'The army came through my village, Chang'an, near Youshan in 1934. I got on very well with the soldiers. They didn't cheat, curse or beat the peasants. When they left, they asked me if I wanted to go with them. I said "yes" and went.'

As simple as that, a snap decision at the age of eleven to join an army he had known for only a day, to fight for a cause he knew almost nothing about. Chen's father was dead. Like Zeng Shaodong, he wouldn't see his mother again for eighteen years.

'I felt like I'd become part of a family,' Chen says. 'At the start, I had no work to do, I just walked. My feet hurt a lot and my unit leader allowed me to ride a horse and made sure my feet were washed. There were many people to take care of me – I was only a child – and so I felt very thankful. I would do anything for this feeling. I would die for it. This was how the soldiers felt about the army. When the leaders called for volunteers to put a bomb in a pillbox [a probable suicide mission], many would volunteer.

'There were Guomindang everywhere – front, back, both sides. I felt very scared every day. The older soldiers told me not to be afraid. Listen to the sounds of the bullets, they said, and you'll know how close they are and whether it's dangerous.

'If we killed landlords and distributed the property, maybe we could get something good to eat. Otherwise we only ate plain rice, which I carried in a small bag by myself. I remember it was very cold, I only had half a thin blanket because I was only a child. My sandals were made for me by adults – I didn't know how to make them myself.'

Chen didn't finish the Long March. He says he was injured in the area around Kangding in Sichuan, where he was left behind in the care of a local family. He eventually rejoined the army to fight the Japanese in 1938, and finally returned home in 1952 to run a state provisions store. His mother was overwhelmed. 'Don't cry, Mama,' Chen told her. 'I'm alive, I've come back.'

He married Li Shuixiang, who at six had been bought by his mother to help around the house. She cost eighteen baskets of grain. Together, they had three sons and one daughter.

After dinner, Chen takes us back to our room at the top of his home. Li Shuixiang brings a bucket of hot water to bathe our feet – it is about 3 feet in diameter, easily big enough for all three young marchers. Chen sits with us a while longer and I ask if he remembers any songs from the days of the Long March.

Chen sings:

'Soldiers
Remember the flag that leads us
Co-operate to go forward
For the Chinese Workers and Peasants Red Army
Begin the counterattack
Create a base
Must strive, must strive.'

As he finishes this song, a single tear runs down from Chen's right eye. While Sitao talks, he turns his head away to wipe it clear.

After Chen leaves, Sitao won't let us sleep.

'He reminds me of my grandfather, you know, the one who died last year,' he says. 'He was always talking about the Communist Party, but I wasn't interested. I thought it was all just bullshit. But I never met a real Long Marcher before. When he said he believed in that, "Serve the people heart and soul" stuff, he really meant it.'

It's fashionable to be cynical about the modern Communist Party. Ordinary people see Party members squandering public money on 'study sessions' that are less socialism than social event; a liggers' world of free banquets and booze, karaoke and ten-pin bowling. Party leaders cruise the streets in chauffeur-driven black limousines with tinted windows. I have never met a member under fifty who said they joined for ideological reasons. They join to gain access to jobs, money and power – though many do see that power as the power to do good. But there was once something about the Party that could conquer hearts and minds. After listening to Chen Jie all evening, the last thing Sitao says to us before bed is, 'I want to think more about this. I want to talk to more old Communists and understand more about them.'

Although we might become the first foreigners to retrace the Long March, twenty years ago a Chinese journalist and former soldier named Luo Kaifu claimed to be the first person to walk from Jiangxi to Shaanxi in the Red Army's footsteps. We met him once in Beijing and made use of his published diary in planning our own journey. No matter how much we might feel we don't know what we're doing, at least we know we're better prepared than Luo Kaifu was. He told us he had the money to buy only one piece of equipment before he left – a brand new bag that was promptly stolen, or you might say 'exchanged', as the thief left a tatty old bag in its place.

Twenty more years of 'reform and opening' also ease our passage through rural China. In the mid-1980s, peasants would most likely have called the police at the sight of two foreigners. Now they ask if we might help bring 'foreign investment' into their area. Standards of living have risen to make many once remote, poverty-stricken areas relatively comfortable.

Nowhere does this seem more apparent than after we cross Youshan Mountain into Dayu County. The first major town is called Chijiang, which Luo Kaifu remembered as a pretty desperate place. 'The windows of the school have no glass,' he wrote. 'What's more, there is no money for electric lights in the classroom. Instead, they use candles and oil lamps. Local people save their eggs and meat for festivals.'[4]

We find Chijiang transformed by the highway that now cuts through, linking the major cities of Ganzhou and Shaoguan via Dayu County Town. For nearly 2 miles, this road is lined with new buildings, cleaner and better than anything we have seen outside the county towns. Most host some form of business, principally restaurants, guesthouses, furniture stores and motorcycle shops. The new school has glass windows. A group of schoolgirls directs us to a four-storey building on the corner of what might loosely be called a 'square'. For 50 yuan, we spend the night in what now seems the height of luxury – a clean room with a hot shower. Across the 'square' is an internet bar.

Twenty years ago, Chijiang was the kind of place you dreamed of leaving. Today, we meet a family who have moved hundreds of kilometres from Guangxi to open a home-distilled liquor store here. Every other young man appears to have a motorbike – and nothing to do but ride it up and down the street with his friends. Everywhere the fields and shops are full of women hard at work. The streets, however, are full of men either riding motorcycles or lounging against them, smoking. Urban Motorcycle Man can also be seen playing pool and mahjong. He chews sunflower seeds and spits them onto the floor. He grows a bum-fluff moustache. He likes to ride around in pairs, showing off to girls and shouting 'HA-LOO!' at foreigners in a comical high voice.

The Dayu County authorities have contacted Jia Ji to say we are not welcome to pass through their area. The Long March route goes through a closed military training zone in Dayu, they say. The county is officially closed.

This emerges as an object lesson in asking the right questions. Our road map of south-east China shows a highway straight through the county – it can't all be closed, can it? Jia Ji calls them back and asks, 'Isn't there some kind of compromise? What if they pass through the county along the highway?'

'Oh, yes, that would be fine.'

We aren't committed to following the 'exact' route of the Long March. We know that will probably be impossible – even if such a thing exists. Not only were there three main columns, but within those columns soldiers also moved along several different paths as they searched for food (with 86,000 people, feeding the First Front

Army was a major challenge) and a safe passage. Reconstructing a route is therefore bound to be a slightly impressionistic business. We're doing our best to follow the central column with which the leadership marched, as that is the best documented and most direct, but we're prepared for mistakes and insurmountable obstacles. Mistakes we'll just have to live with; obstacles we will walk around.

Once in the county town, we find lodgings in 'the first 2-star modern foreign travel hotel in Dayu County'. Dayu, says the Chinglish blurb in the hotel, is the 'World Tungsten Capital'. So much for a 'closed military district'. It seems all we have to worry about is missing the old trail that went over the pass from Dayu into Guangdong Province. First, however, we have to deal with the fact that the daily evening thunderstorm has expanded to an all-day downpour. Previously, we knew the rain as *da yu*, or 'big rain', but the maid in the Mudanting Hotel teaches us a new phrase: *bao yu*, or 'torrential rain'. We hang our sodden clothes under the air conditioner and by a unanimous vote agree to sit out the storm. The next day, Dayu makes the national news for its record-breaking rainfall. I feel aggrieved. Luo Kaifu's diary suggests this should be the dry season in Jiangxi. Since we set out from Yudu two weeks ago, it has rained 11 days out of 14.

On the third day, the *bao yu* eases. As promised, we head south along the highway to Meiguan, the pass into Guangdong named after the plum-blossom trees that adorn the hillsides. Three miles out of town, we spot two policemen by the roadside. Andy ignores them and walks faster into the distance, but the senior officer catches my eye and waves me over. I start rehearsing excuses and explanations, but the cop has no interest in hearing me out.

'Have something to eat,' he interrupts.

'Um, well, I've already eaten, thanks.'

'Where are you going?'

'Meiguan.'

'Are you going by the footpath?'

Ha! Nice try, copper.

'No, no, of course not. We're taking the main road.'

'You don't want to do that,' says the cop. 'That road's still under construction, and besides, you can walk over the mountain by the old footpath Chen Yi used.'

He points down the road to a turn about 50 yards away.

'Look, your friend's already gone past it.'

I call Andy back and together we start up the track only to find our way barred not by a military patrol, but by a ticket office. It costs us 10 yuan each to get into the official Meiguan 'scenic spot', through which we can walk across the border via the path that a tourist guide we meet on the Guangdong side tells us has been in use since the time of Qin Shihuang, China's first emperor, who ruled from 221-210 BC.

Except for the guide and his three-man group, we have Meiguan to ourselves. The plum blossom has fallen and a grey drizzle makes the ancient flagstones treacherous. The guide tells us the path was paved in the Tang Dynasty, 1,300 years ago. And yes, he says, the Red Army walked this way.

It's a puzzle. Where is this military zone and why does everybody say the Long March route lies through it?

We step gingerly down the Tang steps into Province No.2 of the Long March. I don't much care about un-answered questions, because this is our first really im-portant milestone. I reckon the further we go, the easier it will be to explain ourselves. If we have already walked through one province, why should authorities in another province make a fuss?

'They thought it was fine in Jiangxi,' I will protest. 'What's your problem?'

In my imagination, this works every time.

Guangdong

2004 GDP per head: 19,316 yuan ($2,333)
Population: 86,420,000
Ethnic minority population: 1,230,000 (1.42%)
Main minorities: 46.4% Zhuang, 16.5% Yao,
2.3% She, 2.1% Hui, 1.5% Manchu

(China Census 2000, National Bureau of Statistics of China)

Hunan

2004 GDP per head: 9,117 yuan ($1,101)
Population: 64,400,000
Ethnic minority population: 6,575,300 (10.2%)
Main minorities: 40.1% Tujia, 29.2% Miao, 15.5% Zhuang,
12.8% Dong, 10.7% Yao, 1.91% Bai, 5% Hui,
2% Mongolian, 0.1% Manchu, 0.1% Uygur

(China Census 2000, National Bureau of Statistics of China)

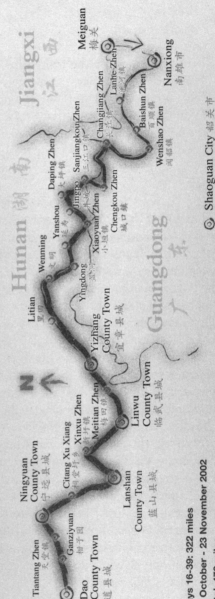

Days 16-39: 322 miles
31 October - 23 November 2002
Total: 473 miles

Chapter 2

A Minority of Two

Guangdong Province is the birthplace of the Guomindang party, founded by Sun Yat-sen in 1912, the year after the last Chinese emperor abdicated. The party immediately became one of the most important contenders to fill the political vacuum. Sun was no left-winger – his political philosophy was based on what he called the 'Three People's Principles': nationalism, democracy and livelihood. But in the early 1920s, Sun fell under the influence of the Soviet Union. Since the Chinese Communist Party had been founded only in 1921 and its membership was just a few hundred, Stalin saw the 30,000-strong Guomindang as his best bet for extending influence into China. For his part, Sun Yat-sen wanted Soviet money and military hardware. He agreed to reorganize the Guomindang along Soviet revolutionary lines and in 1924 persuaded the reorganization congress to accept an alliance with the Communists. Despite their numerical weakness, the Communists accounted for 10 out of 41 members of the Guomindang's new Central Executive Committee. One of them was Mao Zedong.

After Sun Yat-sen died of liver cancer at the age of fifty-eight in 1925, his protégé Chiang Kai-shek came to dominate both the political and military apparatus of the party. Chiang was thirty-seven when Sun died, and soon to abandon his second wife to marry Sun's sister-in-law. As a young man, Chiang had spent a year at military school in Japan. He returned to China to join the republican revolution that unseated the imperial Qing Dynasty in 1911, after which he divided his time between revolution and revelry, carousing around Shanghai with associates from the underworld Green Gang. He became Sun Yat-sen's military adviser in 1916 and by the early 1920s was the party's senior military figure. In 1924, Chiang set up the Whampoa Military Academy, whose graduates formed the nucleus of the Guomindang's regular army. 'If I control the army, I will have the power to control the country,' he said, according to his second wife, Chen Jieru. 'It is my road to leadership.'[1]

Chiang had distrusted Communists at least since a trip to the Soviet Union in 1923. As Chiang saw it, the Soviets' promises of aid were half-hearted and insincere. On his return, he wrote, 'The sole aim of the Russian party is to make the Chinese Communist Party its legitimate heir.' He told Sun Yat-sen's lieutenant, Liao Zhongkai, 'My personal observations lead me to the conclusion that the Russian Communist Party cannot be wholly trusted. I told you that we could believe only 30 per cent of what the Russians had to say. That was really an understatement.'[2]

The united front between the Guomindang and the Communist Party survived for two years after Sun Yat-sen's death. Chiang Kai-shek continued to accept aid and advice from the Soviet Union, but relations began to break down as it became clear that Chiang was fundamentally opposed to the left. In March 1927, Chiang turned on his allies and declared what his secretary called a 'bloodthirsty war to eliminate the enemy within'.[3] On 12 April 1927, soldiers and members of the Green Gang loyal to Chiang began rounding up and executing workers, labour organizers and Communists in Shanghai, where the Party leadership was based. The subsequent 'White Terror' claimed hundreds of thousands of lives, most horrifically in Hunan Province in the wake of the 'Horse Day Incident' on 21 May, when the garrison commander began a three-week killing spree that slaughtered 10,000 people in and around Changsha, the provincial capital. In the four Hunan counties of Chaling, Leiyang, Liuyang and Pingjiang, the terror claimed nearly 300,000 lives.[4]

The violent break from the Guomindang convinced the Communists they needed their own armed forces. As Mao Zedong said less than four months later, 'From now on we should pay the greatest attention to military affairs. We must know that political power is obtained out of the barrel of a gun.'[5]

The early efforts of the Communist army were not encouraging. The first major action was the 'Nanchang Uprising' of 1 August 1927, in which around 20,000 soldiers took the capital of Jiangxi Province and held it for four days before marching south into Guangdong Province. Within two weeks more than half this army was gone, mostly lost to desertion. The leaders ultimately reached the Guangdong coast in early October. There they abandoned the remaining troops and fled by sea to Shanghai and Hong Kong. 'The Nanchang Uprising thus came to a tragic end,' wrote Zhang Guotao, one of those leaders and a founder member of the Communist Party who would later play a major role in the Long March. Only a force of about 1,000 men under Zhu De, the future Red Army Commander-in-Chief, fought on after becoming isolated from the main force in the Guangdong–Jiangxi border region.

Mao was not at Nanchang. He had been placed in charge of organizing the 'Autumn Harvest Uprising' in his home province of Hunan. The insurrection was scheduled for 16 September, but it never got started. Mao's troops were defeated almost immediately and Mao himself was briefly captured. He escaped into tall grass while being taken to local militia headquarters for execution. Mao retreated south with his remaining forces, finally taking

refuge in early October in a poor, mountainous district of
Jiangxi Province called Jinggangshan. In April the following year, Zhu De and his troops arrived in Mao's base
area. The two armies united to form what would become
known as the 'Zhu-Mao Army'.

Although Jinggangshan was an excellent stronghold, it
was too poor to support the forces gathered there. In
winter 1928-9, 25,000 enemy troops from fourteen Guomindang regiments began to converge. The Zhu-Mao
Army did not have enough provisions to sit out the winter.
Mao opted for a tactic he would return to several times in
the future, not least on the Long March – he ran away. On
14 January 1929, the main force of 3,500 men left
Jinggangshan by an obscure mountain route, and the
Zhu-Mao Red Army entered a nomadic period.

It was in southern Jiangxi that they at last began to
build a stable base of operations. Communications were
so poor in this area that it was difficult for Guomindang
troops to move against the Reds, who used guerrilla
tactics to excellent effect. Between December 1930 and
September 1931, the Zhu-Mao Army fought off three
'encirclement campaigns' by Chiang Kai-shek. They were
so successful that the Communist Party leadership began
to retreat from the Shanghai underground to the rural
Jiangxi base area, shortly afterwards renamed as the
'Chinese Soviet Republic'.

At this point, the Communists were completely surrounded by hostile forces. The Jiangxi base was their most
important stronghold, at its peak in 1932 incorporating
four to five million people, but there were two others. One
was in the border region of Hubei, Henan and Anhui
provinces, controlled by around 15,000 soldiers under the
command of Zhang Guotao; the other was on the border
between Hubei and Hunan provinces, where 10,000 Red
soldiers had installed themselves under the former bandit
leader He Long.

After the defeat of Chiang Kai-shek's Third Encirclement Campaign, the Reds were given some respite by the Japanese invasion and occupation of Manchuria (northeast China) in September 1931. But in summer 1932, Chiang put this distraction to one side and returned his attention to the Communists. Zhang Guotao was driven out of his base to a still more remote area in the northwest; He Long also gave way, moving west into Guizhou Province. Wrongly believing he had annihilated these two lesser Red forces, Chiang now turned his armies towards the final target: the Jiangxi Soviet Republic.

This time, the defence was directed by Zhu De and Zhou Enlai – Zhou now in Mao's old position as Political Commissar for the Red Army. Mao had been ejected from this post in October 1932, after which he played little part in military affairs and instead devoted his time to the civil administration of the Chinese Soviet Republic. The new leaders succeeded brilliantly, defeating several Guomindang divisions and taking 10,000 prisoners. The Fourth Encirclement was called off in spring 1933.

The Soviet Republic would enjoy no more great victories. For the fifth and final encirclement campaign, Chiang refined his tactics. Advised by the German General Hans Von Seeckt, he surrounded Red China with half a million soldiers and began to squeeze the life out of the Red base.

I've probably given the impression that Chiang Kai-shek in 1934 was the untrammelled ruler of all China, challenged only by the ragtag Red Army. That would be the wrong impression, because Chiang was a good deal less than that. The Reds could never have escaped him otherwise.

China's government had weakened progressively during the latter years of the Qing Dynasty. Within five years of the dynasty's fall in 1911, central authority disintegrated entirely. Although the Republic of China, declared in 1912, persisted in name, the country fragmented into fiefdoms controlled by 'warlords' who headed independent armies. Chiang Kai-shek's great achievement was to unite enough of these warlords under the Guomindang banner to be able to consolidate a national government at Nanjing in 1928. Chiang doled out titles and positions of official authority to the warlords, but largely failed to dislodge them from their power bases across the country. In many parts, Chiang's writ ran only as far as the provincial bosses permitted. And because the warlords rightly suspected that Chiang would like to get rid of them altogether, many did their best to keep him at arm's length.

One such was the warlord boss of Guangdong Province, Chen Jitang, who in 1934 thought Chiang was a bigger menace than Red bandits. The Jiangxi Soviet Republic lay just north of the Guangdong border, and Chen regarded this as a useful buffer against his ambitious master. He sent a secret message to Zhou Enlai in September 1934 proposing private talks. Zhou jumped at the chance: 'We can make use of General Chen's anti-Chiang Kai-shek attitude,' he allegedly said.[6] (I think of quotes such as Zhou's as more likely correct in spirit than in fact; I prefer to imagine him greeting Chen's message with a colourful expletive of delight.) The upshot was that two Communist emissaries were sent to negotiations in a village in northern Guangdong, where a mutual non-aggression pact was sealed. After the Red Army broke out of the Jiangxi Soviet area one month later, they passed through the Guangdong border regions virtually unopposed, moving through a corridor in the mountains well north of the city of Nanxiong.

I have been promoted to Route-Finder General as Andy can't read the Chinese map. Not that the map is any use. It says the only road runs due south for 17 miles from

Meiguan to Nanxiong – and we're supposed to be head-ing west. I spend much of the morning in head-scratching discussions with toothy old characters, all of whom claim ignorance of any paths over the mountains that corral cars and Long Marchers onto the four-lane blacktop highway. And because I'm a novice at this game, I believe them. As we drift ever further south, I console myself with one gentleman's suggestion that a handful of Red scouts got as far as the suburbs of Nanxiong. Not lost at all then – I declare the revelation that Nanxiong is, in fact, on the Long March trail, which usefully means a trip to the supermarket and a night in a room with hot running water. Andy doesn't challenge my historical revisionism.

The march into town, however, is neither comfortable nor convenient. This is the first time we have been on a long stretch of sealed highway, and the experience gives a stiff two fingers to the armchair advisers who told us, 'all the new roads will make your Long March easier'. If the Meiguan-Nanxiong highway is a measure of things to come, our Long March will mainly be unpleasant, unin-spiring and dangerous. And while it raises blisters on my soles, the road simultaneously sinks my spirits. Officially, Guangdong is the wealthiest province in China, but here the small towns and villages look depressed and depres-sing. The mud brick of the village homes is no longer the rich orange of Jiangxi, but a washed-out yellow. Many stand side-by-side with half-finished brick constructions that are being built in stages, progressing in fits and starts as families receive occasional bursts of income – for example from those members who have gone to the cities to *da gong*. The market in Meiling offers a miserable selection of greying meats and bruised fruits. I pause to consider taking a photo, but the feeling of voyeurism is too strong. As I put my camera away, a stallholder shouts: 'What are you doing here? This place is too poor!'

A giant cement works sits moribund above the village, a

grey hulk with smashed windows on a loop of the old road that has been cut off by the new highway like an oxbow lake. All the cement business is now being done by family-size concerns that line the highway, belching clouds of white dust from shacks and lean-tos. Instead of bringing wealth and modernity, I feel like this road picks up whatever is worth having in this area and takes it somewhere else. Villages half a mile across the valley look marooned, like rusting hulks half sunk in disused channels. Perhaps they were dying anyway, and the road is simply hurrying them out of their misery.

The diverse agriculture of west Jiangxi has given way almost exclusively to rice cultivation in the fields of north Guangdong, for which late October is harvest time. Peasants are spreading their grain across sections of the highway to dry in the sunshine. As if this isn't perilous enough, they cordon these areas off with boulders, obliging trucks and buses to swerve around them.

'Don't you think that's dangerous?' Andy asks a young man raking a yellow carpet of rice across the southbound lane.

'*Mei shi*,' answers the youth.

A lot of things are '*mei shi*' on the Long March trail. Smoke two packs a day? *Mei shi*, Chinese people are very healthy. Drink a bottle of hard liquor and ride your motorcycle home? *Mei shi*, it's not dangerous. Wake you up in the middle of the night to look at your documents? *Mei shi*, we're the police. Andy's Chinese textbook suggests *mei shi* means, 'That's OK'. But in practice, it appears to mean, 'I don't give a toss.'

Although we manage to turn west at Nanxiong, locals continue to frown on our efforts to find the Red Army trail. They point north over more mountains and say no, the old paths aren't there any more. No one goes that way. Why don't you get the bus?

The Guangdong people call this the Beishan ('northern

mountain') region. Not long after the Long March began, these thickly wooded slopes became a sanctuary for those Reds left behind in the Soviet zone. Only around 30,000 soldiers were left to guard the Soviet Republic of China; at least a third of these men were already wounded. The Guomindang took Ruijin, the former Red capital, on 10 November 1934. Yudu fell on 17 November, a month after the main force of the Red Army pulled out. The remaining Reds were scattered, captured or killed. Mao Zedong's thirty-year-old brother, Mao Zetan, was shot dead by a Guomindang patrol and his body was put on public display in Ruijin. Zetan had been looking after his elder brother's two-year-old son, Xiao Mao. Now Zetan's wife, He Yi, placed Xiao Mao in the care of a peasant family. He was never seen again. Only a small band led by Chen Yi and Xiang Ying survived as guerrilla fighters hiding in the mountains. For the next three years, Chen Yi once said, they 'lived like animals',[7] hunted by Guomindang units that sometimes set fire to the forest to try and flush the guerrillas out.

By Chinese – and Long March – standards, the Guangdong mountains are small potatoes. There are no snowcapped peaks among them, and the passes are low enough that we regularly walk over two or three a day. Relatively speaking, they are just hills. By English standards, however, they are enormous and exhausting. Their slopes are still covered in the dense greenery that shielded Chen Yi and his men; there is no way through without a machete, no paths at all that we can see, and so we wind slowly up and down the interminable switchbacks of the modern road. These are lonesome days. The mountains defy cultivation, leaving humans to scrabble for space in small, trash-strewn towns along the narrow valley floors. Not much traffic bothers us here.

At last, there's a change in the weather. After a fortnight of rain and general misery, we roll up our waterproofs and walk in short-sleeved shirts, and each day after lunch we lie down to cool off and sleep for two hours. Every evening, I regret this siesta as the light fades and the road ahead shows no sign of anywhere habitable. The days are growing shorter and five minutes walking in the dark feels like half an hour in daylight. The unpleasantness of night walking is compounded by the uncertainty surrounding the day's two key issues – food and lodging. Since we may be the first foreigners ever to walk through these villages, and since we're each around twice the size of the average local, night-time is definitely not the right time to be knocking on doors and begging for help. We're a bit less intimidating when people can see us coming from a distance.

And since the forest makes camping out of the question, once the sun sets we have no choice but to push on into the night. Eventually, we know we must reach a small town, the administrative centre for the district. There's never more than a day's march between these towns, perhaps because in the days before roads and cars people still shared our aversion to sleeping rough. It's fine to arrive in towns after dark. Almost all of them have some form of guesthouse that stays open until 9 or 10 p.m., and in town a hulking great foreigner's money is just as good as anyone else's.

So it is that we haul our weary selves up and over one last mountain at sunset and behold the mining town of Lanhe laid out along the valley below. It looks deserted as we follow the switchbacks down. Few buildings show any light at all; those that do cast an orange glow like a dying fire. Where the main road reaches the valley floor and enters the town, the buildings are new, but empty – their fronts either shuttered or unfinished. Unlit streetlights line what is suddenly a treacherous, potholed track. It takes another couple of hundred metres for the town to show any signs of life – a hairdresser's, a clothes store and finally a pair of restaurant-cum-guesthouses, one on either side of the street at the point where buses pick up and drop off.

A random choice gives us a 10-yuan room scattered with playing cards and cigarette butts. Yes, says the landlady, we are the first foreigners she has ever seen in Lanhe. But no, she doesn't know anything about Long Marchers. A gaggle of children clusters at the door, pushing to take turns for a peek. The local policeman has to force his way through to make a rather nonplussed and almost apologetic request to see our documents. He's never seen a foreign passport before, and so I give him some Chinese newspaper clippings about our Long March to help him fill out the report he says he has to make to the Nanxiong Public Security Bureau. Although he doesn't seem especially bothered to have two strangers in town, I don't want him wondering where our 'official permission' might be, so while he copies out names and numbers I try some diversionary small talk.

'What's life like in Lanhe these days?'

'Not so good,' he says. 'The mines used to be quite busy in the '70s and '80s, but since reform and opening started the state-owned businesses have lost the government's support. Thing's haven't gone so well since they had to fend for themselves.'

Satisfied with *Jiangxi Daily*'s explanation of our endeavours, the cop warns us that we're still off track. He gestures north as he conjures up a picture of yet more mountains standing between us and the proper trail. I don't care. I've walked 21 miles today, the furthest yet, my feet are killing me and all I want is a bottle of beer and a game of football.

Saturday night is the most important night of the week for Long March morale, because on Saturdays, China Central Television's sports channel, CCTV-5, broadcasts a double bill of German and English Premiership football.

This has become central to our view of the immediate future. Andy badgers me to look ahead in our schedule and calculate when we will next make a county town, or at least a larger *zhen* (the next-biggest urban centre after a county town) where we can get access to a TV. Both of us clutch at these links to former lives. No road is too long if it promises football at the end.

Kick-off is 10 p.m. The only television in our guest-house is downstairs in the main dining room. But when we descend, the lights are out and the door is barred. We reel into the street. It's completely dark. Ten o'clock on a Saturday night and Lanhe has gone to bed. Don't they know there's a game on?

'There's got to be somewhere open,' says Andy. 'We've just got to look harder.'

As our eyes adjust, we perceive a faint glow from the hairdresser's. Lanhe's entire nightlife consists of three friendly ladies delighted to welcome two frustrated football fans. They have a TV, too.

'Sit down, sit down,' says the boss, 'Would you like your hair washed?'

'If we have a hair wash, can we watch your television?' I ask.

'Sure.'

Andy snatches the remote control and starts scanning the channels and . . . *there is no CCTV-5*. Hold the shampoo. Now I know we're in trouble. We have walked so far from civilization, there isn't even football on TV.

Civilized or not, television sets are ubiquitous, and the peasants leave them on from breakfast until bedtime. As far as I can tell, TV schedules in rural China are entirely devoted to two forms of programme: cheesy historical soap operas featuring regular bouts of piss-poor kung fu, or government propaganda. While the peasants clearly prefer the former, the latter is currently in the ascendant thanks to the opening of the 16th Congress of the Communist Party of China (CPC) on 8 November.

I studied in the USSR before the fall of Soviet Communism, but I've never seen anything like this. Day after day, vast outdoor spectaculars extol the Party in song and dance. Even the audiences are choreographed for the cameras. In between shows, commercials are supplemented by songs such as the jaunty 'Without the Communist Party there is no New China', performed by ageing divas in flowing dresses of red or white, standing on the Great Wall or above the crashing rapids of the Yellow River at Hebian, or swirling against a backdrop of marching soldiers and rolling tanks, swooping helicopters and soaring space rockets. The 'news' is a string of reports from around the country detailing festivities in honour of the CPC. One comes from an ethnic minority region of Sichuan Province and is presented by a reporter in full ethnic costume, hat and all. Behind her a parade of colourful characters dance and strike interestingly primitive musical instruments.

Most important of all, however, is something called the '*sange daibiao*', or the 'Three Represents'. It seems the Party Congress has decreed that no one on television can open their mouth without mentioning them. The Chinese people are studying the Three Represents, they are using the Three Represents to solve problems and develop the nation, they are even bringing the Three Represents to bear on the population question. While I pack my rucksack one morning, Andy channel surfs and stops at a quiz show designed to test Chinese students' knowledge of English. The quiz-master's very first question is, 'What are the *sange daibiao*?'

The student recites: 'The Communist Party represents the basic interests of the broad masses of the people, advanced culture, and advanced science and technology.'

The quiz-master says, 'The "Three Represents" would have been sufficient, but well done.'

The Three Represents are with us throughout our journey. Every media organ in the country hammers home the Three Represents message every day. Walls and buildings in every town and village feature yard-high slogans exhorting citizens to 'conscientiously study the Three Represents'. But what do they represent? Unlike the fresh-faced student on TV, no ordinary citizen we meet so far has a clue. They can't even recite them, let alone explain them. This ignorance is extraordinary. It seems this avalanche of political education sweeps over the people without leaving any trace. The best answer any non-Party person can come up with is a sixteen-year-old girl who ventures, 'Chairman Mao, Deng Xiaoping and, er, Jiang Zemin?'

The Party functionaries we encounter are a different matter. They can recite the same formula as the English student on TV, but they also struggle to say why they are obliged to learn it. They know the Three Represents are President Jiang Zemin's brainchild, his theoretical legacy to Chinese Communism, but they can't explain what Jiang has in mind.

It takes us two months and nearly 1,000 miles to find someone who sees Jiang's legacy as more than an empty slogan. This is a gentleman who has studied both in the United States and the Party School in Beijing. The Three Represents, he says, are not meant for ordinary citizens. They are strictly for Party purposes, as a weapon for Jiang and his allies to use against their opponents. Jiang steps down as Party General Secretary at the 16th Congress; in March 2004, he retires as President as well. Putting the 'Three Represents' in the Constitution is his way of ensuring his chosen successor, Hu Jintao, and his supporters have the ideological backing to pursue a course that repels some Party members – opening the country ever further to the outside world and withdrawing the State ever further from the economy, diluting its historical responsibility to the workers and peasants. Where once the Communist Party represented the workers and peasants in the vanguard of the class struggle, now it merely represents 'the broad masses of the people'.

'It's straightforward,' says our Party friend. 'It's like justifying action by reference to the Bible – you find the appropriate text to fit your needs. The Three Represents make this very easy. Say, for example, there is a clash of interests within a local government between progressive leaders – theoretically on the side of Jiang and his supporters – and a group of corrupt officials who want to build themselves a new set of offices.

'The leaders may call a Three Represents study session, at which they will cite the "interests of the broad masses" and argue that government money would be better spent on a new hospital. There's nothing in the "Three Represents" to support spending money on yourself, so how are the opposition going to argue their case? Once upon a time, people cited Mao Zedong Thought or Deng Xiaoping Theory to defeat their opponents. Now Jiang's people have the Three Represents to back them up.'

At Chengkou, on the border of Guangdong and Hunan provinces, our path finally converges with the Red Army's. Twenty years earlier, Luo Kaifu passed this way during his retracing of the Long March. He wrote: 'To welcome the Red Army, the peasants dug a large pool for the local hot spring to allow the Red soldiers to wash. Now this place has become a high-class hot spring bath-house. A local government official tells me I must certainly have a wash there.'[8]

A high-class hot spring bathhouse is just what we need. To reach Chengkou took a 22-mile trek featuring baffling mountain trails and at least one major detour imposed by a rambling bull who – to my mind, at least – had no right to be standing on such a narrow footpath. And besides our generally filthy and dishevelled state, I'd also like to know if there are any old locals who might remember why they should have been so moved by the Reds as to dig them a hot bath.

We are accosted on the edge of the old town by a gentleman named Li Anmin, who laughs and shakes his head at our quest.

'That's not what happened at all,' he says. 'The hot spring was dug for the Guomindang commander here, Mo Furu. He ran away when the Red Army came and the soldiers used it, of course. Mo came back after the army left. That's his bathhouse.'

Li has a splendid head of sticky-up, salt-and-pepper hair, but he can't be much older than fifty: far too young to remember Reds or Guomindang bath fans.

'How do you know?' I ask.

'Follow me,' says Li.

The alleys in old Chengkou are still cobbled, a handful of decaying, two-storey wooden structures giving a faint impression of the town as it might have been 70 years, perhaps 300 years ago. Li leads us into a stained concrete building opposite the last surviving town gate. There are no customers, only a handful of male and female attendants passing the time with a game of cards. The place reeks of neglect, or is that just the sulphur? One man detaches himself from the card game to ask if we want a wash. 'No, no,' says Li. 'I'm just taking them to see Mo Furu's plaque.'

Li points to an engraved slab propped against the wall in the trash corner, where a square of unused space has developed into a general-purpose dump. A mound of empty plastic bottles keeps us at a polite distance.

'See,' says Li. 'That records the digging of the spring and the erection of the memorial plaque by Mo Furu in 1934.'

Propped against the other angle of the corner is a blank, grey slab roughly the same size as the plaque.

'Mo Furu left before Liberation and his plaque was taken down,' says Li. 'Then in the Cultural Revolution that stone was used to cover it up completely. Mo came back to Chengkou in 1984. He wanted to restore the spring and put his plaque back up, but the local government wouldn't let him.'

Li reckons Mo Furu is still alive, in his mid-nineties and living in Hong Kong. This spring must have meant a lot to him. After fifty years, it called him back. But it's hardly surprising the government turned him away. Even in these more liberal times, it would look odd for the local Communists to welcome the old Guomindang commander to restore a symbol of his former status and authority.

Mo Furu made his visit in 1984, the same year the local authorities lied to Luo Kaifu when he asked about the digging of Mo's spring. It wasn't a big lie, but Mo's plaque makes it a poignant one – the truth hidden in a corner and covered with rubbish.

We spend our first night in Hunan Province in the small town of Daping. Andy is itching to get online. I scoff: what a waste of time, there's no way a place like this is going have the internet.

Andy addresses the lady who runs our guesthouse:

'Excuse me, is there an internet bar in Daping?'

'There's one right down the street,' she says. 'I'll get my daughter to take you there.'

My expectations of backwardness along the Long March trail are regularly confounded. I expected access to electricity to be a major issue and consequently packed a solar cell large enough to charge all our equipment. I've decided to get rid of it already. I never imagined that almost every town would have a mobile telephone signal, and I certainly didn't expect so much internet access. In

the months ahead, there will be many places much smaller
than Daping that boast computers and internet connections. I rarely see anyone surf the net, though. The internet
bars are used almost exclusively for male teenagers to
practise smoking and playing violent computer games.

The map says that just west of Daping we will enter
areas inhabited by the Yao ethnic minority. The Yao are
one of fifty-five officially recognized minorities in China.
They number something over 2.5 million, living in mountain communities scattered across five South China provinces and one autonomous region. A friend in Beijing
warns, 'Those Yao are rather wild.' A local calls the area
'Hunan's Tibet'.

In the 1930s, the Communist Party and Guomindang
held very different views on China's ethnic diversity. The
Guomindang took their cue from the Party's founder, Sun
Yat-sen, whose opinion was that, 'we must facilitate the
dying out of all names of individual peoples inhabiting
China, i.e. Manchus, Tibetans etc . . . unit[ing] them in a
single cultural and political whole.'[9] In practice, 'facilitat-
ing' meant imposing a process of assimilation to Han
Chinese culture. The Communists rejected this assimila-
tionist policy. The 1931 Constitution of the Chinese
Soviet Republic stated: 'The Soviet Government of China
recognizes the right of self-determination of the national
minorities in China, their right to complete separation
from China, and to the formation of an independent state
for each national minority. All Mongolians, Tibetans,
Miao, Yao, Koreans, and others living on the territory
of China shall enjoy the full right to self-determination.'

That was an easy promise to make from their belea-
guered stronghold in Jiangxi. The Communists also found
it tactically useful on the Long March, when they passed
through many minority regions and needed to encourage
locals to help them. But once in power in 1949, the Party
no longer found it so appealing to grant 'the full right to

self-determination' to the various peoples living in the territory of China. In September that year in Beijing, the 'Common Programme of the Chinese People's Political Consultative Conference' came up with a new formulation: 'Each national autonomous area is an inseparable part of the People's Republic of China . . . The People's Republic of China will become a big fraternal and co-operative family composed of all its nationalities.'[10]

The country was therefore to be unified (by force, if necessary) into a multinational state, which meant state structures had to be created that reflected ethnic diversity and at least paid lip service to the notion of ethnic autonomy. The question was, how could seats in a People's Congress, for example, be allocated to minorities if no one knew exactly who and where those minorities were? The first attempt to identify the ethnic minorities involved a process of self-registration in the First National Census, which counted more than 400 ethnic groups, including more than 260 in Yunnan Province. From an administrative point of view, 400 separate minorities didn't look very practical. The government decided to ignore subjective identifications in favour of political expediency and 'objective' expert analysis. The result was an 'ethnic group definition' research project that aimed to establish an official catalogue of China's ethnic groups. Thirty-nine were recognized initially (including the Han majority), while another fifteen were reconsidered and added to the list during the period before the Second National Census in 1964. The Luoba minority won recognition in 1965 and a 56th group, the Jinuo people of Yunnan Province, was last to be formally registered in 1979.[11] The remaining groups from the original 400-plus were either classified as Han or placed in subgroups of 'official' minorities like the Yao. About a million Chinese people are still 'unidentified', as the government can't make up its mind what ethnicity they should be.

Andy told me he once visited an exhibition in the Drum Tower in Beijing devoted to the fifty-six nationalities of China. Every nationality was represented by a photograph of one of its members wearing traditional costume – every nationality but the Han, that is, who were represented by a picture of a man sitting at a computer wearing a suit and a large pith helmet, sorry, yellow hard hat. Andy was accompanied at the exhibition by our friend and former colleague Wu Wenzi. She was troubled by the suit-sporting Han gentleman, but for reasons she found hard to explain.

'You know I can't really say what he should wear. Han don't really have any identity of their own,' she said.

At the time, this struck Andy as an extraordinary statement from someone taught from the cradle to have pride in '5,000 years of civilization'. Yet given that the notion of Han nationality is a relatively recent invention that covers a diverse group of approximately 1.2 billion people, he shouldn't have been so surprised. The idea itself that there is a single Han race dates back only to the late nineteenth century, when European nationalist theories of blood and belonging began to filter into Chinese intellectual life. Sun Yat-sen was among those convinced there was one Han race bound by blood, history and a common culture, and he concluded that the Han's numerical superiority should translate into political primacy as well. Although Sun recognized five distinct peoples in China (Han, Manchu, Mongolian, Tibetan and Muslim), his anti-Manchu republican nationalism was supported by a mythical narrative showing how China had developed, 'a single state out of a single race' since the Qin Dynasty was founded in 221 BC.[12]

But the factors that fostered coherent national identities in Europe were largely absent in China. While European nations coalesced basically around language groups, with a standardized form of the 'national' language enforced by government-directed education systems, China's linguistic diversity persists even today. The local tongue spoken by Han people in Beijing is as different from those of Han residents of Shanghai or Hong Kong as Russian is from Polish, or Spanish from Italian. Mandarin is based on the language of the Beijing region, and its national role as a lingua franca was traditionally reserved for the educated classes. It has only begun to function as a true 'national' language for China's lower classes as a consequence of industrialization (leading to mass movements of labour around the country), mass education and television. Without a simple marker like language to cling to, many people share Wu Wenzi's uncertainty about what it means to be a Han. They have no obvious characteristic to distinguish themselves, not even a national costume or a single national cuisine – China has eight officially recognized national cuisines, each hailing from a different part of the country.

China's sheer size and economic backwardness have also held back the development of Han identity. In the smaller nations of Europe, education and mass communications combined much earlier to create a sense of shared experience, culture and history, all of which could be interpreted as elements in a single national identity. Those factors of economic development have only very recently come into play in China.

A particular feature of the Communists' minorities research project was the ethnic hierarchy it formalized. Each group was ranked on a scale of social development that began with 'primitive' and ended at 'socialist'. The Han at the time of the Communist land reform (1949–51) were deemed to be at the stage of 'late feudalism', while most minorities were classed lower down the scale of development. Minorities were thus officially declared 'backward', while the Han were the most progressive nationality and therefore the vanguard for other ethnic groups to catch up with.[13]

As in the 16th Party Congress news report we'd watched on TV, minority peoples in the Chinese media are generally portrayed wearing traditional costumes, and are almost always singing and dancing or engaged in some colourful customary activity. The media propagates a romanticized stereotype of 'primitive' society that appeals to a Han majority sense of cultural superiority. I've always suspected this TV image of the minorities was a fake, cooked up for the benefit of Han viewers, an image of primitive societies within China against which the Han can define themselves by way of contrast. I thought maybe it was comforting to the ill-defined majority that minorities were visibly different and 'backward'.

Wu Wenzi herself told Andy a story that fuelled my suspicions. Some friends of her uncle were Yao minority and she once went to visit them in Dao County in Hunan, not far from where we are now. She was interested in their background and minority customs, and was disappointed to find it was not like TV. Everyone looked the same as anywhere else. There were no colourful costumes, no strange languages and definitely no singing and dancing.

'I asked people there why they weren't wearing their traditional clothes,' said Wu. 'They said, "We don't do that anymore. We only get them out for special occasions. If we wore them into town, people would stare and point at us, so we don't bother." '

Wu badgered the grandmother of the family: can I see the clothes?

'They got them out, and then the grandmother said why not put them on? I got all dressed up and went for a walk around the village, where I bumped into a film crew from the county TV station.

'The director rushed across and asked me to join them.

He said, "We are filming a documentary on local economic development,"' and asked me if I would help. I said, "But I'm not local! I'm a Han, a Beijinger! I'm just here visiting."

'The director said that was no problem – it didn't matter. He already had got another girl dressed up in traditional costume, and they put us both in a pigsty and told us to pretend to work.

'So there I am – a city Han girl in Yao costume, working in a pigsty in the countryside to demonstrate local development. My friends back in Beijing thought it was hilarious.'

The Yao have clearly lost out in the struggle for land. The Han villages immediately west of Daping sit in a broad and fertile valley and are among the most attractive we have seen. We have walked up on to a higher plain, where the seasons are a couple of weeks out of sync. Where previously all labour was manual, here the fields are full of the sound of petrol engines driving the rice threshers. Beyond these, however, the path rises into mountains where farmland is scarce and poor. Passing an impossibly small paddy field, we bump into Qu Nianghua. He has holes in his clothes and wears cheap sandals. We offer him a mandarin. Most Han Chinese would refuse, then finally accept, but Qu accepts the fruit immediately. This is the only real cultural difference we can find: no customs or colourful clothes, just relative remoteness and poverty. In speech, physical appearance and dress, there is nothing to choose between the Yao and the Han around Daping. I wonder at first if I'm just oblivious to the differences because I'm an outsider, but the Yao themselves can find little to fix their own 'identity'.

'About 80 per cent of the people here are Yao,' says Li Ling'ao, seventy-four and a Yao himself. 'I know who's who so here I can tell Yao and Han apart, but I can't if I go somewhere else.'

Yanshou has been connected to the outside world by road since the 1950s, but it still feels cut off. It's the first urban *xiang* centre we've seen without a mobile phone tower, though locals say one will be built soon. To continue west from here means trekking straight over the mountain to Yindong Yao Minority Xiang – only 10 miles away by the Red Army trail, but 25 or 30 miles by road.

Everybody in this area treats us with great courtesy, to the point where it becomes too embarrassing to continue shopping. We are looking for fruit to buy for the next stage, but all anyone in the grocery shops has are a few mandarins they are reluctant to sell – but happy to give away as gifts. I notice an old woman giving a younger man a bag of mandarins and I ask if she will sell us some. She reaches into her bag, pulls out two of the best – and they are largely of poor quality – and hands them to me. 'Please take them,' she says.

I give up after that. I don't want to spend all my time in Yao country refusing the kindnesses of its wild inhabitants.

Jia Ji meets us in Yizhang to replace broken and worn-out equipment and bring Andy his heart's desire: a cup of fresh coffee. Her best intentions almost backfire when she discovers she has forgotten the cafetière, but I invoke the spirit of Gear Guy and create a coffee maker using a piece of filter paper and two chopsticks.

Home comforts apart, it's a great boost to have Jia Ji to share our experience with. I can already feel myself becoming ever so slightly jaded. I notice I'm retreating into myself to guard and conserve my emotional strength. When we set out, I was open to everything and everyone, absorbing and observing every possible new experience. I'm not like that anymore. I'm more wary and selective about who and what I interact with. Jia Ji brings a fresh perspective and undimmed enthusiasm. I sense an opportunity to give myself a good kick up the arse.

Jia Ji spends one day with us on the road, walking the 15 miles from Yizhang to Meitian, a flourishing coal town and by far the biggest *zhen* we have seen. It's easy marching all the way. Such hills as exist are gentle rollers. There isn't a rice terrace in sight. Village homes are strong and straight, mostly red brick instead of mud. Among these are new buildings covered in gleaming white tiles. We see children picking flowers and skipping instead of labouring. This is the wealthiest area we have passed, but the extra development brings familiar stresses – noise, filth, traffic, casual discourtesy and urban danger (our reunion dinner is interrupted by a chef chasing another guest out the door with a meat-cleaver). And although Jia Ji sets out full of positive thoughts, amused and gratified by the attention we receive on the road, by evening she announces, 'I hate men on motorcycles'.

It's reassuring to find common ground here. When Andy or I criticize some aspect of Chinese life, friends and colleagues tend to respond that the problem is that we're foreigners, and therefore don't understand China. But Jia Ji also doesn't like being yelled at from behind her back. She also notices that the shouts of 'ha-loo' rarely come from single people, but mostly from groups of men, or Motorcycle Men in twos and threes. She realizes that they're not being friendly at all – they're just showing off to each other. She notices this doesn't often happen in villages, that this juvenile peacock culture belongs to the towns. And the people who stop and talk to us and make friends with us don't yell and laugh. They don't put on funny high-pitched voices to cry, "Ha-loooOOOoooo" as they ride past, never to return.

We leave Jia Ji in Meitian. Our next meeting is fixed for Tongdao County Town in Hunan, about five weeks away. Beyond Tongdao, our next rendezvous point will be the most famous city in Long March history: Zunyi. Both of us feel that if we can make it to Zunyi, then everyone will have to start taking our effort seriously. But it's all too far down the road as we plod through Hunan. We're treated as objects of suspicion, yet tolerated. Police stop us on the street to inspect our documents and interrogate us on our intentions. We are tailed by unmarked cars with darkened windows. On the way to Citang Xu, we ask a peasant woman how far we have to go. A green Jeep passes, heading the other way back towards Lanshan County Town, but as we set off again we notice it slow, turn around and pull up next to the same woman. It follows 50 yards behind us for the 3 miles to Citang Xu and parks directly outside the guesthouse where we seek shelter. About a minute after we enter, the telephone rings. The landlord admits to us that he has been ordered to 'guarantee our safety'. His solution is to bolt the door, refuse to let us out of his sight and charge us double for the service.

The provincial welcome sours still further on the edge of Tiantang after lunch. A minivan empties a group of unsmiling policemen. After seizing our documents and telling us this isn't a 'tourism area', they order us into their van.

'We'd rather walk, if you don't mind,' says Andy.

'We're doing the Long March, you know,' I say for the fourth or fifth time.

'Get in the van,' says a man in a suit. He stinks of booze. I assume he's the leader.

'I think we should record what these guys say, just in case,' says Andy, switching on the digital recorder in his pocket. The recorder is called a Voice Pen and does indeed bear a passing resemblance to a very large fountain pen. From our seat in the corner of the grubby station, I can see the leader making phone calls. When he finishes, the atmosphere magically changes. The Long March is on everybody's lips. Here are your passports, handshakes all round, have a cigarette! We respect you!

Thanks for your warm welcome, we say, but we can't rest because we're heading for the next county.

Ten minutes down the road, the police minivan catches us up. We tense. What now? The cop in the passenger seat leans out and hands Andy his digital recorder.

'You dropped your pen,' he says.

While no one is openly hostile towards us, the hand of friendship does seem to have been put back in its pocket. Half a day beyond Tiantang, just over the county border in Ganziyuan, we can't find anywhere to stay – not even the guesthouse, which the owner says is closed.

'So what are we supposed to do?' I ask.

'*Mei banfa*,' he replies – 'There is no solution.'

If there's one thing I've learned about China, it's that there's always a solution, even if it's a tent in a turnip field – a sign across the road into Ganziyuan boasts that this is a 'Turnip Production Base'.

I hate turnips and Andy hates tents. It's one thing to put a tent up in a secluded spot, but quite another to put it up in a well-populated area, where you can guarantee a crowd of sightseers and no rest at all. We decide to do something we've never done before, although it's a course of action people advise us to take almost every day. We head for the local government to ask for help.

In Beijing, I remember friends and colleagues doing their best to avoid having any dealings with the local government, which was a byword for bureaucratic time wasting and frustration. But on the Long March trail, people seem to have great faith in the ability of the local government to solve the problems of two foreign strangers. 'Have you been to see the local government?' is often the third question we hear (after 'Where are you from?' and 'What are you doing here?'). Given the last few days, I half expect to be arrested, but as Andy points out, at least that way we might get a bed for the night.

In each town, there are usually three relatively new, shiny, white-tiled buildings – the school, the police station and the local government office. But Ganziyuan is a most unusual place. Not only are the people unfriendly and uncooperative, but we find the government and police station away from the centre, located in an abandoned schoolhouse at the end of a muddy track. No one's at home except one young policeman and the equally young Party Secretary. Both are in their mid-twenties, graduates from the Hunan Provincial Public Security Bureau College in Changsha, the provincial capital. They invite us to stay.

After ten minutes' chat over a cup of hot water (no one drinks hot tea in this part of Hunan), the policeman, Tang Hongyun, asks if we have identity documents.

'Sure, I'll go and get them,' I say.

'Oh, it's OK, we trust you,' says Tang.

We eat together, a simple meal cooked by the one old fellow who looks after the compound, a kind of multi-purpose cook/cleaner/gardener. He prepares a stewed fish, a plate of stir-fried green vegetables called *cai xin*, and a bowl of pickled hot peppers. No one drinks alcohol. Andy asks Tang what life is like as a policeman.

'Hunan is short of police,' he says.

If this was a TV show, Andy would gag on his *cai xin* and I would do a comedy double-take. I've seen more policemen in ten days in Hunan than I might see in ten years in England. That's misleading, according to Tang, who calculates that Hunan has fewer police per head than wealthier provinces such as Guangdong.

'We only have four policemen in this station, and one of them is chronically ill and stays at home, so really there are just three of us, but the population we have to look after is 30,000. Being a policeman on the Chinese Mainland is hard work. We don't really have "working hours", as we're always on call, and we don't get any holidays, not like police in Hong Kong, for example.'

I'm used to seeing policemen riding up and down the highways in large four-wheel drive vehicles – brand-new Toyota Landcruisers or, more often, Mitsubishi Pajeros. I've noticed that these vehicles are always gleaming, and that I never, ever see them off road. Usually, they are escorting government officials, or are packed with people who look less like criminals and more like family members – unless there are a lot of criminal gangs in rural China made up of grandma, mother and two kids. Identifying the best restaurant in town is easy – it's the one with the police Pajero parked outside. In the villages off the main roads, however, there is almost no police presence at all. Maybe Tang is right and what I've noticed on the highways is just expensive window dressing.

Tang leaves us to sleep in our shaky dorm beds and retires to his own accommodation – a single tiny room in the police building. It is furnished with a rickety wooden bedstead, one wooden chair and a desk. He possesses a scattering of books and a cheap stereo with four or five CDs. He is a soft-spoken, serious young man, and we like him very much indeed.

Breathless, He Xia catches us up during a roadside break. After spotting us in the distance, she has run half a mile from her home in the village of Hejia, clutching her school English textbook. She is fifteen, a bundle of hope, energy and frankness, and she plies us with questions on that week's English text. She likes English, but thinks her teacher is no good and complains that her school has no tapes to help with pronunciation. Her dream is to go to the upper middle school in the county town, but she fears the cost will be too high for her family.

The Chinese school system begins with primary school, which pupils typically attend from the ages of five to eleven. They then enter lower middle school, which lasts three years. These nine years of basic education are theoretically compulsory. Upper middle school also lasts three years, after which students may sit the national university entrance exams. For most rural children, upper middle school is out of reach, while even the 'compulsory' years of lower middle school are denied to many because of the expense. With very few exceptions, even the most basic primary school charges at least 120 yuan (US$15) per year, while it takes at least 400 yuan (US$50) to pay for a year at lower middle school. This might not seem much, except that rural families usually have two children and we pass through areas on the Long March trail where total family income is 400 yuan a year. Charges for upper middle school start around 800 yuan a year and go up into the thousands depending on the location and quality of the school.

'You're not much like the other girls we meet,' Andy tells He Xia.

She nods. 'I'm more like a boy,' she says. 'The other girls don't play sport, but I like ping pong and basketball.'

I wonder about her future. How old does He think she will be when she gets married?

She shrugs. 'It's better not to get married too early. You should see something of the world first. After I leave school, I might leave the village and go to *da gong* in Guangdong.'

'Will your parents choose your husband or can you choose yourself?' asks Andy.

'Most people find their own husbands and wives now, though sometimes parents still choose for them. I've heard the adults talking about some places where people still buy wives. I heard of two men who bought them from Vietnam.'

'How much did that cost?' I ask.

'Four, five thousand yuan.'

Probably more than an extra child, then, but He doesn't know anything about that.

Recent experiences prompt another question about local life. 'Is there a lot of crime around here?' asks Andy.

'This area is very chaotic,' says He. 'There are groups that stop you and demand money and they beat you up if you don't give it to them. It's not safe to go out alone at night.'

I bow mentally to Officer Tang. Being followed around by cop cars might not be such a bad thing after all.

Guangxi

2004 GDP per head: 7,196 yuan ($869)
Population: 47,442,000
Ethnic minority population: 17,211,000 (38.3%)
Main minorities: 84.4% Zhuang, 8.7% Yao,
2.8% Miao, 1.8% Dong, 1% Mulao,
0.4% Maonan, 0.2% Hui, 0.1% Jing,
0.1% Shui

(China Census 2000, National Bureau of Statistics of China)

N ←

湖 南

Hunan

Guangxi
广 西

Wejiang River

Tongdao
County Town
通道

Pingdeng
平等

Shijing
石径

Sishui
泗水

Jiangdi Xiang
江底乡

Liangshui Xiang
两水乡

Fengmu
枫木

Shaoshui Zhen
绍水镇

Mao'ershan
猫儿山
7,024ft

Huajiang
华江

Xing'an
County Town
兴安县城

Tieshou Zhen
太兽镇

Quanzhou
County Town
全州县城

Xiang River
湘 江

Lianghe
两河

Xianzijiao Zhen
仙子脚镇

Dao County Town
道县城

Days 40-60: 244 miles
24 November - 14 December 2002
Total: 717 miles

Chapter 3

The Xiang River

As we approach the biggest killing ground of the Long March, the folk memory the Red Army has left behind consists of stories of skirmishes and tales of soldiers who paid for things instead of pillaging them. It's a staple of Long March mythology that Red soldiers adhered strictly to Mao's instruction that 'nothing must be taken from the peasants, not even a needle'. Those old enough to remember swear this is true. Younger locals point out battlefields where they played as children, sometimes finding relics of weapons – just as London children collected shrapnel from German bombs during and long after the Blitz. On the border of Hunan and Guangxi, we meet an old man who points to the village below the road and tells how his mother gave him words of comfort, 'Don't cry, don't be afraid,' as the battle raged outside. He remembers trying to talk to the Red soldiers, but he couldn't understand their dialect.

The border has no sign but is clear nonetheless. On the Hunan side, there is no development at all; on the Guangxi side, the highway is being widened all the way to Quanzhou County Town. Roadworks are good news. They bring services that would otherwise be unthinkable in a village like Wulipian, where a shanty-style construction has been erected to take the road workers' business, selling food, drink, cigarettes and karaoke. Three pretty girls imported from the county town encourage the drinking and karaoke. They apply to join our Long March, even though it's 12 miles to our destination for the day, Lianghe.

'You'll have to pay the boss to get us out of here, though,' says Liu Guihua.

Sadly, our Long March doesn't pay for recruits – even ones bold enough to walk 12 miles in high heels.

Guangxi is officially an 'autonomous region' of the Zhuang ethnic minority, the largest minority group in China. Here in Quanzhou County, however, we are still in Han country, a pleasant and relatively prosperous region just outside the orbit of the popular tourist areas around Guilin about 60 miles to the south-west. The paths are easy and relatively flat. Twenty-plus miles in a day is no problem, and necessary sometimes to keep pace with the Reds, whose advance units were racing ahead at this stage.

It was easy for Chiang Kai-shek to predict the First Front Army's movements. The Reds' reconnaissance mission had marched the same way three months earlier on their way to a chance encounter with the bandit-turned-Communist He Long, whose forces had been roaming north-east Guizhou since abandoning their base in summer 1932. Writing in Beijing at the end of 1934, the young American journalist Harold Isaacs cited a telegram from a group of Guizhou landlords: 'The [Guizhou] armies certainly cannot suppress [He Long] . . . There is no hope in asking them to do so. When [He Long] came . . . he had only 3-4,000 men, many of them sick and wounded . . . He relieved the poor, abolished harsh requisitions . . . Within two months, his army expanded to 10,000 men.'[1]

To combine forces with He Long, the First Front Army had to cross the Xiang River, the last major natural barrier between Guangxi and Guizhou Province. Here, Chiang Kai-shek planned to finish the seven-year civil war once and for all. He positioned provincial troops on both flanks of the approaching Red Army, while regular Guomindang forces came up behind. When the Reds reached the river, Chiang would trap and kill them all.

The Reds' most important crossing was at Jieshou, 27 miles downriver from Quanzhou. Jia Ji says she has heard there is still one old man in Jieshou who helped build the pontoon bridge for the Reds. Since this is now a town of several thousand people, Andy and I decide our best shot is to see if the local government knows where he is.

We find a roomful of officials taking life easy. They act as if it's quite reasonable and natural for two foreigners to walk in out of the blue, announce they are retracing the Long March, and ask for help in locating a man who built a pontoon in 1934. Within half an hour, Liu Faxiang has been found and we have two officials to help translate his thick local dialect into comprehensible Mandarin. I'm rather stunned and very grateful for this public service, although I can't help a sneaking feeling that it's a sign they don't really have enough work to do.

Every house on Liu's street dates back to the pre-Communist era. This is where the old folk live, the only part of town to have survived the modern urge for concrete and white lavatory tiles. It's mid-afternoon, but little daylight penetrates even Liu's main room, where we sit on wooden stools with our host and two helpful officials, Liu Yongrong and Jiang Hongwei. A single bare light-bulb casts an orange glow on the scene.

Liu was nineteen years old in November 1934. He was working as an apprentice to a blacksmith, a Jiangxi man from Ruijin named Zeng Xiangqiu.

'I didn't know anything about the Communists then,' recalls Liu, 'except that the Guomindang officials said they would murder us all. When we heard they were getting close, other peasants ran away. My master, though, he told me not to be afraid. He said the Red soldiers were good people, they didn't kill the peasants because they were peasants themselves.

'An advance unit came to my master and asked him to forge chains to build a pontoon bridge. He told me to help him and we worked on the chains in secret.'

Liu's pontoon was ready in time for the 1st and 3rd Army Groups, which crossed without difficulty. For three days from 25 November, the Xiang appeared to present no great obstacle. But on the fourth day, 28 November, General He Jian brought up four divisions to attack the Reds' right flank. Guangxi warlord Bai Chongxi moved in on the left and the situation changed dramatically. The Red Army was now cut in half by the river, with its first-class divisions on the north bank while the slow-moving supply column struggled on towards the crossing points. It was the beginning of the most disastrous battle of the Long March.

Nie Rongzhen, political commissar of the 1st Army Group, and group commander Lin Biao telegraphed the Central Military Committee just before midnight on 30 November:

'. . . If the enemy attacks tomorrow with their superior position we cannot guarantee that we can hold out with our available equipment and existing level of troop capability. The Central Military Committee must move all troops on the east side over the Xiang River today.'[2]

The answer came back at 1.30a.m.:

'The 1st Army Group must remain in position and eliminate the enemy troops . . . which are marching south-westward . . . No matter what happens, we have to control the road and the branches to the west of it.'[3]

Two hours later, the Central Military Committee sent a further telegram to emphasize the seriousness of the situation:

'Today's battle has great significance to the campaign to march west. Winning the battle will clear the way for the future . . . The commanders of the 1st and 3rd Army Groups and also their Political Departments should send political instructors to encourage our soldiers to engage in the battle and make them aware of the significance. Either we are victorious, or we are defeated . . .'[4]

Several months before we began the Long March, Andy and I approached one of the senior editors at *Beijing Youth Daily* to see if his newspaper would help us identify and interview Red Army veterans. He politely refused to co-operate, but liked the idea so much he commissioned his journalists to go ahead with the project themselves. The results were collected into a two-volume publication called *My Long March*. One of the interviewees, a propaganda soldier and guard in the artillery battalion of the 1st Army Group, recalled the battle at the Xiang:

'[It] was very, very cruel,' said Liao Dinglin. 'The clear water turned into a black river of blood.'[5]

More than half the army was lost, according to Liu Bocheng, chief of staff of the First Front Army.[6] Chinese histories usually give the toll on the Communist side as 30,000, but this almost certainly includes injuries and desertions. A survey published for the 60th anniversary of the Long March counted 8,400 deaths in three separate battles around the Xiang.[7] Only twenty-six of their names are listed at the enormous memorial in Xing'an, because the Reds kept no records of enlisted men at the time. As far as I know, no one has ever bothered trying to count the Guomindang dead, who are not commemorated at all, even though they were largely drawn from the same poor peasant stock as the Reds and knew even less of the politics and ideologies of their leaders.

Although the Reds never made it within the walls of Quanzhou County Town, today there is a small memorial cemetery on a low hill behind a dirt playing field in the centre of town. The field is occupied by a group of men and women involved in a game of croquet. I've always thought of croquet as a game of upper-class English imperialists, to be played on summer lawns in period movies by ladies in long white dresses. I don't expect to find it on a public square of dirt in the middle of a little-known Communist city, below a cemetery that commemorates heroes of the Red Army.

There are seven tombstones by the path through a tiny park. The path is turning to mud in drizzle that will not relent for three days. Occasional couples pass. They check out the foreigners, but pay no attention to the graves. The black stones are brand new, an inscription in white at the bottom right of each recording their erection in 2002. Each has a red star at the top. Two belong to soldiers of the Long March, one of whom fell in nearby fighting. He occupies the central grave. The inscription gives his name as Yi Dangping, born in 1908, entered the Communist Party in Changsha in 1926 and joined the Red Army in 1927. In April 1934, he was awarded the Red Star (second class) by the Central Revolutionary Military Committee. He was safely with the Central Military Committee and the main force of the Red Army during the crossing of the Xiang, but then fought and died in the 'Dangshan defensive action' trying to keep the passage open for the rest of the army.

The gravestone in Quanzhou doesn't record the story of Yi Dangping's death. During fighting on the west bank of the river, Yi was badly wounded – so badly that he believed he would not be able to escape the battlefield. Rather than face capture by the Guomindang, which probably meant execution and perhaps torture for an experienced officer like himself, he ordered one of his own men to shoot him.

The man refused to obey. Yi took his gun, put it to his head and blew his own brains out. He was twenty-six years old.

About 12 miles down the west bank of the Xiang from Quanzhou, Andy and I stop at a village called Jiaoshan, where Luo Kaifu wrote there was a 'martyr's cemetery'. A local man leads us across the Quanzhou-Xing'an highway and into some orange trees. About 50 yards from the howl of the main road, he points to a hole in the ground.

'What's this?' says Andy. 'Why are we being shown a hole?'

There must be some misunderstanding – not surprising given the trouble we're having understanding and being understood by the Jiaoshan man, whose dialect is among the strangest I've ever heard. We talk back and forth, trying to make sense of each other, until I catch two key words and realize what we're being told: we are standing over Yi Dangping's grave.

His remains were disinterred six months earlier and moved to the site we visited in Quanzhou. This is the spot where he shot himself and where his comrades risked the danger of burying him so close to the battlefield. Now, all that's left is a hole in the ground next to a pile of trash in an orange grove, the drone of traffic in the background.

I grew up in a peaceful world. The Second World War was already more than twenty years in the past by the time I was born; compulsory service in the army had ended long before I even started school. The most conflict I ever saw was the Saturday-night punch-up outside my local in Manchester. I sit by Yi's empty grave for an hour, trying to imagine this man, ten years younger than me, pull the trigger and take his own life. But I can't empathize. Both his life and his death are too extreme.

A measure of disbelief surrounds our passage through rural China. For some people, it seems Andy and I phase in and out of reality. In a tiny restaurant in Fengmu, we eat a simple dinner, chatting all the while to the family who run the place – a forty-something lady and her three daughters, all in their early twenties. It's late even as we start our meal and so we finish up quickly and ask for the bill. The lady looks hopefully at her eldest (I've noticed peasant parents often defer to their children in matters of business) and mumbles something to the effect that, 'they're foreigners, shouldn't I ask them for a bit more?'

It's as if suddenly we aren't there, as if the last forty-five minutes of conversation have never happened. The daughter is appalled and mutters, 'Mum, they *can* understand Chinese.' We phase back into reality and the mother looks mortified. She undercharges us by about 10 yuan.

The further we walk, the more these oddities in people's attitudes emerge. For example, I'm beginning to notice there are many more Red Army footpaths than I first suspected. At first in Jiangxi and Guangdong, I simply believed what people told me: the paths don't exist. But lately I've realized that the reality is much more complex. Often, the peasants won't admit they don't know the way or are simply unwilling to tell the truth.

Andy and I argue about why people appear to conceal information. Is it because they want to protect us, because they believe the main road is safer and we will surely get lost if we stray from it? Or is it because they simply can't understand why we would want to walk over the mountains? Perhaps they conclude that they must have misunderstood and therefore answer the question they think we should have asked. If a peasant does admit the existence of a footpath, he tends to add, 'It's very hard going'.

There's no way of knowing in advance what 'hard going' means. It might mean a perfectly flat dirt track that even trucks can negotiate with ease. As we climb away from the easy paths of the Xiang River plain, however, it means a slippery mountain path no more than 8 inches wide in places. And since we end up walking down a riverbed, I assume the peasant was right and actually we couldn't ever expect to find the path. But we make it on to the valley floor just before sunset and join a group of men returning home from their day's labour in the heavily forested mountains. One carries a large and lively rat tied to the end of a stick.

'What are you going to do with that?' I ask.

'Eat it,' says the man, visibly astonished at such a stupid question. 'It's very good.'

'Ah, um, so you'll stir-fry it, then, will you?'

He's delighted at the thought. 'Yes, stir-fry.'

'Add a bit of hot pepper?'

'Mmmmm . . .'

Our restaurant that evening has several large 'mountain rats' hanging from the wall. The boss is very proud of them. 'They taste better than pork,' she insists.

For once, I think Andy would be quite happy to see me try a local meat dish. I plead poverty – the rats cost 25 yuan each, as much as a whole chicken. No wonder that mountain man looked so pleased.

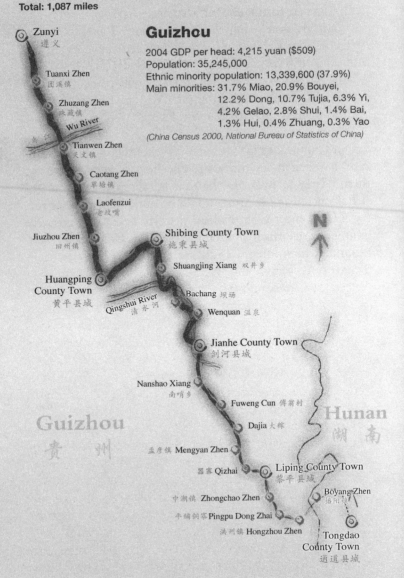

Days 61-86: 370 miles
15 December 2002 - 9 January 2003
Total: 1,087 miles

Guizhou

2004 GDP per head: 4,215 yuan ($509)
Population: 35,245,000
Ethnic minority population: 13,339,600 (37.9%)
Main minorities: 31.7% Miao, 20.9% Bouyei,
　　　　　　　　 12.2% Dong, 10.7% Tujia, 6.3% Yi,
　　　　　　　　 4.2% Gelao, 2.8% Shui, 1.4% Bai,
　　　　　　　　 1.3% Hui, 0.4% Zhuang, 0.3% Yao
(China Census 2000, National Bureau of Statistics of China)

Zunyi
遵义

Tuanxi Zhen
团溪镇

Zhuzang Zhen
珠藏镇

Wu River
乌江

Tianwen Zhen
天文镇

Caotang Zhen
草塘镇

Laofenzui
老坟嘴

Jiuzhou Zhen
旧州镇

Shibing County Town
施秉县城

Shuangjing Xiang 双井乡

Huangping
County Town
黄平县城

Qingshui River
清水河

Bachang 坝场

Wenquan 温泉

Jianhe County Town
剑河县城

Nanshao Xiang
南哨乡

Fuweng Cun 俘箐村

Dajia 大稼

孟彦镇 Mengyan Zhen

器寨 Qizhai

Liping County Town
黎平县城

Bóyang Zhen
摆阳镇

中潮镇 Zhongchao Zhen

平浦侗寨 Pingpu Dong Zhai

洪州镇 Hongzhou Zhen

Tongdao
County Town
通道县城

N

Guizhou
贵　州

Hunan
湖南

Chapter 4

The Tongdao Incident

We're arrested for the first time within two hours of stepping back into Hunan Province. It's 8.20 p.m. on 15 December, 3 miles south of Tongdao County Town.

Thanks to a geographical quirk, we pass twice through Hunan. Tongdao Dong Nationality Autonomous County occupies the south-western toe of the province, poking in between Guangxi and Guizhou. We've spent the last fifteen days picking our way across obscure trails along the northern Guangxi border; this morning we followed a footpath over the last mountain and walked back into Hunan. The map suggests two days should be enough to cross Tongdao and enter south-east Guizhou Province – the very place the words, 'What would it be like to try and follow the whole March . . . ?' first popped into my mind nearly three years before.

On first acquaintance, this looks like the poorest county yet. Even the *xiang* centres are little more than jumbles of wooden shanties, and when we try to beg some dinner at one of the newer buildings in Chuanxu Xiang, the lady of the house apologizes and says she has nothing but rice and cabbage. We're taken in by the kind couple who run the shop attached to the local government building. They possess the luxury of eggs, which they stir into some fried rice for us. Although after sunset we reach a sealed highway to the county town, its two lanes are devoid of traffic –

except, that is, for the enormous, beige four-wheel drive vehicle that slows behind us, then stops. Two men get out. One wears a badass leather jacket; the other sports a less threatening brown corduroy top. Leather Jacket demands to know who we are and what we're doing.

'Never mind that,' I say. 'Who are you?'

At moments like these, I think it's important to stall for time and act like you're in charge. Chinese policemen are obliged to show their documents before they harass you, and it's surprisingly easy to bluff officials by acting like you're more important than they are.

But these cops aren't impressed. Quite the reverse: they have IDs at the ready. 'Police. What are you doing here? Foreigners aren't allowed on this road. Get in the car and we'll take you into town.'

'Actually, officer, we're doing the Long March, you know . . .'

My appeal to Long March spirit is waved away. First comes the 'safety' refrain. We can't walk along this road at night, insists Corduroy Top.

I hope my winning smile translates into Chinese. 'OK,' I say, 'Thanks for your concern. You're quite right. We won't walk at night. We'll go back to the local government at Chuanxu Xiang and ask them to put us up for the night. We can carry on in the morning.'

'No, you can't do that. Just get in the car. It's not far.'

After marching 17 miles over the mountain from Pingdeng in Guangxi, Andy is in no mood to be pushed around by a man in a cheap 1970s jacket. 'Well if you're that worried about our safety, why don't you just drive behind us while we walk the last few kilometres into town?'

Badass takes over. 'This is a closed area. Foreigners aren't allowed here. Get in the car or we'll put you in it and drive you back to Guilin.'

A trip to one of China's top tourist resorts at this

gruelling stage of the Long March wouldn't be such a bad idea – except that it's 60 miles in the wrong direction. I wonder if Andy's rolling eyes translate. He doesn't want to give up. 'Look! You don't understand,' he says.

'We're . . .'

'Get in the car!'

'But . . .'

I interrupt Andy in English. 'I don't know if we should argue this any more. These don't look like regular cops, and if what they say is true, we don't have any choice.'

OK, I admit it. I'm chicken. A free ride back to Beijing is not the way I want to finish our mission. Andy bows to my logic and so we squeeze into the back seat with Corduroy Top – the front passenger seat is occupied by someone's grandmother. She twists around to inspect us. 'They speak very good Chinese,' she says.

I try appealing to reason again. 'Listen,' I say. 'We don't understand. We called the government and they told us it was OK to come through this county.'

Corduroy says, 'They don't know.'

What? 'The government doesn't know this county is closed?'

'That's right. Outside, they don't know.'

'What do you mean, "outside"? We called the county government.'

'You will get on the first bus to Guizhou tomorrow morning.'

The real problem is that we can't be sure if these policemen know what they're talking about, or if they're just bluffing to be on the safe side. Chinese officials aren't above inventing regulations if they think it will help keep them out of trouble, and we've already had plenty of opportunity to see how nervous our presence makes policemen in Hunan.

We're held at the police station for about an hour of perfunctory questions about our movements and previous jobs in Beijing, then placed under guard in the Tongdao Hotel. Andy tries to book the cheapest room, but they oblige us to pay for more expensive accommodation. It's 'safer'. Jia Ji and two friends, Sarah Bai and Nicole Gardner, are due to meet us in Tongdao the next afternoon. We're told we cannot wait for them. Nicole's an American. I don't mention this to the policemen and I wonder – silently – how she will get on. Next morning, the police are in such a hurry to get rid of us, the bus – uniquely – leaves fifteen minutes early. Leather Jacket spots a rebellious gleam in Andy's eye.

'Don't even think about it,' he says, or words to that effect.

We make a final bid to overturn our expulsion order while changing buses an hour later in Xianxi. We call as far up the government ladder as we can reach, all the way to the Huaihua City Public Security Bureau, which oversees the police in Tongdao. Bureau Chief Wu Kaiyi is sympathetic. It's a matter of military jurisdiction, he says, and he will call the military office and ask them to contact us. Three minutes later, a gentleman from the military office does call. He is also friendly. But then the phone appears to be grabbed away from him.

'If you carry on phoning people trying to get permission to go through this county, you and any of your friends are going to be in serious trouble,' says an unidentified voice. 'You will all go to prison.'

We board the next bus to Guizhou. The border is 40 miles away to the north-west.

It's particularly galling to be thrown out of Tongdao because the county plays such an important part in Long March and Maoist mythology. Some Chinese historians go so far as to say this is the place where Mao began his rise back to the top.

'The rank and file of the army [had begun] to voice doubts and dissatisfaction and earnestly call for a change of leadership,' Red Army Chief of Staff Liu Bocheng wrote later. 'This sentiment increased with our army's setbacks and reached its highest point during the battle along the [Xiang River].'[1] In his autobiography, Otto Braun took a more sanguine view of events at the Xiang. He argued that most of the losses were suffered among the support columns and recent recruits, while the veteran combat divisions came through with relatively light casualties.[2] But even if that was the case, many leaders were clearly unhappy and ready to consider a change of direction. On or around 12 December 1934, the Red Army commanders and Communist Party leaders met in Tongdao. Mao was among them, and for the first time since 1932 his views were accepted in a military council. He reportedly proposed that the Red Army abandon its efforts to reach the base area controlled by the 2nd and 6th Army Groups. That area lay around 200 miles north of Tongdao, and to continue along this obvious path would play into Chiang Kai-shek's hands. Instead, Mao argued, they should shift direction by moving north-west into Guizhou, where provincial troops were reputed to be weak.

'You know if we wanted, we could still go back,' says Andy. 'All we have to do is avoid the main road and we could sneak through Tongdao without anyone in authority ever knowing . . .'

'Forget it,' I say. 'It's not worth the risk.'

While preparing for the march, a friend, William Lindesay, who in the 1990s retraced a few stretches of the Long March and was the first foreigner to hike the length of the Great Wall, gave us some practical advice. 'Of course you want to be 100-per cent successful, but with a project this big if you manage to complete 80 per cent, it's an achievement. If you manage 90 per cent, it will be fantastic.' He was right. We would have to roll with the punches. Ninety-nine per cent of the Long March will have to do.

Guizhou is a notoriously poor province. It is rarely mentioned in travel guides or newspaper features without reference to an old saying that the province has 'no three *li* without a mountain, no three days without rain, and no man with three coins to rub together'. Watching peasants plough rice terraces by hand or, for the lucky ones, with the help of a water buffalo, it's easy to think nothing here has changed for decades, perhaps centuries. But seventy years ago, life was much, much worse. In the 1930s, Guizhou's staple crop was opium. Even the peasants of the Red Army were taken aback by the nakedness and starvation of the people. Commander-in-Chief Zhu De wrote, 'Peasants call landlords "rent gentry" and themselves "dry men" – men sucked dry of everything . . . Corn, with bits of cabbage, is the staple food of people. Peasants too poor to eat rice; sell it to pay rent and interest . . . Poor hovels with black rotten thatch roofs everywhere . . . One family of ten persons here. Two board beds, one for husband, wife, baby; one a shelf for grandmother. Others sleep on earth floor around the fire, without covering.'[3]

The region we are entering is also minority country, chiefly inhabited by the Dong and Miao peoples. The Red Army leadership issued special orders instructing the soldiers on how to deal with the minority people they encountered, but in most places we ask, the locals say they simply ran away when the Reds approached. Dong villagers in Pingpu Zhai, about 10 miles into Liping County, tell us they watched from the hills as the army passed for seven days and seven nights. They weren't afraid of Communists, but of Han people in general and soldiers in particular. Under the Guomindang authorities, they were often forced to labour for Han masters from two weeks to a month at a time.

Around 3 million Dong people live mostly in mountain villages along the Hunan–Guizhou–Guangxi borders. I'm greatly taken with these areas. Despite their relative lack of contact with outsiders, the people seem more open and direct than before. Although the Han peasants have been generous and hospitable to a fault, they are often slow to get to the point and depend on us to break the ice. Since we're English, this can make it hard to get along – at least initially. The Dong suffer fewer inhibitions. They are spontaneous with their friendship and finding food and lodging is easy.

'Just knock on anyone's door and ask,' we are told. I'm incredulous. But at dusk in Pingpu, we're out of options. Jia Ji, Sarah and Nicole have caught up with us from Tongdao (on arrival Nicole bumped straight into a police-man – who bought her dinner and helped her find a hotel where he bargained the price down on her behalf) and our tent certainly can't host five people. I stop the first man we meet and get straight to the point, 'Excuse me, but we're looking for a place to stay.'

This is only the second time foreigners have ever been seen in Pingpu. We learn later that two French tourists once arrived, took some pictures, and then left again immediately. But Teacher Wu (Chinese people usually only give their surname when asked; it's then common to address them according to their job status) reacts as though foreigners stop him for advice every day.

'A place to stay? Follow me.'

And within five minutes we're arranging our bags in a pleasant room in the two-storey wooden home that be-longs to the village head. We have a charcoal burner for warmth and a stream of visitors for conversation. They are all men. Although Dong women appear more forceful than most in rural China, they still take a back seat when it comes to entertaining visitors – except in the kitchen, of course. Jia Ji, Sarah and Nicole, however, all join the circle for dinner.

We sit around a communal pot of boiling water, into

which go mushrooms, cabbage and pork. As guests, we are presented with a special dish that none of the locals touches. It is a cold fish preserved in a spicy marinade that is the most delicious taste of the Long March (for non-vegetarians). Sarah is a notorious food fanatic and her eyes widen as she reaches for more. 'Mmm, this is *so* good! How do you make it?'

It's the only question our hosts refuse to answer.

I ask how relations are with the Han these days. Wu says there are no problems and besides, they are quite cut off here in Pingpu. No one pays much mind to them.

'I can believe that,' I say. 'We met two Han ladies on the main road over the mountain and they directed us here but said, "They're Dong people over there, they can't speak Chinese."'

Our hosts roar with laughter. Although they speak Dong among themselves, we have been chatting in Mandarin for the last three hours.

By the time we reach Pingpu, Andy and I have abandoned most of our 'only-for-tourist' suspicions about the reality of minority cultures. In village after village, we see evidence of vibrant cultures quite apart from the Han majority – in architecture, dress and language. The wooden architecture of Dong villages is especially recognizable. Each village has at least one *gulou* (literally 'drum tower' although there's no drum in it), a tower whose base is open and used as a place to meet, talk or just sit. Rivers and streams are crossed by the Dong's signature 'wind and rain bridges', covered wooden bridges that, in wealthier districts, feature ornate towers similar to the *gulou*. Pingpu has two, one of which dates back to the late nineteenth century. The village meets there once a week to discuss business. A drum tower meeting also elects the village head.

Near midnight, I stroll outside to pay a visit to the family horse, who watches over the toilet around the corner. There is a gentle drizzle, but I stop to listen to the music that spills from a single lit window at the end of the lane. It's an eerie sound to the Western ear, a four-string *pipa* lute being plucked while a group of young female voices sing harmony. And there isn't a tourist or TV camera in sight.

'No three days without rain' seems optimistic. Next time I meet a Long March veteran, I'll have one question – were you ever dry? And if he answers, yes, then how on earth was that possible? Andy and I are wearing waterproofs developed with the aid of space-age technology, but after half an hour outside we're wet through and miserable, anyway.

Christmas is only four days away when we leave Liping. We have asked friends to box up some food and gifts and send it all to a hotel in Jianhe, the next county town en route. Neither of us can bear the thought of celebrating in a tent up a sodden and freezing mountain, and so even though there are 100 miles to go, we agree to march for Jianhe, double-time if necessary, to secure Christmas at all costs.

We walk deep into the night, mostly along mud tracks with only a half-idea where we are. Worst is the claustrophobia of the mountain trails, where thick mist cuts visibility to a couple of metres at best. Only the odd distant dog bark disturbs the stillness. On 23 December, we plan to stay in Gaoyang, close to the north-west border of Liping County, but the mist is so thick we walk straight through the village, never even realizing that it's there. Instead, we sleep in a solitary drum tower below the dark village of Fuweng.

Our drum tower isn't nearly so lonely in the morning. First to call, at about 7 a.m., are the local schoolchildren on their way to class. Next come peasants heading to work. They all carry wooden-handled knives with an 8-

inch blade curved like a scythe. Some also bear single woven baskets; others have two, one at either end of a carrying pole. Most go about their business without stopping to talk, but a group of three ladies can't contain their curiosity. They inspect the fabrics of our clothes and equipment. Wasn't it cold last night, they wonder? It was fine, we lie. They are especially fascinated by our cooking gear. I demonstrate the camp stove, making what I'm fairly sure is Fuweng's first-ever cup of coffee, though our ladies' curiosity doesn't extend to trying it.

Owing to the drum tower, I assumed this was a Dong village, but the ladies say they are in fact Miao. The Miao are the fifth-largest of China's official nationalities. About half their population of 9 million live here in Guizhou, but they are also scattered through Hunan, Yunnan, Sichuan, Guangxi and Hubei. There are another 2 million or so in Thailand, Laos, Vietnam and Myanmar, where they call themselves the Hmong. Miao subgroups are commonly named according to a particular characteristic of their traditional dress. My guidebook suggests that this being south-east Guizhou, these women must be members of the Black Miao subgroup, as opposed to the Red Miao of north-east Guizhou and west Hunan or my personal favourite, the Flowery Miao of north-west Guizhou and north-east Yunnan.

I can't tell who's who from the way people dress. Styles change from village to village and even within the same ethnic group. From Liping to Fuweng, the dominant colours of the Dong have changed from dark blue to emerald green to sky blue. These ladies are mostly in grey, dressed for work, yet still find space for splashes of green and red around hems and waistlines. I've never seen Han peasants embroider in colours like this. After we've chatted for a few minutes, I ask the ladies if they'd mind having their photo taken.

'Oh, no,' says the eldest. 'We look terrible. We'd have

to go back and put on our nice clothes if you want to take a picture.'

Moments like this make our journey seem so banal. Some phrases could belong to any time or place, and that is one of them. For a second, it's like there's nothing at all different, certainly nothing 'inscrutable' about the remotest places and people. I don't want to make them go all the way back up those stairs to get dressed up just for us, and so I drop the photo request. I'm reminded of one of Luo Kaifu's stories from this region, a tale I used to regard with some suspicion. He spent the night in a Miao village and the next morning was seen off by a crowd of beautifully dressed girls. Luo was consistently hosted and helped by local governments and his description of this scene sounded so much like a tourism write-up that I wondered if the authorities might have set it up especially for his benefit. Now I see that suspicion was probably unfair. This is not the first time, and it certainly won't be the last, that we meet people delighted to get dressed up and show off for our benefit. No one has to organize them. It's a rare, in some places unique, event for a stranger to be a guest, and it's clearly a matter of pride and pleasure for the hosts to show their best things.

Although we have left the Dong behind, the rules of hospitality remain the same. The shopkeeper in Fuweng directs us west along a stream to a village called Wumeng, from where we must cross the Laoshanjie range into Jianhe County. We can have lunch in Wumeng, he says. 'Just go into anyone's home and ask.'

It's true. This remarkable system appears universal in this part of Guizhou – all the more so as we discover Wumeng is a Han village. It takes some time before we realize this, as there is no perceptible difference in the behaviour of the people, and their Chinese is just as hard to understand as that spoken by the Dong and Miao.

The Wu family lends us their kitchen, which doubles as a living room in winter as it's the only room with any warmth. Andy solves his vegetarian problem with some tea oil from the village's one tiny shop (peasants here mostly cook in animal fat), and I entertain the crowd by making fried rice in a wok on the iron stove in the centre of the room. It's a large house and several men from outside the village live here, working as loggers on the slopes of Laoshanjie. A couple of dogs and one puppy also hang around and Andy notices that they are treated with some kindness. This is unusual. We're more used to seeing dogs cursed, beaten and eaten. We often wonder why the peasants bother keeping dogs around at all. They don't name them and rarely treat them as anything other than a nuisance. Andy turns to one of the loggers, Li Rusen, and asks, 'Would you eat these dogs?'

'Oh yes,' says Li.

'What if a child had made friends with one,' Andy persists. 'Would you still kill it and eat it?'

Li ponders. 'No, not in that case,' he concludes.

'What kind of dogs taste best?' I ask.

'Old dogs, young dogs, they both have their good sides,' says Li.

'How do you kill them?' asks Andy.

Li points to a log by the fire. 'Beat them to death.'

'Could you do it with one blow?

No,' says Li, who then mimes repeated blows saying – in English – 'One, two, three, four!' He laughs, as do Wu and his wife.

Andy doesn't laugh. I'm sure he's wondering what Li and the others could possibly find funny about beating an animal to death. But I don't think they're laughing in a funny-ha-ha way. Their giggling is the same sound as often follows shouts of 'ha-loo!', the product of a childish delight in daring to try something new – like speaking English – to show off in front of others. There's also an undercurrent of nervousness to it, as if to say, 'Was that right? Did I do OK?'

City life used to insulate Andy against this kind of casual cruelty, but now he is faced with violence against animals on an almost daily basis. In the city, you never hear a pig scream. It's an extraordinary, unforgettable sound, like a human baby with bellows for lungs. In the village, it can take half an hour to prepare a pig for slaughter. The pig screams the entire time, until the butcher silences it by slitting its throat.

To simplify matters, I gave up eating meat at Yudu. Trying to explain that we have different dietary requirements is just too tiring. It's difficult for rural Chinese to understand why someone with plenty of money should choose not to eat meat. Even after a careful explanation, scraps of pork are still likely to feature in everything, as if vegetarianism is a brand of Western *politesse* to which the courteous response is an extra helping of meat. Peasants also seem to have trouble grasping that foreigners might not all eat the same things. It's hard enough for most people to come to terms with our presence in general, let alone separate us into individual, distinct characters. I can't help being reminded of that old racist cliché that all Chinese people look the same. When Andy and I are apart, we're often mixed up and mistaken for one another. After washing the laundry in Liping, Andy set his socks on fire while experimenting with a miniature hair-dryer. Later that day, a maid stopped me in the hotel corridor. 'I'll bring the towels in half an hour,' she said.

'What?'

'After that fire in your room you asked me for towels. I'll bring them in half an hour.'

'I didn't . . . oh, I see, yes, the towels. Thank you very much.'

We wake on Christmas morning in the most attractive lodgings of the Long March so far, a wooden Miao home that descends in five stages from the road level down to the riverside. Directly outside our bedroom, the coldest day of the year awaits on an open walkway overlooking the water. The toilet at the end of the walkway invites the occupant's extremities to experience the icy breeze coming off the river 50 feet below. Although there are plenty of regulation concrete boxes, Nanshao Xiang also has older wooden buildings perched on stilts all the way into the centre of the town, which stands on the confluence of two rivers, closely surrounded by lush hills just inside the border of Jianhe County.

Christmas Day is also market day. The streets are filling with Miao and Han peasants from all over the area. The men of both ethnic groups are nondescript beasts of burden, but the Miao women are a fine sight, their basically sombre attire transformed by vivid interruptions of scarlet and burnt orange in their headdress and around their sleeves and shoulders. Some have painted light red dots about an inch across in the centre of their foreheads. Others also wear heavy earrings that have distended their ear lobes by up to half an inch.

Andy and I toy with the idea of staying and spending the day here, rather than face the 20 miles of imponderable blank space that are all the map promises between Nanshao and our goal: Christmas dinner in the county town. I step outside into a fine drizzle to call Jia Ji on the satellite phone.

'It's OK,' she says, 'I've spoken to the mayor. He says he can find you a guide over the old Red Army trail, which will take you to the county town by sunset, no problem.'

Given the uncertainty of our relationship with the authorities, we avoid guides and governments wherever possible. Today being Christmas Day, however, we make an exception.

At the government building, the mayor is busy. Instead, we explain our situation to Hu Bingwen, a young man who tells us he studied in Beijing before returning to Nanshao to enter government work. It's important to understand the normal procedure in a situation like this. First, you must sit down, have a rest – '*xiuxi*'. How about a cup of tea? Something to nibble? You explain your problem and what you want. You add, again, that you're in a hurry. The first person you speak to disappears, apparently to address your request. They never come back. In the meantime, you explain your situation to more people, who offer more tea and more snacks. Perhaps one or more of them goes out to see what has happened to the first person. They come back with others. Before you can say 'Qiu Jiulong', it's lunchtime and someone suggests, 'Maybe you should just stay here for the day?'

Hu Bingwen says, 'Christmas, yes, I understand. Come with me.'

Hu takes us up the street to a small tea shop, where he leaves us while he finds a man to guide us. In the meantime, we chat to Li Yingmo, who tells a story from his father, who saw the Reds pass through Nanshao around this time in 1934. Units came off the hills along two different paths, mistook each other for the enemy and started fighting. I'm pleased with this tale. In the books, it all seems so straightforward. Mao gives an order, the army moves here, there, wherever it's told. No one gets lost, no one makes mistakes. The soldiers are like pieces on a board game, and the only question is what choices the players, i.e., the leaders, make. I imagine the Long March as more often chaotic, confusing and full of spontaneous action – such as the decision to shoot at those soldiers over there in Nanshao. Li's story brings my imaginings to life, but it also underlines what an extraordinary effort it was to co-ordinate the movements of such large numbers of people, along so many different paths in such difficult country. Not every unit had the luxury of a local guide. When they reached a fork in a mountain trail, like us they just had to take their best guess. Unlike us, however, their best guess might be a matter of life and death.

Within half an hour, Hu introduces us to our guide, a sixty-one-year-old Miao gentleman named Wang Fanghe. For today's 20-mile trek, Wang has equipped himself with: one fur hat; one home-made pipe, which he actually uses as a holder for hand-rolled cigarettes; one rolled-up umbrella. Wang says we can be in Jianhe in six hours and with preparations like that, we believe him.

The trail goes almost due north, mainly along a ridge that rises three times to peaks where the drizzle freezes instantly on our hair and clothes. The villages in this area have no communication with the outside world except along this footpath. The peasants wear cotton shoes with rubber soles that somehow grip the mud far better than our state-of-the-art boots. We step slowly and gingerly, while old ladies heading for market lose patience and push past. In two and a half months and 700 miles, I have never seen a peasant fall over.

If the Dong people had fewer inhibitions than the average Han, the peasants here take openness still further. In Miao village after Miao village, we see few men. Instead, we're greeted by groups of women who laugh and wave us over, calling, 'Come and *wan'r* [play] with us.' They often have designs painted in blue dye on their faces – a sign, we're later told, that they've been drinking and having a good time. In Wuku, one thirty-something lady breaks off from her group of comrades, strides up to me and lays her hand on my arm while she invites us to dinner.

I'm greatly struck by this because previously on the Long March trail, physical contact seemed all but illegal.

The only exception was among young men, who Andy reckons compensate for not being allowed to flirt openly with girls by hugging each other instead. I've seen groups of teenage boys indulging in what to the English eye look like open expressions of homosexuality, yet Chinese people (straight ones, at least) are inevitably mortified when I make this observation.

How can I explain why we cannot stop? What do these people care about our Christmas dinner? I can only smile, say thank you and move on. But I only get a few steps further along the footpath before I'm halted by an even more remarkable character. He is wearing an off-white, pinstripe jacket and trousers, and I take him for some kind of trader from the county town. 'Hello,' he says in English.

Well, so what, I think. Anybody can say that. 'Hello,' I smile.

But then this man continues in quite passable English – where are we from, what are we doing, where are we going? He asks vocabulary and pronunciation questions. I goggle.

'Where are you from?'

'From Wuku,' the man says, 'I'm a farmer here.' He's even been studying politically correct terminology.

'Have you ever met anyone English before?'

'No, I've never seen a foreigner in Wuku. I studied English myself. I listen to the radio. My dream is to go to Beijing to study at university. Goodbye, I go home.' And with that, he's gone.

I'm staggered. This man lives in a village that doesn't even have a road, and that's never seen a foreigner. And yet somehow he has been inspired with this dream not just to leave, but to go all the way to the capital, enter university and study the language of a country halfway around the world. And instead of just sitting around daydreaming, he has studied all by himself to make it possible – no teachers to encourage him, no fellow students to support him. I'm so taken aback by this encounter that it's several hours before I realize I forgot to ask this remarkable individual his name.

Wang Fanghe is as good as his word. We reach Jianhe County Town just after five, the first time in a week we have made any destination before dark. We unpack the goodie box our friends have sent and carry a few choice items across the street to a Hubei-style restaurant, where each table has a charcoal burner underneath that keeps you warm all the way up to your knees. As we mix Chinese vegetarian stir-fries with Australian red wine, cheddar cheese and Christmas pudding, rain begins to beat a tattoo on the iron roof. By the time we leave at 10 p.m., the rain has turned to snow and the city is already buried. There's no traffic and even the karaoke bar has closed early – saving us from our drunken plan to sing a cappella Christmas carols to the locals. I pad across the empty street and admire the snowflakes falling past the orange streetlamps. After a lifetime of disappointment in England, I celebrate my first White Christmas with only my best friend for company. I hardly miss home at all.

By New Year's Day, we're so exhausted that even Andy admits the need for a big breakfast. We find a small restaurant on the main street in Shuangjing, where the boss, Zhang Jianyuan, is busy practising his calligraphy. He hands Andy a basket.

'I haven't got anything to cook. Go buy what you want and I'll prepare it for you.'

We arrived in Shuangjing at 10.45 last night after a truly terrible evening that began with the realization that we were marooned on a rocky outcrop on the north bank of the Qingshui River. There was no way forward and, with only an hour until sunset, no time to retrace our steps to safety. Our only hope was a group of women washing cabbage on the opposite bank, apparently oblivious to the plight of two foreign adventurers.

'Help! Help! Save us!' shouted Andy.

'Shut up!' I said. 'Waving's enough.'

I was right. It took only a quarter of an hour of gesticulating before two women rowed to our rescue in a wooden boat. On the way back, we realized why they were hesitant – the river was full of rocks that reached almost to the surface, and with our extra weight it was a tricky business navigating back to the pebble beach that ran the length of the ladies' village. Our saviours looked fairly relaxed about the near-misses and the imminent danger of capsizing. When we reached the beach, the other ladies greeted us enthusiastically.

'You're Miao, aren't you?' I asked.

'Yes. It's getting late, why don't you stay with us?'

'Sorry, but we've got to move on.'

'But it's nearly dark . . .'

And so we declined a pleasant evening in good company, with hot food and an early night. Instead, we risked our lives re-crossing the Qingshui 3 miles downstream in a torchlit ferry piloted by three morons, got lost in a muddy maze of paddy fields somewhere outside Pingzhai and finally waded through double mud over the hill to Shuangjing. We woke up the only guesthouse in town, shared a nourishing supper of dried pineapple chips and kicked ourselves to sleep.

Andy grabs Zhang Jianyuan's basket. A man who offers a solution unprompted is not to be scorned. Besides, there are plenty of Miao peasants trading along the main street and within five minutes we have filled the basket with bamboo roots, carrots, eggs and Andy's staple: dried tofu. Zhang puts his calligraphy aside and sets to work washing, chopping, frying and wondering what we're doing here.

'Ah, the Red Army,' he nods. 'My mother used to tell

me about that. She was a child when they came. She said all the Miao people ran into the hills when the Reds approached, so the soldiers slept in their empty houses.'

But if the Miao thought they were playing it safe, says Zhang, they reckoned without the Guomindang militia from nearby Taijiang. After the Reds left and the Miao came back home, the militia arrived and executed five or six villagers for collaboration.

'It's a pity you missed Pingzhai,' says Zhang. 'You can still see slogans written by the Red soldiers on the walls of some of the homes there.'

I can see from Andy's face that he is also thinking of the mud heap we trudged over last night between Pingzhai and here. Forget it, says Andy's face.

'But never mind,' Zhang continues, 'There are also some right here in Shuangjing.'

'Can you show us?' I ask.

Of course he can. In fact, he'll shut his shop in order to take us to the house. I'll never get used to this kind of behaviour, the effusive goodwill and generosity that occasionally, no, frequently overwhelms Chinese people once we've spent a bit of time talking.

The Long family's home is in an old part of town below the high street, just beyond an outdoor, communal laundry where at least two dozen women are washing and pummelling clothes in and around a group of stone pools. A small, handwritten notice from the county cultural bureau hangs by the front door, announcing the presence of 'Red Army slogans'. Inside are three examples, which have all been restored in black paint. It's a crude preservation job, but Zhang says there used to be other slogans that have been lost entirely. One reads simply, 'Red Guizhou'; another exhorts, 'Unite with the Miao to bring down the bandits and evil rich'. The latter seems rather hopeful if, as Zhang says, there were no Miao people around with whom to unite.

Except that in 1934, things weren't exactly as Zhang's mother said. In her experience, 'everyone' ran away. But in the Long household there is a woman named Wu Laoxiu who was a little girl when the Red Army came. Her memory is quite different.

Wu produces a dusty black-and-white photo of her father-in-law, Long Qianchen, but as she begins to talk our friend Zhang looks bemused. Although his mother tongue is also Miao, he cannot understand this woman's old-fashioned speech. One of Wu's granddaughters translates into Mandarin. A dozen family members gather round to listen. For the very youngest, I sense it's an unusual event to hear a story from the past from their great grandma. Our presence has, if only very briefly, bridged the generations and brought past and present together.

Wu says her family did not run. Quite the opposite, in fact – Long Qianchen not only welcomed the soldiers into his home and looked after the injured, he also guided one unit up to Shibing County Town. Wu says he was rewarded with the gift of a saddle, but no one in the family knows what happened to it.

At least once, then, the Reds did 'unite with the Miao'. And what about Zhang's folk tale of innocent villagers butchered for collaboration by the Guomindang militia? Long Qianchen *was* collaborating, but he got away with it. From now on, whenever I hear that 'everyone' did this or that, I will think of Long Qianchen, who stayed when 'everyone' ran away.

Beyond Shuangjing we gradually move out of Miao country into a vague multi-ethnic borderland, an area of transition before the Han take over again completely just south of the Wu River. As we walk south-west from Shibing to Huangping County Town, the mountains relax into hills and the farming land grows broader and more fertile. Horse and cart, a rarity in the mountains, become a common sight. Houses turn from wood to red brick. To judge from the sudden proliferation of restaurants from Huangping to Jiuzhou, dog is the meat of choice in this region.

The closer we approach to the Maoist shrine of Zunyi, the more frequently we find memorials to the Red Army's passage. Like the concrete red flag that illuminates the road into Jiuzhou, most were erected to mark the 60th anniversary of the Long March in 1994–5. Yet although less than a decade old, many are already in a state of decay, shrouded by an air of neglect and irrelevance. The thrusting obelisk in Caotang Zhen is covered in graffiti; 2 miles down the road in the village of Xiasi is the shell of a memorial hall to commemorate the 'Houchang Meeting', at which the leadership finalized plans to cross the Wu River, the last major obstacle to their march on Zunyi. Villagers tell us it was started five years ago but remains unfinished because 'there's no money'. For now, all that records the event is a small white tablet in a cabbage patch.

There is an especially incongruous sight at the bottom of the main street through Jiuzhou – an abandoned stone church, whose architecture would not have looked out of place in early twentieth-century England. Once, it must have been the most impressive building in town. Today, it is empty and crumbling, shut behind a rusting, padlocked gate, surrounded by a high brick wall covered in advertising slogans and obscured by electricity and telephone cables. Next door is a new church building, smaller and built largely of wood in a contemporary Chinese style – i.e. a style-free box with a turned-up 'traditional' Chinese roof stuck on top. This is locked up, too, and so we ask passersby if they know anything of the old building's history.

'It used to be a church,' is the best anyone can do. No one knows that this church was where the Swiss missionary Rudolf Bosshardt was kidnapped by the 6th Army Group in August 1934. Fifty years later, the leader of the 6th Army Group, Xiao Ke, told Harrison Salisbury, a writer researching the Long March story in 1984, that a map of China was also discovered in the church. It was a priceless find, but the place names were written in French, which none of the Reds could read. Bosshardt was brought to Xiao's headquarters to translate.

'The two men spent all night over the map, wrote Salisbury. 'To Xiao Ke it was an unforgettable occasion. His face lighted up as he spoke of it.'[4]

Bosshardt would stay with the Reds for 560 days. Soon after his capture, the 6th Army Group united with He Long's 2nd Army Group and together they established a Communist base area in north-east Guizhou and north-west Hunan. One year later, they would make their own Long March from Hunan to north-west China, reuniting with Mao's men in October 1936. Bosshardt marched with them as far as Yunnan Province, where he was finally set free.

I wonder at the windswept and lonely monument at the edge of town. What would make more sense as a memorial – a beautiful building that is both part of the town's history and a meaningful witness to the Long March, or a big, red, concrete flag?

Sichuan

2004 GDP per head: 7,514 yuan ($907)
Population: 83,290,935
Ethnic minority population: 4,148,292 (4.9%)
Main minorities: 51.2% Yi, 30.6% Tibetan, 7.3% Qiang, 3.6% Miao, 2.7% Hui, 1% Mongolian, 1% Tujia

(China Census 2000, National Bureau of Statistics of China)

Days 87-124: 321 miles
10 January - 15 February 2003
Total: 1,408 miles

N

Guizhou 贵州

Sichuan 四川

Yunnan 云南

Chishui River 赤水河

遵义 Zunyi

Banqiao Zhen 板桥镇
Sidu Zhen 泗渡镇
Loushan Guan 娄山关
Tongzi County Town 桐梓县城
Jiuba Zhen 九坝镇
Guandian Xiang 官店乡
Shuanglong Xiang 双龙乡
Liangcun Zhen 良村镇
Xishui County Town 习水县城
Minhua 民化
Erlong Zhen 二郎镇
Taiping Zhen 太平镇
Tucheng Zhen 土城镇
Deyao Zhen 德耀镇
Jianzhu 蔺竹
Huangjing Xiang 黄荆乡
Jin'er 金鹅
Xuyong County Town 叙永县城
Daba Zhen 大坝镇
Jiusicheng Zhen 九丝城镇
Shibie 石碑
Guandou 观斗
Luobu 落卜
Weixin County Town 威信县城

Chapter 5

Zunyi

We approach the city like a pair of peasants.

I used to work in Beijing on Wangfujing Street, which the capital's tourism promoters like to call the city's own 'Champs Elysées'. Every day I'd notice new arrivals from the countryside gaping in wonder – not just at my 6-foot-4-inch frame, but also at the extravagance of the shops and offices. They walked slack-jawed up and down the pedestrianized area, then wandered into traffic perfectly oblivious of oncoming buses, their eyes glued to two-storey billboards of models and make-up. Now I think I know how they feel.

Even the sight of a white-tiled building is enough to provoke excited pointing. It's a signal that perhaps we've arrived somewhere that might have, say, a shop, a restaurant or – praise the Lord! – hot water. In the city there are bright lights and pretty girls, markets with at least three different kinds of vegetable, toilets that flush and shops that sell chocolate. I also wander out into the middle of the street without looking at anything but the shiny glass and tall buildings.

One steep, steep hill guards the southern entrance to Zunyi. Once over that, we move into a suburban industrial sprawl. The sun is setting through air choking with factory dust and reeking of rotten eggs. On the horizon, just a few hundred yards away, sulphurous flames belch out of brick monoliths. In the valley to our left sprawls an electricity substation the size of a football field. Straight ahead, there is nothing but soulless buildings, white tiles galore, multi-storey concrete tower blocks everywhere. It's choking with people, with traffic, with noise.

It's the most beautiful thing I've ever seen.

The Red Army's entry into Zunyi on 7 January 1935 was so unexpected that the population, which Otto Braun estimated at 10,000, had no time to flee. 'Even Guomindang officials, big landlords, and rich merchants were still there. Enormous stores of food and textiles fell into our hands,' wrote Braun. The Politburo issued orders to establish a new base. 'Agitprop brigades were formed, mass meetings were held, revolutionary committees were founded, confiscated provisions and work tools were distributed to the needy, and self-defence units were organized. Even the first stages of land reform were contemplated.'[1]

After nearly three months of marching and fighting, for the first time since leaving Yudu the Reds were free of immediate pressures. The Guomindang had been shaken off temporarily and the soldiers could eat, rest and even get new clothes.

Mao used this breathing space to make his play for power. His two most important supporters were Wang Jiaxiang and Zhang Wentian, who together with Mao formed what Otto Braun referred to as the 'Central Triad' that led 'the faction which waged a subversive struggle to take over the Party and Army leadership'.[2] Both Wang Jiaxiang and Zhang Wentian were members of the Communist Party's highest body, the Politburo; both had studied in the Soviet Union, and Zhang had also spent time in the United States. Wang was twenty-eight, Zhang thirty-four, and while the two of them initially identified with the other Soviet-educated leaders headed by Bo Gu, during the course of 1934 Mao drew them to his side.

Until September 1934, Zhang Wentian lived in the same building as Mao, a small temple at Yunshi Mountain outside Ruijin, where Mao had daily opportunities to convince the younger man of his case. Wang Jiaxiang suffered a severe shrapnel wound in 1933 and had to be carried in a litter for the whole Long March. He had become addicted to the morphine he used to dull his pain. Weakened by an attack of malaria, Mao also spent the early stages of the Long March in a litter. When they camped together in the evenings, Mao and Wang passed the hours discussing what had gone wrong in Jiangxi and what should be done now that the Red Army had veered off course.

As the 'Central Triad' approached Zunyi, the Red Army counted no more than 45,000 left of the 86,000 who started the Long March. The soldiers had already walked 1,100 miles in 12 weeks; rations had run out after a fortnight, after which they had to survive on whatever could be bought or expropriated along the way (hunger is the common thread in all Long March veterans' reminiscences). The plan to establish a new base with the 2nd and 6th Army Groups had been abandoned, while the Reds' only major engagement with the enemy had led to shattering losses at the Xiang River.

With Mao's influence on the rise after the Tongdao Meeting, Wang Jiaxiang and Zhang Wentian instigated the calling of an 'enlarged conference' of the Politburo, at which ten political leaders were joined by seven senior Red Army men, plus Otto Braun and his interpreter, Wu Xiuquan, and finally Deng Xiaoping, editor of the *Red Star* newspaper and secretary to the Central Committee. They met for three days, 15–17 January to discuss the failed struggle against Chiang Kai-shek's Fifth Encirclement and the events of the Long March so far. The Zunyi Meeting would be the most important of the Long March.

Some say it was the most significant meeting in modern Chinese history.

The leaders gathered in the home of a local warlord, Bai Huazheng. Bai's house still stands about 300 yards from our lodgings in the Zunyi Guesthouse. It's a two-storey structure, restrained and relatively small by wealthy European standards, built of black brick with white mortar, with a wraparound balcony. Red Army Political Commissar Zhou Enlai and his wife, Deng Yingchao, took one room on the upper floor, as did Commander-in-Chief Zhu De and his wife, Kang Keqing. Downstairs was used as the headquarters of the military staff. The meeting room itself is upstairs, and while the chairs have been lost, the original table is still there. Eighteen men sat around this table. Otto Braun and his interpreter sat away to one side in the corner close to the door.

As far as anyone knows, no notes were taken of the discussions. All we know of the Zunyi Meeting comes from two documents and the testimony of a handful of participants, all now dead. These sources, however, are suspect. The documents were written some weeks after the meeting and reflect a pro-Mao political bias, while no witness can be taken to be objective. Braun wrote his account thirty years later, at a time when he was busy penning anti-Mao diatribes, while the others all wrote or gave interviews in a China where history served the Party rather than the truth. Everything I'm about to tell you, therefore, may not be true.[3]

Twenty-six-year-old Party leader Bo Gu made the opening speech, followed by Zhou Enlai. Both reviewed the failure against the Fifth Encirclement and the trials of the Red Army on the Long March, but they differed in emphasis. Both Braun and Chinese witnesses suggest Bo Gu emphasized objective factors such as the strength of the Guomindang and relative weakness of the Communist movement, whereas Zhou Enlai stressed subjective factors such as tactical and operational mistakes. Zhou criticized himself – a shrewd move in a situation where others were lining up to do the criticizing. Wu Xiuquan remembered Zhou's speech as going down well with the comrades, while Braun characterizes it as subtly distancing Zhou from Bo Gu and himself, 'thus providing Mao with the desired pretext to focus his attack on us while sparing him.'[4]

Mao was third to speak. He went straight for the throat, denouncing military strategy and tactics from the time of the Fifth Encirclement, for which he singled out two scapegoats: Bo Gu and Otto Braun. He drew a line between 'we', i.e. Mao and his supporters, and 'them'. 'They' had lost the Soviet Republic through their mistaken leadership and then taken the Red Army to the brink of disaster on the Long March. The implication was that 'we' would correct these mistakes and rescue the Red Army.

Braun faced particularly sharp criticism. He wrote, 'I was accused of having "monopolized work in the Military Council" and of "abolishing collective leadership" . . . How a single foreign advisor without power to command, knowledge of the language, or contact with the outside world was supposed to have accomplished this feat remained [Mao's] secret.'[5]

But I don't believe Mao was interested in setting the facts straight. His mastery of propaganda and myth-making was already hard at work in Zunyi. He knew the Red Army was in a desperate position. It had lost half its men, the Guomindang was still at its heels and there was no end in sight to the Long March. To look objectively at the past risked igniting a free-for-all of mutual recrimination. Instead, Mao declared that the political line of the Central Committee, the Chinese Communist Party's supreme policy-making body, had been 'irrefutably correct' throughout the Fifth Encirclement and Long March.

This was convenient for Mao, since he was a member of this Central Committee. On the subject of military policy, however, Mao reeled off errors that he laid at the door of Braun and Bo Gu. Wu Xiuquan told Harrison Salisbury that Mao explicitly rejected Bo Gu's excuse that the Red Army had been defeated because the Guomindang had numerical superiority. 'It was not numbers, it was tactics. The military direction was wrong [Mao] insisted . . . The Bo Gu-Braun policy had been based on "conservatism in defence", "adventurism in attack", and "flightism in retreat".'[6]

It was particularly easy to make a scapegoat of a foreigner who did not really matter to the Party, while Bo Gu was also a convenient fall guy. He was intimately associated with Braun (they even shared a house in Zunyi) and – unlike Zhou Enlai – had no background and little apparent backing in the army. Both Bo Gu and Otto Braun had been appointed by the Comintern and both ultimately relied on Moscow for their authority. Now they were on their own. Communications with Moscow were broken in September 1934 when police seized the Comintern wireless transmitter in Shanghai. There would be no contact between the Red Army and Moscow for the entire Long March. By pinning the blame firmly on Braun and the Party leader, Mao's speech to the Zunyi Meeting absolved the Chinese military men of all responsibility for past defeats. No wonder they went along with it.

Braun wrote that Mao's speech, 'was approved by acclamation afterwards, if one can describe passive acceptance in this way. But there can be no doubt that most of those present were in agreement.'[7] Wu Xiuquan said that Zhang Wentian and Zhu De openly pledged their support for Mao, while Zhou Enlai made a second speech accepting Mao's criticism of Bo Gu and Otto Braun and proposing that Mao be made commander of the Red

Army. In Braun's words, Zhou 'went over to Mao's side with flying colours'.[8] General of the 1st Army Group Nie Rongzhen also laid into Braun. In his memoirs, Nie wrote that Wang Jiaxiang spoke to him beforehand. 'Let's throw them out of the meeting,' Wang said, 'Drive [Braun] off the stage!'[9]

Otto Braun was never as all-powerful as Mao and subsequent Chinese histories made out. If he punched above his weight before Zunyi, it was mainly because of the influence he wielded over Bo Gu. Bo Gu had been trained in Moscow and was wedded to the idea of Communist internationalism. In the Communist hierarchy of the time, the Communist International (Comintern) ranked above the Chinese Party leadership. As Braun was the Comintern's appointed military adviser, the Chinese were obliged to take him seriously. And as Bo Gu had no military experience or training, he not unnaturally leaned on the German, who was eight years his senior. But other Chinese commanders also treated Braun's advice with respect – to the extent that Braun had the impression they abdicated responsibility to him. When things went badly, this put the Chinese in the happy position of being able to blame it all on the outsider.

Zunyi saw the end of Braun as a significant influence in the Red Army, although he was not frozen out altogether. He was present at several important meetings later in the Long March and continued to associate with senior Party and army leaders. He survived the Long March and attended his last high-level military meeting in January 1936. For the next three years, he taught tactics, trained a cavalry unit and performed various tasks for the general staff. In 1939, he returned to the Soviet Union, where he became a translator and member of the Soviet Writers' Association. In 1954, after twenty-six years in China and the Soviet Union, he went home to East Germany, where he died in 1974 at the age of seventy-three.[10]

In the immediate aftermath of the Zunyi Meeting, Braun came to the conclusion that Mao was made either Chairman of the Politburo or of the Chinese Communist Party as a whole, (neither post had previously existed). He also believed Mao had displaced Zhou Enlai as the Red Army's chief political commissar. Neither was the case. For the time being, Mao was only raised to the Politburo's executive body, the Standing Committee, while Zhou remained chief political commissar alongside Zhu De at the head of the Red Army. But Braun's belief reflected the deeper reality. Mao had emerged from the Zunyi Meeting as the predominant figure, whatever formal positions he and others occupied within the Party and army hierarchies. By accepting his critique of Bo Gu and Otto Braun, the Zunyi Meeting signalled a crucial shift in power to Mao and his supporters. The only documents recording the proceedings of the Zunyi Meeting were written by two of those supporters, Zhang Wentian and Chen Yun. By casting Mao as the leader of the 'correct' line at Zunyi, they sowed the seeds of the myth that would eventually enshrine him as the single-handed saviour of the Red Army.

Andy and I contemplate the meeting room in near silence. There is only the occasional soft tread of a guard or shuffle of a random tourist. Outside, beyond the high walls of the compound, there is a bustling, peaceful and relatively prosperous city. It's a thoroughly modern place, with large and well-stocked supermarkets, fashionable shopping malls and broadband internet bars. Somehow, what happened here affects every person out there – every person, indeed, in the country, and many beyond. The men who argued here in this tiny room touched the lives of billions. For good or ill, every one of those life stories has a thread that runs through this empty room.

There is a famous painting of the Zunyi Meeting by Shen Yaoyi. Most of the participants are depicted in plain style, though Bo Gu looks rather harried as he reads a document that presumably details his incorrect leadership. I think the representation of Mao, however, is the finest there is. The future leader dangles a cigarette in his right hand and looks into the middle distance, just catching the eye of the viewer. He is a man apart and his expression seems to say, 'Gotcha!'

I realize in Zunyi that I am living life with an intensity I've never felt before. Constant movement piles on new sensations. At times, I rebel against the fullness of this experience. 'Please don't let anything happen this afternoon,' I say to myself. People come and go with bewildering frequency. I make friends and move on, often several times a day, knowing that I will never see these people again. This instability deepens my attachment to old relationships. Friends arrive to visit us in Zunyi and our reunion is emotional beyond any ordinary meeting. One week later, the sense of loss when they leave is, if anything, even more acute.

While aping the Reds' efforts to feast and rest, we also have a mass meeting to prepare for. Our Long March has turned upside down. Two weeks ago, we were under 'hotel arrest' in Tongdao; now we're the toast of Zunyi. TV crews lie in wait for us, local officials shepherd us around historical sites, the mayor invites us for dinner . . . And it's all thanks to a deceased American journalist.

When Harrison Salisbury was researching the story in Guizhou, he and wife Charlotte were chaperoned by a young woman named Yang Shengming. Eighteen years later, Ms Yang has risen to head the Guizhou Provincial Tourism Bureau. Salisbury obviously left a good impression, because when Yang hears two more foreigners are heading for her province to retrace the entire route of the

Red Army, she declares the Tourism Bureau will support us throughout our stay. But it's not only nostalgia that prompts Yang to become our first 'official' sponsor. She is planning a 'Red Trail' promotion to open up parts of the Long March route to tourism, and she spies a splendid propaganda opportunity in the unexpected advent of a foreign vanguard unit.

So it is that we find ourselves behind a long table on stage in a meeting room of the Zunyi Guesthouse. Beside us are five comrades: Jia Ji, who is really responsible for this, having called up Yang Shengming in the first place, the deputy mayor of Zunyi, Yang Shengming and her deputy, Fu Yingchun, and an eighty-eight-year-old veteran of the Long March named Wang Daojin. Above us hangs a red banner that reads 'Celebrating the 68th Anniversary of the Zunyi Meeting and Two Young British Scholars Retracing the Long March Press Conference'.

In front of us are more than 100 people drawn from tourism agencies and provincial and national television and newspapers. But despite this rather startling crowd, my attention is continually drawn back to Long March veteran Wang Daojin. Wang is wearing a baseball cap. I am wearing a Red Army uniform. I feel ridiculous. Yesterday, I was normally dressed, sitting in Wang's living room, and asking the veteran roughly the same questions as the reporters are now putting to me and Andy.

'Why did you walk the Long March?' I asked.

'I was sixteen when I joined the revolution in 1930,' said Wang. 'My family were peasants from generation to generation, the fields were owned by landlords. The harvest was very bad. There were mountains all around and transportation was very inconvenient. Still, if the transportation had been convenient, it would have been difficult to revolt. We felt we worked the whole year and still hadn't enough to eat. We had to give all the rice to the landlords as rent. All we ate was sweet potatoes and *feng mi* [a kind of brown rice]. We used to say, "With *feng mi* and pumpkin soup to eat, the Red Army will win victories every day." At that time, if we wanted to eat our fill and wear warm clothes, we had to solve the "three mountain" problem. The three mountains were feudalism, landlord exploitation and bureaucratism. Revolution was the only way to solve these problems and joining the Red Army was the only way to revolt.'

'What was the most difficult thing about walking the Long March?' I continue.

'Food and clothing,' said Wang. 'These became difficult after we left the soviet zone. We had to send good units to raise food from landlords, but this reduced our fighting force. We had the principle that we couldn't eat the poor peasants' food, so to raise food from landlords and wealthy people the units had to travel a long way. At the time, if we could get enough to eat, that was already pretty good. To find guides [was also a problem]. It wasn't usual to ask for guides and so we had to pay high prices or else the locals wouldn't show us the way.

'After we lost the battle of Songpan [in northern Sichuan], we had to cross the Swamps. It took us nine days. It was very difficult. There was no food, it was freezing cold, we couldn't make a fire or drink the water. Hailstorms began after one in the morning. Small ones we could bear, but big ones could kill people. At that time, we sat back-to-back in our units holding our guns erect. Every unit had one soldier who carried a two-layer cloth, and everyone tied this cloth to their guns and we held it above our heads. This was fine for small hailstones, but big ones couldn't be stopped.'

Back at the press conference, a lady from Guizhou Television asks: 'What's the meaning of the Long March for China and Chinese people today?'

That one wasn't in our questionnaire for Wang Daojin. I hate this question, and not just because I don't yet feel qualified to answer it properly. I hate it because I'm convinced that if I try to give a serious answer, the journalists will smile and nod politely and then write a heap of trash they made up themselves. As for the TV, I'll be reduced to an out-of-context sound bite that could be used for just about anything.

Chairman Mao instantly recognized the propaganda value of the Long March. Within a week of arriving in Wuqi in October 1935, he made a speech in which he said, 'The Long March is a manifesto. The Long March is a propaganda unit. The Long March is a seeding machine'.[11] Mao didn't only mean that the Red Army had spread the word of communism throughout China during its year on the run, sowing seeds of revolution that would later flourish across the nation. He also meant the legend of the March would continue to inspire recruits to the Communist cause. But the Long March is more than a propaganda masterpiece – it is an inspirational event quite apart from its Party political associations. Throughout our trip, hundreds of people, mostly young Chinese, write to us about our journey and their feelings towards the Long March. Only a couple even mention politics; the rest focus on their dreams and aspirations, and how they seek encouragement and inspiration from the struggles and achievements of others. An émigré Chinese academic writes from the USA, 'Please hang in there. The Long March may not mean communism to a lot of people. But I am sure it means courage and hope to all.'

Yet the Long March *is* very much about politics, the politics that have shaped modern China. It is about a dream of liberation from oppression. It is about the Maoist seizure of the Party and all that meant for the Revolution and every aspect of Chinese society since.

The Guizhou Television reporter is still waiting for an answer. Andy nudges me. I improvise, 'I read at school back in England that Zhou Enlai was once asked the significance of the French Revolution. Zhou said, "It's too soon to say." '[12]

I nudge Andy back. 'At least they won't have to make up a quote from Zhou Enlai,' I whisper. (The next day, one newspaper reports that I said all English schoolchildren have Zhou Enlai's picture in their schoolbooks.)

I'm accustomed to being misquoted, but I can't get used to looking like Otto Braun. When our Red Army uniforms arrived yesterday as a gift from the Zunyi Meeting Memorial Museum, neither I nor Andy could think of a face-saving reason to refuse to wear them to the press conference. It seemed insulting to our hosts and, particularly, to Wang Daojin.

None of them sees what we're afraid outside observers will see – when a photo is indeed published the next day in Hong Kong's *South China Morning Post* – two naïve clowns dressed up for the glorification of the Communist Party. The local media see only a nice photo opportunity that will help achieve the press conference's aim, which is not to promote communism, but to raise the profile of Zunyi and encourage tourism in Guizhou. And so we rationalize: a picture of us dressed up as Red soldiers isn't likely to convert anyone to communism, but if it helps encourage more people to visit Guizhou, that is probably a Good Thing.

Only 'probably', because in other poor parts of China I've seen tourism areas where the local cultures have congealed into a parody of their former selves. What is left is a kind of human zoo, where people are exhibits rather than individuals. The flipside is that for many such communities, tourism is the only way to attract investment and raise standards of living. All along the Long March trail, I have heard people speak of their desire for

'investment'. In Guizhou, this desire was specifically connected with tourism even in isolated places like Pingpu,
where our hosts spoke of their wish to open a guesthouse
for the tourists they hoped would one day follow us via
Liping. They don't want to be cut off. They want to feel
part of a wider world and I think similar feelings account
for the warmth of our welcome in many places, as if our
arrival is a signal that the wider world just got closer. And
besides, the land in minority areas especially is so poor
that there is no other industry they could reasonably
expect to develop. Whatever we look like in our Red
Army uniforms, if we're promoting tourism, we're doing
what our friends in Pingpu want. And that's good enough
for Andy and me.

We're on a footpath allegedly heading for Jiuba Zhen,
about 6 miles west of Tongzi County Town. The villages
we've seen today have been dismal, and we are just
wondering what Jiuba will be like when a young man
with trousers like a pantomime sailor's breezes round the
corner.

'Yes,' says Xiong Gang, 'There's a place you can stay in
Jiuba.'

Is there an internet bar, wonders Andy. 'Oh, yes,' says
Xiong. Food? 'No problem.'

Everything a Long Marcher needs, then; but we've had
enough false dawns not to get carried away just because
someone tells us what we want to hear. And besides, as
Andy says, look at those trousers.

Xiong leads us to a nondescript home near the top of
the village and leaves us in the front room while he looks
for the owner. (Rural China is like the Good Old Days in
England, when no one locked their front door.) Most of
our crowd of thirty spectators joins us inside; the rest
press up against the window. We sit on an L-shaped black
leather cushion sofa that hugs a black iron stove. The

stove is a comfort-object for us, a familiar character in our ever-changing lives. Wherever we come in from the cold, those already inside indicate the stove and say, '*Kao huo*'. Even the sound of this in Chinese is reassuring, almost warming by itself. Because we are cold practically all the time, we are obsessed with opportunities to *kao huo*.

Later, after the boss has arrived, ejected most of the rubberneckers and shown us to a spartan back room with two beds, Xiong Gang takes us to another home across the street where we eat a simple dinner of smoked tofu, potatoes and fried rice. Again, there is no sign to announce this is a place of business. Without Xiong, it would be invisible.

Xiong sits with us while we eat. He is twenty-four and worked a couple of years in a factory in Guangdong before coming home to try his hand at the hairdressing business. He is a mild-mannered, courteous young man and he helped us out of a spot without any particular reason to do so. I promise never to judge anyone by their trousers ever again.

Beyond Jiuba is the mountain range that lines the border of Tongzi and Xishui counties. At 4,500 feet above sea level we are surrounded by mist and confusion. We were led over the pass into Xishui County by a twenty-two-year-old primary school teacher named Luo Liwei. Before our ways parted, he put us on a dirt road and told us to follow it to Hecun, from where we could reach Guandian, our next destination. He said we'd be in Hecun in an hour. That was two hours ago.

A wooden house looms out of the mist to our left. I glimpse a woman in the doorway; as I catch her eye, she shuts the door. The silhouette of a man appears on the other side of the road. Andy hails him, but he fades away. There is nothing beyond that first house, but the mountain falls away from the road to our right – perhaps Hecun is down there, shrouded by the mist. I stay with the bags by

the roadside while Andy turns back to conduct reconnaissance.

A girl no older than fourteen approaches, carrying firewood strapped to a wooden frame on her back. She stares
at my enormous foreign frame in the ghostly mist and her
step slows. I can see she's afraid and so I remain seated,
smile and greet her in my best Chinese. 'Hello,' I say.

The girl stops, staggers backwards, slips the frame from
her shoulders and drops the firewood against the side of
the mountain. Then she turns and runs screaming for her
father into the murk: 'Baba, Ba-baaaaaaaaa!'

Daddy never comes to investigate the devil by the roadside. Andy returns without finding anyone to ask where we
are. He says windows and doors slammed shut on his
approach and nobody would answer their door. Before we
leave, I try picking up the girl's firewood. It weighs half as
much again as my backpack, 70 pounds or more.

We find Hecun about half an hour later, just below the
mist line. With a clear view, the spectacle is astonishing. I
expected the village to be on the valley floor, but instead it
clings to the mountain perhaps 500 yards up. The valley is
too deep and narrow to see the bottom. Opposite, the
ground is too steep for cultivation, but far below Hecun
on our side are paddies of brilliant emerald and above
them, in the starkest of contrasts, is a great opencast coal
face mined mostly by children and teenagers. Their eyes
and teeth shine through black faces.[13]

The road ends here – something Luo Liwei neglected to
mention – and so a young man named Yang Xiong leads
us down through the village as far as the mine, from
where the path into the valley is clear against the mountainside. It takes another hour of toe-crushing descent
to reach the stream that takes us the final mile into
Guandian, where a concrete obelisk in memory of the
Red Army dominates the twilit town and the river is filled
with trash.

That night we make friends with a crowd of children, half a dozen of whom follow us back to our lodgings, keen to carry on talking, practise a few words of English and take some photos. Two return the next day at breakfast time. Hu Xue and her friend Dai Huahua are home for the Chinese New Year holidays. They are sixteen-year-old upper middle school students in Xishui County Town. Today, however, they announce they are joining the Long March.

'We'll go with you as far as Shuanglong and we can get the bus back from there,' says Hu.

'Do you know how to get to Shuanglong?' asks Andy.

'No.'

'Do you know how far it is?' I ask.

'No.'

'What experience do you have in mountain trekking?' asks Andy.

'None.'

Who are we to say no?

Shuanglong is less than 6 miles away as the crow flies, but four hours as we march. Although it's right on their doorstep, the girls have never walked up the old footpaths and through the mountain farms. They're thrilled and totally undaunted by the mud and exertion. The land rises in stages and each time we reach the top of one climb and feel, surely, we must have come to the peak, we find we are actually on the edge of a small, flat space tucked between the folds of the range. There is only room for one farm, sometimes just one small field, and then the muddy path starts upwards once more.

As we're leading two schoolgirls on the Long March trail, I feel we should test their political education.

'Chairman Mao walked along this path, you know,' I say to Hu Xue. 'What do you think of him?'

'He was great,' says Hu, 'But then he turned stupid.'

'Why do you say that?'

'Because of the Cultural Revolution. He had that cult of personality, his picture was everywhere.'

'How do you know about that? Did your parents tell you?'

'No, I read it in my history book.'

'How about Zhou Enlai?"

'Great, definitely.'

'So how do you rate Jiang Zemin compared to Mao and Zhou?' I ask.

'Well, you can't say Jiang is great because he isn't dead yet. Right now, I think he's too soft and his glasses are too big.'

'How about Li Peng?' (As Premier, Li declared martial law shortly before the Tian'anmen massacre on 4 June 1989.)

'He's the same as Jiang – big glasses.'

'With Mao in command, the troops felt at ease,' wrote Harrison Salisbury. 'At last the political commissars could tell them why they were marching and where.'[14]

Actually with Mao in command after the Zunyi Meeting, the troops blundered straight into one of the most dangerous battles of the Long March.

After leaving Zunyi on 19 January, the plan was to move north-west to the Chishui River, cross and press on north to the Yangtze River in Sichuan Province. Once across the Yangtze, the First Front Army would seek out and unite with the Fourth Front Army, the force commanded by Zhang Guotao that had been driven out of its base area in 1932 during the early stages of Chiang Kai-shek's Fourth Encirclement Campaign. Zhang Guotao's army had enjoyed remarkable success since then. It had grown to well over 100,000 men (plus a 2,000-strong women's combat regiment) and established a soviet in the Sichuan–Shaanxi border area.

The plan started to go wrong as soon as the Red

Mao Zedong in Yan'an circa 1937

Mao's wife He Zizhen in Yan'an circa 1937

Mao's rival Wang Ming presided over his first Politburo meeting in Yan'an in December 1937. Pictured are Politburo members Zhang Wentian, Kang Sheng, Zhou Enlai, Kai Feng, Wang Ming, Mao Zedong, Ren Bishi and Zhang Guotao. All bar Wang Ming and Kang Sheng were Long March veterans

The Zunyi Meeting by Shen Yaoyi.
Left to right: Li Fuchun, Wang Jiaxiang, Zhang Wentian, Mao Zedong, Zhou Enlai, Bo Gu, Kai Feng, Zhu De, Chen Yun, Peng Dehuai, Nie Rongzhen, Liu Shaoqi, Deng Xiaoping, Li Zhuoran, Lin Biao, Yang Shangkun, Liu Bocheng, Wu Xiuquan, Otto Braun, Deng Fa

A Red detachment in the Central Soviet Area pre-Long March

Mao with Bo Gu, Zhou Enlai and Zhu De in Yan'an circa 1937

The Red Army crossing the Snow Mountains at the time of the Long March in June 1935

The Swamps by Shen Yaoyi

Mao with three unnamed Red soldiers in Jiangxi pre-Long March

Otto Braun in Yan'an
in 1939

Luding Bridge

A Red Army camp on the swamps

These sketches were made on the Long March by Huang Zhen, a 25-year-old former art teacher. Only 24 of Huang's Long March sketches survive – the only contemporary artistic record of the March

Experimenting with herbs in place of tobacco, which Red smokers had particular difficulty finding in the Tibetan region

The end of the Long March as depicted by Huang Naiyuan and Zhan Beixin

vanguard approached Chishui County Town, from where they hoped to cross the Chishui River and continue north to probe the Yangtze crossings. They found the town too well defended and, after fighting in vain all day, gave up and retreated south towards the main force, which was about to get into even bigger trouble.

At dawn the next morning, 28 January, with the Red vanguard still 20 miles away, the main body, under Mao's direction, turned on an enemy force that had been at its heels for the last couple of days. It was assumed that this was a small and typically unmotivated provincial unit that could be defeated easily and quickly, freeing the Reds to speed ahead, unmolested from the rear. This intelligence was completely wrong. The enemy consisted of well-armed Sichuanese regiments that were up for the fight and matched the Reds man for man. As the day progressed, losses mounted and fears grew that the Red Army might not hold out. At 3 p.m. an emergency meeting of the Central Military Committee was called – the only time this ever happened during a battle. It decided to break off the engagement at dusk and retreat immediately back across the Chishui at Tucheng, a mile-and-a-half west of the battlefield.[15] Instead of marching north to the Yangtze, the Reds fled west into the most remote, mountainous region of the Long March so far. They would spend the next two months walking in ever-decreasing circles.

West of the Chishui, Andy and I follow a tributary along a dirt road that we share with vans and motorcycles. The first village, Baicun, has a sprinkling of white tiles and even a couple of shops. But by mid-afternoon, there are only isolated farmhouses and a narrow, mud trail that divides and then divides again as the river breaks up into ever-smaller streams. Beyond Baicun, our route information doesn't tally with anything we can find on the Guizhou map and so we interview local peasants.

'Did the Red Army go this way?'

'Yes.'

'Which way did they go?'

'To Sichuan.'

The peasants make a characteristic gesture, an airy wave in no particular direction. Just carry on, says the wave, you'll be fine.

The records we carry suggest some Red units passed a town called Huangjing the day after crossing the Chishui. According to the map, Huangjing is more or less due west across the border. We meet two peasants at 3.30 p.m. who tell us they are from Huangjing and it's only '20 *li*' away.

In his book, *Marching with Mao*, William Lindesay writes:

'The Chinese peasantry are the last bastion of the *li*, a bizarre and uniquely Chinese distance which is flexible. A flat *li* is half a kilometre [550 yards]; but an uphill one, being more difficult, is shorter, and a downhill one, being much easier, is longer! For a unit to be variable seems quite contradictory until one realizes that the *li* is an indication of not only distance but the effort needed to cover it, a logical and ingenious measure conceived specifically for travellers on foot. Through ignorance I had initially ridiculed this unit but with experience I began to trust it in the knowledge that a *li* was about five minutes' walking irrespective of terrain.'[16]

In that case, we have less than two hours to go. Plenty of time to reach Huangjing before sunset. An hour later, a herd of black goats edges past us, followed by half a dozen men. We ask: are you going to Sichuan?

'No, we're from Guizhou. We're going home, but come with us and we'll show you the way. Where are you going?'

'Huangjing. How far is it?'

'Twenty *li*. Maybe you can't make it before dark.'

We thank the goatherds and they leave us to climb to a

ridge perhaps 100 yards above, where their village is hidden in lush forest. Follow the lower path, they tell us, and it will take you over the mountain and into Sichuan.

Like the *li*, the definition of 'path' is also a flexible concept. To begin with, it's a familiar, slightly uphill trail well marked by man and goat. Gradually, its edges blur as the forest encroaches. The river that runs alongside diminishes to a trickle fed by the very highest points of the mountain. A fine drizzle doesn't so much fall as hang in the air and drape itself over the deep green vegetation. And then the trail turns at right angles – straight up. The 'path' is now a 50-yard staircase of mud and stone. Sichuan is at the top.

The sun is already setting by the time we sit, gasping, on the soil of Province No.6 of the Long March. There is a sound like heavy rain in the distance. To our left is a valley that is more like a crevasse. It mocks our recent climb. Opposite, a sheer stone face falls from a forested toupee into spaces beyond our field of vision. We pick ourselves up to hurry towards the noise of falling water, looking all the while for flat, open spaces that might allow a tent. There are none, and as we round a bend and a gap opens up through the trees, we see our prospective water supply is also well out of reach.

They are twin waterfalls, bursting straight out of the mountainside opposite our path, which now runs along the edge of a cliff that allows us to see all the way to the valley floor. One waterfall begins about 30 feet above the other, making it at least 300 feet high. They are stupendous, awe-inspiring, and profoundly irritating. Why do they have to be here, now? It's nearly dark, and we are almost immediately driven from contemplation and appreciation of the wonder of our journey by another sight – a cultivated field, which sits above the higher fall and close to the line of our path. Agriculture = people = food and beds.

Within ten minutes we are in the darkening courtyard of a large, well-lit building. Through the open doorway I can see a fire and a row of thermos flasks. The man of the house, a thirty-something farmer, appears. I apologize for our intrusion, explain that we are heading for Huangjing but that it seems we have run out of daylight, so would it possibly not be too much trouble . . .

'There's plenty of homes that way in Longba,' he says. 'Why don't you go and stay there?'

'But it's getting dark,' I say. 'If we can't stay here, could you at least show us the way?'

We get that wave again. 'That way, only ten minutes.'

'How can we find it in the dark? Won't you help us?'

Silence. Andy takes charge.

'Well, it's too late now,' he says. 'We'll just put our tent up here in your courtyard. We won't bother you. Is that OK?'

Silence.

If travel is supposed to broaden the mind, why do I immediately feel so hostile towards Sichuan? Both Andy and I are increasingly jumping to conclusions, making snap judgements about places and people. We can't seem to help it. For good or bad, one person can colour attitudes to a village, a town, a whole province even.

'That's Sichuan people for you,' says Li Mingxia after hearing about our first night in the province. Li Mingxia is from Henan, the province with the worst reputation in all China – at least as far as people in Beijing are concerned. Before we set out on the Long March, Beijing was in a panic about a gang of Henan peasants who were allegedly roaming the city injecting passers-by with HIV-infected blood. It was rubbish, of course. Henan is more properly notorious for the thousands of HIV infections caused by uncontrolled blood sales in the province. Local governments connived at the blood-collection programmes and, with the support of the provincial authorities, did their best to cover up the disaster. Entire communities are being devastated by AIDS, but no one has been held responsible or punished – except victims who have been harassed, beaten up and imprisoned for protesting about their treatment.

Andy and I are the first foreigners many people on the Long March route have seen. Some days I worry our behaviour will dictate their impression of all foreigners, perhaps for all time. I don't relish the role of ambassador for the rest of the world, especially first thing in the morning, packing a tent away in the rain while our host makes conversation.

'Where are you from?' he tries. I give him the silent treatment. I don't want word to get out that England is a nation of bad-tempered weirdos. Besides, right at this moment I can't think about home except in the person of another Englishman, William Lindesay, and his trust in the 'flexible' *li*. Huangjing, it has emerged, is still 20 *li* away.

It's still 20 *li* away six hours later. We arrive at five, just before sunset.

There is no warning as we pick our way through a village whose name I never discover. We have lost track of the main path, meaning we are now passing through the kitchen gardens and back yards of peasant homes. This is risky. Dogs are becoming more aggressive the further west we go. Before Zunyi, we paid little attention to them. They were a nuisance only for the noise; they rarely dared approach, and the slightest aggressive move was enough to send them scurrying. This one, however, doesn't make a sound as it slinks up behind Andy and takes a bite out of his calf.

Dog bites vegetarian. Andy says later that if he is ever forced to eat meat, dog will be the first animal in the pot. While I apply first aid, a fifty-something woman and a pre-teen girl come out of the nearest house, seize the dog and tie it up. The woman then approaches us in a dreadful state of shame and apology. She cannot stop apologizing, '*Dui bu qi, dui bu qi,*' and after a few moments I realize she is deaf and her granddaughter must have drawn her attention to the commotion outside. I also come to realize we are standing next to a fresh grave, which belongs to the woman's father, and that she is about to walk to the next village to visit her eighty-year-old mother.

We can't help ourselves – we wind up apologizing for upsetting this lady. Andy gives the granddaughter an orange. But he's still sore and annoyed and when he says, 'I can't even have the satisfaction of being angry at the dog's owner,' he is only half joking.

Andy digs out the satellite phone and calls our doctor in Beijing.

'I've been bitten by a dog. What should I do?'

'Where are you?' asks the doc.

'Sichuan.'

'In that case, you go to the nearest major city immediately and get a rabies injection.'

'Are you sure?'

'Well, we regard rabies as endemic in Sichuan, so yes, I'm sure.'

The nearest city is Chongqing, a full day away by bus assuming we actually get to the highway by evening. Even though Andy had rabies shots in Beijing, they buy him only an extra 48 hours before he needs a follow-up jab. We call an official Long March Meeting to resolve what to do. To begin with, Andy is inclined towards the local peasant viewpoint on the risk of getting rabies: '*Mei shi.*' I point out that, in the event of that dog being mad – and it certainly looked mad – in three days he will start to froth at the mouth, his brain will disintegrate and he will die in unthinkable agony.

Andy touches his forehead a moment. 'I'm going to Chongqing,' he says.

It takes until dusk to reach the highway at Daba and by the time we get there, Andy is also deprived of the satisfaction of being the injured and suffering party. He only has a sore leg, whereas I am so sick I can hardly walk. I have had diarrhoea for the past forty-eight hours, but this afternoon it worsened as the trail grew in difficulty. We have been following steep footpaths almost all day, cutting directly through great switchback sweeps of road over stony mountains that grow nothing but scrub. Over the final 3 miles, I have had to rest every half hour. I am bathed in sweat and every step is an effort of will.

Why bother? Why not just flag the first car and go straight to the county town 12 miles away? I have no life-or-death reason to continue. I'm not a Red Army soldier. Yet I am driven on, it seems, by a determination not to cheat myself.

Andy and I often protest that our goal is not to experience what the Reds experienced, but there are times when I sense the knife edge on which they walked. I have never paid much attention to diarrhoea. I suffered it frequently in Beijing, especially after a red-hot Chongqing hotpot, and it never got much in the way of normal life. I couldn't connect when I read about what a killer it is in the developing world. I can now. In Daba, I'm too wasted to move. Despite all the medicine and high-tech support available to me, I know I can't carry on. I see how in extreme circumstances a chance sickness, even a minor tummy ailment, could be a death blow. I see how the survivors of the Long March were not only strong and courageous. They were lucky, too.

'No sickness,' veteran Zhao Yuxiang told the reporter who interviewed him for *Beijing Youth Daily*'s 'My Long March' oral history project. 'I mean you didn't get ill. Conditions didn't allow it . . . At that time, there was no concept of wounded or sick, only life or death."[17]

Liao Dinglin told *Beijing Youth Daily* he saw sick men begging their leaders to shoot them.[18] Li Kaiyou, a propaganda soldier in the 6th Army Group, was responsible for finding safe houses. 'We left money for wounded soldiers with local people. We didn't expect that some of the seriously wounded soldiers would be killed by local people for the money. After realizing this, we didn't give money to wounded soldiers in front of locals. We warned them to use the money only at crucial times and sometimes told them not to tell locals they had money.'[19]

I can't go to Chongqing with Andy, who must leave immediately for his jabs. Two days later, I take my first steps outside. I hail a ride into the centre of town, send a fax to Andy, then return to bed and spend four hours recovering from my exertions. We're a long way behind the Red Army now.

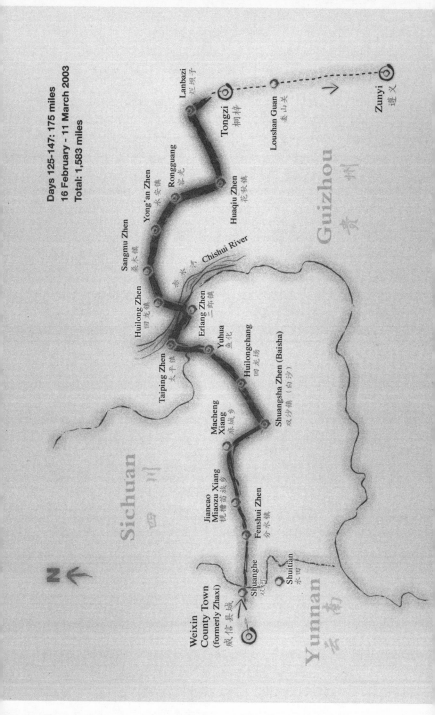

Days 125-147: 175 miles
16 February - 11 March 2003
Total: 1,583 miles

Lanbazi 岸坝子
Tongzi 桐梓
Zunyi 遵义
Loushan Guan 娄山关

Rongguang 容光
Yong'an Zhen 永安镇
Sangmu Zhen 桑木镇
Huaqiu Zhen 花秋镇

Chishui River 赤水河

Huilong Zhen 回龙镇
Erlang Zhen 二郎镇
Yuhua 鱼化
Taiping Zhen 太平镇
Huilongchang 回龙场
Shuangsha Zhen (Baisha) 双沙镇（白沙）

Macheng Xiang 麻城乡
Jiancao Miaozu Xiang 枧槽苗族乡
Fenshui Zhen 分水镇

Guizhou 贵州

Sichuan 四川

N

Weixin County Town (formerly Zhaxi) 威信县城
Shuanghe 双河
Shuitian 水田

Yunnan 云南

Chapter 6

The Lost Daughter of Chairman Mao

The Red Army Memorial Museum overlooks Zhaxi from the hill above the remnants of the old town. Little is left from the Long March era. There is a single street of misshapen wooden houses and, directly below the museum, a fine pair of red-lacquered halls that once served as a kind of club for people from Jiangxi Province – an appropriate venue for the Red leaders to convene the last in a series of gatherings now known collectively as the Zhaxi Meeting. The halls are beautifully restored and preserved in a quiet compound that also features the house where Mao and Zhang Wentian stayed. This is a small building, just one room for each man either side of a tiny central room where museum guide Luo Hongfen tells us they ate. Mao and Zhang lived together on Yunshi Mountain outside Ruijin even before the Long March began, and I have noticed they were regular housemates on the Long March itself. Three days before reaching Zhaxi, Zhang got his reward for supporting Mao at Zunyi. At a meeting in Huafangzi on 5 February – the first of the 'Zhaxi Meeting' series – Zhang formally took over Bo Gu's position as 'Person with Overall Responsibility for the Party' (in theory, the most senior Party position at the time).

This episode of the Long March turned out to be the pinnacle of Zhang Wentian's political career. Within weeks of the Zhaxi Meeting, Zhang and Mao were already starting to drift apart. Otto Braun claims Mao told him in late April that Zhang had 'panicked' and begun 'intriguing' against him.[1] Whether or not that's true, Andy and I see no more joint lodgings for Zhang and Mao on the Long March. And while for the time being there was no open break with Mao, Zhang never quite reached the heights he seemed destined for in 1935. He remained a leading member of the Party, but the top jobs eluded him. After the final Communist victory in 1949, he entered the Foreign Ministry, becoming ambassador to the USSR in 1951 and Deputy Foreign Minister in 1955.

Zhang's career went right off the rails in 1959, when he was identified by Mao as part of an oppositional 'clique' led by Peng Dehuai, general of the 3rd Army Group on the Long March. Mao's Great Leap Forward had been launched the year before. This was a quixotic effort to apply mass political mobilization to economic development. Mao decreed that the countryside should be industrialized rapidly, to the point where the value of industrial output matched agricultural output. He declared it was the task of the whole Party, 'to lift the lid, break down superstition [about the possibility of overcoming difficulties] and allow the initiative and creativity of the working people to explode'.[2] The main effects of this campaign were to divert resources away from farming and provoke the worst famine of the twentieth century.[3] At a Party meeting in August 1959, Peng Dehuai delivered Mao a confidential letter in which he detailed the results of an investigation he had made in Hunan. Peng concluded that the Great Leap Forward was going badly wrong. Mao didn't want to know. He had been at odds with Peng several times since they first met on Jinggangshan in 1928, and now he treated Peng's letter as a treacherous attempt to overthrow his authority. Peng was purged, along with those suspected of sharing his views. Zhang Wentian was kicked out of his job at the Foreign Ministry, but things got a lot worse after the Cultural Revolution began in 1966.

Zhang was accused of spying for the Soviet Union and spent time in prison before being exiled to Guangdong, then Jiangsu, where he died in obscurity in 1976. Peng Dehuai had already died in a prison hospital two years earlier. In 1967, he had been interrogated more than 130 times and beaten repeatedly. He spent the rest of his life in prison, where he was interrogated and tortured again throughout most of 1970.[4] The reputations of both men were officially 'rehabilitated' in 1978, two years after Mao's death.

'After Zhang was brought down, his role in history was glossed over, so because the meetings in this area were strongly associated with him, documents relating to them were censored, "lost" or ignored,' says Luo Hongfen. 'The Zunyi Meeting got all the attention, but that meeting still left important questions unresolved. It was the Zhaxi Meeting that tied up the loose ends.' As a result of Zhang's downfall and persecution, however, the meetings in this area were effectively struck from Chinese history.

Luo leads us through a museum full of detail and original artefacts. She knows the local stories inside out and recounts them with verve. There is a whole room devoted to slogans written by Long Marchers, all on original wooden boards that have been taken from the homes where the soldiers stayed. Luo says Mao ordered everything not absolutely necessary to be jettisoned in Zhaxi. One display case houses an X-ray machine that was buried in a peasant's home. In the meeting hall, the back of Chairman Mao's chair has been worn smooth by visitors touching it for luck, just as pilgrims rub the marble animals in the Taoist Baiyunguan Temple in Beijing.

But there is one thing conspicuously absent, one exhibit that occupies pride of place in every other major memorial hall we have seen. It is the picture of a central government leader visiting the site. Once a museum receives a visit of this kind, the door is open for funding and for attention and publicity across the country. Zhaxi has never received such a visit.

Over roast potatoes in her office, museum head Guo Zhangxiong ponders how and why her town missed out on Long March glory.

'Mao was the kind of man who liked others to be below him, to be less important than himself. That's why he brought Zhang Wentian down, because he saw Zhang as being on an equal footing to him and he couldn't accept it. To us, Zhang is a model character, but it's because of his association with Zhaxi that it took many years for historians to begin researching events here.'

Now, however, Guo and her colleagues think they have stumbled on a story that could put Zhaxi back on the map – a story so unlikely that Andy and I initially laugh it off as a joke.

Mao Zedong's wife, He Zizhen, was around five months pregnant when she began the Long March. She gave birth to a daughter after the first crossing of the Chishui and the child was immediately given away to a peasant family. It was impossible to care for a baby under the conditions of the Long March.

Zhong Yuelin, the youngest woman in the First Front Army, was with He Zizhen when she gave birth. Sixty years later, she told American scholar Helen Praeger Young:

'I didn't understand what was going on. I'd never had a baby! I just helped her a little. Once in a while I brought some water. The birth was quite easy. She had already had several babies and it went pretty fast. She had a girl. Qian Xijun carried [the baby] that night and found a local family.'[5]

Qian Xijun went on to tell Praeger Young:

'[We found] an old, blind lady, fifty or sixty years old . . . There, in the minority areas, they needed labourers. I said, "We'll give [this baby] to you. You can raise her as your daughter."

'She said, "I'm too old [to nurse her]."'

' "Never mind. You can find some rice porridge for her to eat. She will be your daughter and can help you work."

'She agreed, because there was no alternative. "There's no one else around and you're going off to fight. Just leave her here."

'Because she was very poor, we left her ten silver dollars.'[6]

All trace of the child was lost. When Harrison Salisbury interviewed Long March survivors in 1984, he was unable to pinpoint even the place of birth. Mao's bodyguard Wu Jiqing said he was uncertain of the location. Wu told Salisbury it may have been Baisha in Sichuan, Fengxiangba in Guizhou, or Zhaxi in Yunnan.[7] Qian Xijun thought it was in Guizhou. The mystery has never been solved.

Our guide Luo Hongfen brings us to a small section of the Zhaxi museum devoted to the women of the Long March. Among the grainy black-and-white pictures is one outstanding image, a full-length photograph of He Zizhen, taken in Yan'an perhaps two years after the end of the Long March. We both pause to study the picture: she stands smiling and relaxed, her hair cut boyishly short under a Red Army cap. Luo recounts the familiar story of He's lost Long March baby, throwing in a graphic and probably fanciful portrayal of a tearful He being ordered by Mao to leave the child behind. And then Luo adds two extra pieces of information I've never heard before.

One is that museum staff are certain the child was born in their area, in Huafangzi, the same village where Zhang Wentian was chosen to take over Bo Gu's duties as 'Person with Overall Responsibility for the Party'. Guo Zhangxiong has interviewed old villagers around Huafangzi who say the Red Army left a baby girl behind when they pulled out. The villagers never thought much of it, because they never knew what Guo knew: Mao's wife was the *only* Red Army soldier to give birth anywhere near this time.

The second is that six months ago in a mountain village

some 20 miles from here, an old woman was identified who might be that child.

Just after 7 p.m., Andy and I are sitting in the kitchen of a modern apartment in the centre of Weixin County Town, as Zhaxi is now known. On the other side of the stove are – possibly – Mao Zedong and He Zizhen's granddaughters, Yang Tingyan, thirty-eight, and Yang Tingyu, thirty-two, plus Tingyan's husband, Xiong Minghu.

Right at this moment, I'm still extremely sceptical about the 'lost Mao child' story. Mao and He lost three children altogether – two left behind in Jiangxi together with the Long March baby – and there have been numerous rumours and phoney claimants. 'Yeah, yeah,' I thought when Luo Hongfen started telling us the story, until I realized she wasn't talking about old news, but about something no one outside this county even knows.

Yang Tingyan begins the tale.

'I first heard about it last year from a local official named Tao Yunxian. He had been researching the Long March in this area and he was particularly interested in finding Mao and He's baby. He believed the child had been given to a family of the Miao minority. Early last year, he interviewed an old man in Shuitian [a small town half a mile or so above Huafangzi] called Zheng Mingquan. Zheng was living in Huafangzi in February 1935. About 400 yards up the hill was a Miao family headed by a man named Xiong Zhikui.

'In 1936, Xiong Zhikui came to see Zheng. Xiong was distressed and quietly told Zheng he had been given a two-year-old baby girl. He asked whether he should adopt or not. Zheng told him, "You've got the baby. You raise the baby." In a Miao village, people don't give babies away. No one will give babies to other people to raise.

'The Xiong family raised a girl nicknamed "Maomei". Zheng said she still lived nearby and had visited him once in the early 1990s. It was the first time he had seen her since she moved away in the 1940s.'

Yang Tingyan passes us a blue-tinted photo of a young woman in Miao minority dress.

'This is my mother,' she says, "Maomei."'

'Maomei' could be interpreted as meaning 'Mao's little sister'. I look for resemblances – large facial moles, for instance – in the photo and in the faces of the two daughters, but I'm sorry to say I can't find any.

'There must be more,' I say. 'How can you even be sure Maomei and the child given to Xiong are the same?'

Son-in-law Xiong Minghu (confusingly, half the people in Weixin seem to be called Xiong) takes up the story.

'One day when they had no salt at home, Maomei went to get some from her aunt. After she gave her the salt, Maomei's aunt told her she was adopted. Her elder brother teased her about it. And then there's the thing about her birthday. Her father asked her to memorize her birthday as 1936. He didn't ask his other children to remember their birthdays. Her father died in 1944 and soon afterwards her mother told Maomei she had been told to memorize the wrong date. Actually, she said, the real date of birth was February 1935.'

On 5 February 1935, the Reds were in Huafangzi. This is the same village in which Guo Zhangxiong and the museum staff believe He Zizhen gave birth and the place Maomei spent the first ten years of her life as an adopted child. So, the right time, right place, and adopted.

'Do you think we could go and see your mother? I ask Yang Tingyan.

She is thrilled. 'Of course, we can go tomorrow. My mother's never met a foreigner before.'

'*I've* never met a foreigner before,' says Yang Tingyu.

'Let me ask you one thing,' says Andy. 'What do you think? Do you believe your mother is Chairman Mao's daughter?'

The women shrug. 'I can't say,' says Yang Tingyan.

Yang's twelve-year-old daughter, Qisu, is standing behind us. She has followed the whole conversation. She whispers, 'Yes.'

Even by Long March standards, the Miao village of Tianchi feels remote. We are far up in mountains so high and so steep, the view into the valley is like looking out of an aircraft window. In the 1950s, a team from Beijing came to Zhaxi to look for the Mao child. Tao Yunxian had seen their report during his research, hence his belief the child had been given to a Miao family. But in the 1950s, the searchers could not have found Maomei in this area because she and her family weren't there anymore. They had moved away after the father Xiong Zhikui died in 1944. In 1947, two years before the Communists won the civil war, Maomei was given to the Yang family in Tianchi to be the second wife of their son, Yang Hongming. She was twelve years old. She was sent to tend the goats. She still can't write her own name.

Maomei's proper name is Xiong Huazhi (Chinese women retain their maiden names after marriage). She meets us at the gate to her home, a typical dark-wood, single-storey Miao home with one wing on either side off a central porch. Her skin is pallid and drawn tight against the bones of her face, which looks older than her sixty-eight years. Although only just out of hospital, she walks without aid. She leads us into the front room of the right wing and sits herself in a purple padded armchair on the far side of the black stove. On the wall behind her is a poster of the '10 Marshals of the People's Republic of China' on horseback, a Cultural Revolution-era pewter relief of Chairman Mao, and a picture of TV star Zhao Wei as Princess Huanzhu in one of China's biggest hit shows of recent years. Xiong smiles and waves us on to benches around the stove. We ask after her health and she grimaces, 'Not good.'

Yang Tingyu sits to her mother's right. 'After my mother heard [the theory about her parentage], she went into hospital straight away,' she says. Not for the first time, I wonder why the children thought it would be a good idea to tell their mother they suspected she might be the daughter of the most powerful and important Chinese man of the twentieth century, perhaps of all time. I don't think this is the right time or place to put this question, though.

There are sticky rice cakes heating on top of the stove. Xiong's second daughter, Yang Tinghua, thirty-four, serves everyone tea and Xiong encourages us to eat the hot snacks. We can barely understand her speech and so Yang Tingyan, who sits opposite her mother, interprets into Mandarin.

'These are a Miao tradition at Spring Festival,' she says. 'The festival is over once they are all eaten.'

Xiong tells what little she knows of her family background: how her mother moved her to Sichuan after her father died and then returned to Tianchi in 1947, and how she was told of her true birth date.

'Did your mother ever explain why you were given the wrong date?' I ask.

'No.'

'You never asked?'

'No.'

'Do you think you are Mao's daughter?'

Xiong answers without hesitation, as if she has thought this question over many times. 'Don't want to pretend to be something I'm not. I just want the facts.' She points to her wrist. 'It should be simple to do a blood test, shouldn't it?'

Xiong Minghu (Yang Tingyan's husband) has already told us how he has tried to raise his mother-in-law's case with the local government. He has asked them to find a way to perform a DNA test that would establish the truth and set his mother-in-law's mind at rest. To do that would require agreement from the only known surviving child of Mao Zedong and He Zizhen – Li Min, born in Bao'an in 1936. Li lives in Beijing, serves as a deputy in the National People's Congress and might be Maomei's younger sister. The only answer the family has received is that the matter has been 'passed to a higher level' for consideration.

'I ask every day if there's an answer,' says Xiong Minghu, 'and every day my mother-in-law asks me if there's any news.' His voice rises, 'They say we are talking nonsense and that we have no evidence. But nobody comes to our door to investigate this. I asked the government if I could invite foreigners here. The government said: "Don't you dare do that." We are not doing this for us or others. It's for the older generation. If there had been no revolution, then no child would ever have been lost like this.'

At Andy's instigation, I ask, 'Do you think your problem is that you are poor peasants, while Mao's family is rich and powerful?'

Yang Tingyu says – quietly – 'Thank you', and then steadily loses control of her emotions as she describes Xiong Minghu's daily efforts on behalf of her mother, how they have all tried to find an answer, but no one will help them. Her mother comforts her with a tissue. I've never seen the humiliation of powerlessness laid bare like this.

As we leave, Xiong Huazhi gives us a hand-embroidered jacket, one of those she made for special occasions when she was a young woman. It's a beautiful piece of work and we try to refuse the gift. 'Take it,' she insists. Finally, I accept it on one condition.

'We'll bring it back when you find out who you are,' I say. Xiong smiles and accepts the promise.

We're under no illusions why we have been told this story. Xiong Huazhi's family has no *guanxi*, as the Chinese call the networks of personal connections that are vital in such a bureaucratic country. No one outside

Weixin County will listen to them. They obviously hope that we will spread word of Xiong's dilemma and that someone might listen to us – someone important enough to be able to help them. We're being used, but now that I have heard the whole story, I don't think it's a joke anymore. The museum people had independent corroboration from local witnesses that the Red Army left a child in Huafangzi in February 1935. He Zizhen was the only Red Army woman to give birth around that time. Zheng Mingquan, who lived a few hundred metres from Xiong Huazhi's home, testified that Xiong was an adopted child and was living in Huafangzi from at least 1936. An elderly aunt of Xiong Huazhi confirmed Xiong was adopted. If Xiong is making up the story of her birthdate, then she's a magnificent actress.

If the search team from Beijing had found Xiong Huazhi in the 1950s, they would certainly have taken a close look at her. Unlikely though it seems after all these years, I do believe she might be Mao's lost daughter. It would be easy enough to prove it, of course, but how does a family of Miao minority peasants convince Li Min, Deputy to the National People's Congress and eldest known daughter of Chairman Mao, to take a blood test that might oblige her to call an illiterate peasant, 'Big Sister'?

I believe Xiong Huazhi when she says all she wants is to know, one way or the other. She is old and sick and feels she may not have long left. Her children are another matter. For all their protestations that they just want to help their mother, they can't be blind to the implications if it could be proved they were Mao's descendants. The prestige of the Mao name could be worth a great deal – if only as a tourist attraction. The museum staff certainly see it that way. If it turns out that Maomei really is the Mao child, says our guide Luo Hongfen, 'We hope journalists from all around the world will come to Zhaxi. Zhaxi will be famous.'

But cynicism and an eye to the main chance don't alter the facts. Whatever the rights and wrongs of the situation, whatever reasons the authorities and the Mao family may have for ignoring Xiong Minghu's pleas, Andy and I walk out of Weixin obsessed with one question: what could we do to persuade Li Min to take that blood test?

Two days after the birth of his seventh child, on 7 February 1935, Mao and the Red Army leadership continued the Zhaxi meetings in the village of Dahetan. They discussed the defeat outside Tucheng, the retreat across the Chishui River and the necessity of a new plan of action. Mao's plan to go north across the Yangtze had failed. Instead, the Red Army had been chased into a remote, poverty-stricken corner inhabited by Miao and Yi minorities as well as Han. It was difficult for the troops to find food. Chiang Kaishek was mobilizing forces to surround them. The outlook was as bleak as at any time since leaving the soviet republic nearly four months before.

The meeting at Dahetan agreed to a radical change of course. The plan to cross the Yangtze was cancelled. It was decided to establish a base area in the Yunnan–Sichuan–Guizhou border region, and to attempt to expand this area eastwards across the north of Guizhou. The Red Army would therefore turn around and fight its way back to Zunyi.

The same meeting also approved Zhang Wentian's summary of the debate at the Zunyi Meeting, which was in fact a summary of Mao's speech in Zunyi. This document would enter history as the Zunyi Resolution, Exhibit No. 1 in the Maoist history of the Long March. According to this official version, the Zunyi Resolution restores Mao to command, corrects the strategic errors of Bo Gu and Otto Braun, and allows Mao's genius to lead the Red Army to glory. Hence our museum guide's belief that the meetings in her county deserve greater attention: the Zunyi Resolution was actually passed not in Zunyi, but in Dahetan, and it was written by Zhang Wentian, who replaced Bo Gu as top Party man not at Zunyi, but at Huafangzi, where Mao's daughter was born the same day.

Otto Braun saw this period as one of 'exhausting and fruitless wandering'.[8] He thought the return east from Zhaxi was dictated by circumstances and basically unplanned. But after the criticism heaped on him during the Zunyi Meeting, either Braun was not invited or he chose to boycott the discussions of the leadership. The records of the Zhaxi meetings show that strategy was not entirely made on the fly. In the final meeting in Zhaxi itself, on 10 February, it was confirmed that all units would move east, cross the Chishui River a second time and retake Zunyi.[9] A major battle was predicted.[10] Just over two weeks later, this plan would be fulfilled to the letter.

On 20 February, Andy and I leave Weixin County Town past a billboard that assures us in English, 'Welcome to Our Town Usually.' Andy can barely raise a smile. He developed a cough almost as soon as we reached Weixin four days ago, but while he initially dismissed this as a temporary inconvenience, his condition has continued to deteriorate. At night, he now coughs so hard neither of us can sleep. I call a doctor in Beijing, who takes a guess at bronchitis. Andy takes the recommended drugs, but they have no impact. His appetite vanishes and his strength begins to fade. By evening each day, he only wants to go to bed. I can see him weakening all the more because he is eating so little. Andy no longer has the energy to share the load of organizing and dealing with the daily questions of route-finding, accommodation and supplies, let alone give time and attention to the many people who want to talk to us. I'm usually a fairly easy-going person, but my temper begins to buckle under the strain of organizing, forging friendly ties and looking after Andy all at the same time.

Every day I tell myself I will be more patient, I will not lose my temper, but it only takes one young man to yell 'Ha-loo!' in a comedy accent from a passing motorcycle and I'm off again, shouting at peasants like a TV Otto Braun, abusing shopkeepers for their prices, haranguing waitresses for putting ham in Andy's fried tofu. I celebrate my 35th birthday in Taiping Zhen by yelling at a meek policeman who unwisely wakes us up to check our documents. After Jia Ji meets us in Zunyi again six days later, she christens me 'King of Quarrel'. It's not a compliment.

After leaving Zhaxi on 11 February, the Red Army marched around 220 miles back to Zunyi, which it captured for the second time after routing provincial forces north of the city on 27 February. The Reds captured 2,000 prisoners and 1,000 rifles to record their first major victory since setting out on the Long March.[11] But whereas they had entered Zunyi in grand style the month before, greeted by curious and friendly crowds and banners and slogans hung up by advance propaganda units, this time they found a desolate city. Otto Braun wrote: 'Shops and warehouses were empty; the homes of the rich landlords and merchants, including the governor's summer residence, were boarded up or half destroyed and plundered. Here and there shreds of posters and defaced slogans of our political workers hung on house walls. These were the only traces of the sovietization that had been so ambitiously started at the beginning of the year.'[12] Nevertheless, confidence was high after finally winning a battle, and the Reds prepared to set about building their new base area.

Andy has exhausted every ounce of strength to reach Zunyi, where he hopes a few creature comforts will help him shake off his mystery illness. Unfortunately, while he convalesces in bed there's nothing to watch on TV but the National People's Congress, at which the 'Third Generation' leadership of the Chinese state – principally Jiang Zemin, Li Peng and Zhu Rongji – will step aside for new faces, making Hu Jintao President as well as Party Secretary.

We kill time watching the nation's leaders parade in Beijing. This is a unique event. I can't think of another example of a Communist country changing its leadership in this way. Traditionally, Communist leaders either die in their posts or are replaced in a palace coup. But during Jiang Zemin's time as Party General Secretary, the top Communist Party posts became synonymous with the leading positions of state. Previously, the state presidency was a prestigious but not especially powerful post given to Party elders as a kind of long-service award. But after Jiang took the presidency as well as the Party's top job, the presidency began to assume greater weight in terms of public perception. As China's global status rose during the 1990s, Jiang met, say, Bill Clinton in his role as President of China, not Party leader. The Jiang administration wanted China to look more modern, and one part of looking modern meant having state institutions and leaders that looked similar to their Western counterparts.

This was one of Jiang's most remarkable innovations. He committed himself and other leaders to fixed tenures as state servants, and by doing so created pressure for change throughout the Communist Party hierarchy. To divorce the presidency from the Party leadership after so many years would demean the office of president at a time when that office was more globally significant than ever. As Jiang's term as president drew to a close, he had little choice but to give up the Party leadership as well. By the same logic, the other leading comrades also had to make way for new blood.

We watch nine men in identical suits emerge at a press conference, complete with English interpreters. We study their glasses carefully. Yes, definitely smaller than Li

Peng's or Jiang Zemin's. The congress is a triumph of modernization.

In between sessions of the National People's Congress, we decide that since we don't know anyone especially important, the best way to find the truth about Maomei is to tell as many people as possible about her. A scattergun approach, we reason, might hit at least one worthwhile target. We therefore write up Maomei's story and email it along with Xiong Minghu's phone number to every TV and print journalist in Jia Ji's bulging contacts book.

Only one picks it up. A short feature by a good friend of ours, Bill Smith at the German Press Agency, DPA, appears at the bottom of a page of National People's Congress news in the Hong Kong daily *South China Morning Post*. The Chinese mainland press is completely silent – with the exception of our friend Hector Mackenzie, who writes from his office at the English-language *China Daily* in Beijing:

'I nearly spat my coffee out when I read your story,' says Hector. 'I showed it to my editor and said, "Don't you think that's a good story?" He said, "Yes, that's a *very* interesting story."

' "So are we going to run it?" I asked. He said, "A-haha-haha," and changed the subject.'

I shouldn't be surprised. At my last job at a magazine called *China International Business*, one of my colleagues was especially fond of writing pieces quoting Chairman Mao. These references were inevitably cut out by the censor. Mao is still a dangerous and divisive figure. The authorities are content to exploit him as an icon, the sanitized 'Great Helmsman' who led the Party to victory and liberated China. They are less happy to expose people to the extreme radicalism of his thought and action.

Mao not only advocated violence, he appeared to lust after it. He compared himself to China's first emperor,

Qin Shihuang, a byword for cruelty and extremism. Qin executed hundreds of Confucian scholars and had all books predating his reign burnt (with the exception of medical texts). 'You accuse us of acting like Qin Shihuang,' Mao once told a group of liberal intellectuals. 'You are wrong. We surpass him a hundred times. When you berate us for imitating his despotism, we are happy to agree!'[13]

The leaders who today promote 'socialism with Chinese characteristics', who have opened Party membership to wealthy private entrepreneurs and sold state enterprises to Japanese companies – these people don't mind peasants hanging Mao's portrait in their front rooms, but they don't want the peasants pondering Mao's words. 'If our children's generation goes in for revisionism,' Mao told the Central Committee in 1962, 'so that although they still nominally have socialism, it is in fact capitalism, then our grandsons will certainly rise up in revolt and overthrow their fathers.'[14]

Sensitivity about Mao, it turns out, extends even to tales of offspring heroically born and tragically abandoned on the Long March. No one except Hector replies to our emails. No one calls Xiong Minghu. As far as the press is concerned, Maomei is already dead.

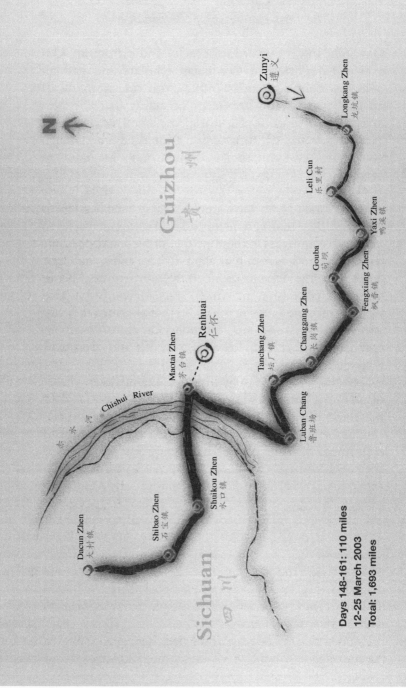

N

Guizhou 贵州

Zunyi 遵义

Longkang Zhen 龙坑镇

Leli Cun 乐里村

Yaxi Zhen 鸭溪镇

Gouba 苟坝

Fengxiang Zhen 枫香镇

Changgang Zhen 长岗镇

Tanchang Zhen 坛厂镇

Renhuai 仁怀

Maotai Zhen 茅台镇

Chishui River 赤水河

Luban Chang 鲁班场

Shuikou Zhen 水口镇

Shibao Zhen 石宝镇

Dacun Zhen 大村镇

Sichuan 四川

Days 148-161: 110 miles
12-25 March 2003
Total: 1,693 miles

Chapter 7

The Four Crossings of the Chishui

Although the fields of Zunyi County are swathed in yellow rape flowers, the air is chill and wet with drizzle. The damp seems to have settled in Andy's lungs. He coughs twenty-four hours a day. It's affecting his stomach too – he wakes with stomach ache most mornings and his appetite has never been so poor. Even after ten days' rest in Zunyi, he is still barely strong enough to march even the flat roads that lead to the third crossing of the Chishui River. Jia Ji joins us to help out for a few days, but falls over heavily in the mud of Yaxi Zhen and injures her knee. Our Long March limps on through villages decked with lines of yellowing cabbage leaves. When they are dry, they will be salted and wrapped in plastic, then sealed in pottery jars for preservation. By roadsides we see stone posts carved with faces and capped with red cloth. The peasants put them there to ward off ghosts. There are ghosts everywhere on the Long March trail.

'The Guomindang rounded up all the sick and wounded they could find and executed them,' says Pan Keming. 'They were hacked to death and their bodies were thrown into a cavern.'

Pan is sitting on the edge of my bed. It is eight o'clock in the morning in Gouba, a village about 30 miles west of

Zunyi, where Andy, Jia Ji and I have been taken in by the family of a local schoolteacher. Pan works with our host at the primary school in nearby Huameng. He says he likes to listen to the old people tell tales about the Long March.

'Two weeks later, a local Guomindang man was out hunting. He heard noises from below ground, and found the entrance to the cavern. The noises sounded human, but he shouted down, "Are you a ghost?" Finally, he was convinced it was a man and he went home to get a rope. He hauled up two survivors, both almost dead from injuries and starvation. One died when his stomach burst after eating, but the other recovered and went back to Jiangxi. No one knows what happened to him.'

Pan reaches for a cigarette. I ask him not to. I can take a breakfast-in-bed of blood and guts, but not washed down with a lungful of cheap tobacco smoke.

'Why would a Guomindang man save them?' I ask.

'It's not so unusual. One of my colleagues, Zhang Chuan – he's retired, actually – is the son of a Long Marcher named Zhang Jiacai. He was only a boy at the time and was lost by his unit near Ganxi, about 12 miles north-west of Gouba. He was taken in by the Guomindang head of the Ganxi government, Mu Zhiqing, who hid him in a cave for two weeks. Guomindang soldiers came looking for survivors, but Mu said he didn't know anything about any Red Army members left behind. After they left, Mu took the boy into his home and gave him work tending the cows and goats. After Liberation, he even helped Zhang find a wife in Huameng. Because he was a Guomindang leader, Mu was in danger after Liberation, but because he was known as a "Red Army saviour" he escaped. His family are still in Ganxi.'

It's refreshing to get away from stereotypes for a moment. They have dogged us all the way. Long March histories and museums show stereotypical Red heroes fighting stereotypical Guomindang villains in a battle where one side is always right and the other always wrong. People see us as stereotypical foreigners and express amazement that we can speak Chinese, use chopsticks and eat spicy food. My powerful temper also comes as a shock, since Englishmen are supposed to have good manners. But that evening in Changgang Zhen, we discover a new and unwelcome development in the image of the typical foreigner.

A pair of tourism officials from the nearby city of Renhuai meets us on the road, accompanied by a crew from Renhuai Television. They lead us to the local Long March site, which consists of a tiny room where Mao narrowly escaped a Guomindang bomb (the hole it blew in the wall is still there). A middle-aged man and elderly woman now live in this room. They squeeze into one corner to make space for us and the TV people, who begin their interrogation with the usual questions about 'Long March spirit' but then add one entirely new poser:

'What do you think about the fact your country and the USA are about to attack Iraq?'

We've actually been thinking of little else these past few days, but we certainly weren't expecting to be asked our opinion on Chinese television. I can't imagine why anybody would care what we have to say about international affairs, but there surely aren't any other representatives of the 'Coalition of the Willing' on Renhuai TV this week.

Andy improvises: 'Let's make one thing clear. In this matter, we don't represent our country and our country doesn't represent us. We don't want anyone in China to think that just because someone is English, or American, they naturally support war on Iraq.'

I don't know if this plea ever gets broadcast. Whatever the outcome, it doesn't make any difference. Everywhere we walk now, I hear muttering as we pass: '*Laowai . . . da yi la ke*' ('Foreigners . . . attacking Iraq'). I think of a German I met once in a Beijing bar. He told me how depressing it was that no matter where he went, he could not escape his country's history. He had thought that in a distant country such as China he might get a break. Just after arriving, however, he got into a taxi and was asked where he was from. 'Germany,' he replied. 'Ah,' said the taxi driver, 'Heil Hitler!'

The peasants are unanimous. No war, they say. We want peace and development. China is a peaceful country.

This particular corner of China also happens to be hard-liquor country. The economy is fuelled by the distilleries that line the Chishui River, producing numerous versions of the Chinese liquor known as *bai jiu*, literally 'white alcohol'. Andy and I are heading for the home of the most famous of them, Moutai, served at state banquets and sold all over the world. A giant red-and-white Moutai bottle sits proudly on a hilltop above the highway that leads to the town which makes it (while the liquor preserves the old spelling, the town is now written in English as Maotai). Close by we meet a middle-aged woman who works at the elite school patronized by the children of Moutai company officials. She says it costs 4,000 yuan a year to study there and the school has its own fleet of three shuttle buses. At that particular moment, we are looking at a peasant working his field behind a brown cow and wooden plough.

'How much would he make a year?' asks Andy.

'Probably about 1,000 yuan [US$120],' says the school lady. 'The peasants in this area are very poor. But the cost of living in Maotai is very high, higher than Zunyi or Guiyang.'

Whenever we are on a road, we always calculate levels of development by traffic volume, especially by frequency of buses and taxis. By this measure, Maotai and the neighbouring city of Renhuai are off all previous scales. This must be the richest place on the Long March trail, and yet peasants still have wooden ploughs and must pay 120 yuan, more than 10 per cent of their annual income, to send one child to the ordinary primary school.

We turn left at the Big Bottle along a dirt shortcut over the mountain. As we rest at the top of a half-hour climb, a middle-aged woman named Jiang Ming stops beside us.

'You're doing the Long March, aren't you?' she asks.

'How did you know?' I ask.

'I saw you on the local news last night. Are you walking to Maotai? I'm going there, too. Can I join you?'

Jiang loves to talk and she speaks in equally upbeat tones about hardships and happy times. She describes the local flowers, the vegetables, the cost of living and her difficult life as a divorced woman with two children, both boys. She has worked locally in a menial job for the last two and a half years, earning 500 yuan a month.

'I don't have much choice about jobs at my age,' says Jiang.

'If you've only been working here two and a half years,' I say, 'what did you do before?'

'I was a planned birth official,' she says.

Our conversations in the countryside vary little. They revolve around certain key themes, all of which touch directly on the daily life of the peasants. Nothing intrudes into their personal life quite as much as *jihua shengyu*, 'planned birth'. Yet every peasant has a different version of how planned birth works. I find it very puzzling.

'Tell me, then,' I ask Jiang, 'What were the actual

rules in your area? How many children could people have?'

'State employees could have one child. It was more flexible for peasants, but still the aim was one child. They could have two without being punished, though.'

'How were people punished if they broke the rules?'

'State employees would lose their jobs. It's more difficult with peasants, though. We fined them 3,000 yuan for extra children.'

'That's a lot of money. What did you do if they couldn't pay?'

'We would demolish one room of their house for every extra child they had. But it wasn't always easy to catch women who broke the rules. Many who became pregnant illegally would go to other villages to give birth.'

'What did you do if you did catch them?'

'We would take them to hospital and make them have an abortion.'

'Don't you think that's going a bit too far?'

Jiang's cheery demeanour is 100-per cent proof against self-doubt. 'What can you do?' she grins.

Never let it be said that propaganda doesn't work. For the first thirty years of Communist rule, population policy was inconsistent. A birth control campaign was instituted in the early 1960s but then abandoned after the beginning of the Cultural Revolution; a new campaign was launched in 1971 that recommended a maximum of two children for urban citizens and three for peasants, but this was not supported by enforcement measures. Since the advent of the 'planned birth' policy in 1979, however, the government's relentless message that, 'China has too many people' has brainwashed even educated people into closing their minds to any alternative population policies – unless they happen to be thinking about themselves, that is.

'You've got two boys,' I say, 'How did that happen?'
'I was an official,' says Jiang, 'It was my decision.'

Jiang and her colleagues didn't have to apply the policy the way they did. In many other places on the Long March trail, peasants have described a relatively tolerant planned birth regime and have rarely expressed resentment. But the Chinese system makes officials responsible only to those above them. Those below can only hope their leaders are decent people.

Four red fingers salute us from the far bank of the river, high above the modern bridge that carries traffic west just a few metres from the point where the Reds crossed in boats. Falling steeply down the east bank of the river is Maotai Zhen. The highway twists down to the riverside via multiple switchbacks, passing the Moutai distillery itself, plus sundry lesser rivals. The *zhen* is enormous, the size of a small county town, and we can't find a single footpath to cut out the loops of the road.

It feels like Andy and I have been getting nowhere – slowly – for more than two months since first arriving in Zunyi on 10 January. We have walked in a 460-mile circle that took us back to Zunyi on 1 March. Today we are exactly on schedule, arriving in Maotai on 16 March, the same date as the Red vanguard, but we are still only around 60 miles west of Zunyi and find ourselves looking at the Chishui River for the third time.

Phase one of the plans laid at Zhaxi succeeded when the Red Army recaptured Zunyi. Phase two, the project for a new base area in northern Guizhou, went wrong almost immediately.

An issue of the Communists' *Red Star* newspaper printed in Zunyi announced that the recent victory provided a base on which they could build the 'Northern Guizhou Soviet District' and then, in co-operation with the 4th, 2nd and 6th armies, turn the whole of Guizhou red.[1] Encouraged by their success at Zunyi, the Reds decided they would try to consolidate control of north-west Guizhou by taking on the enemy. They chose to seek battle at Luban Chang, 50 miles west of Zunyi, on 15 March.

Just as at Tucheng at the end of January, the Reds had picked the wrong fight. They were heavily defeated – the memorial cemetery at Luban Chang records 489 dead – and retreated north to Maotai, where they immediately crossed the Chishui for the third time. They found circumstances no more favourable on the other side, where Sichuan forces again blocked the route north. Five days later, the Red Army turned around and made the fourth and final crossing of the Chishui – the four fingers above the river at Maotai belong to the Long March memorial, symbolizing the four crossings.

The 'Four Crossings of the Chishui' are now legend. The phrase is routinely trotted out to burnish Mao's reputation as a great military strategist and tactician. The military poet Xiao Hua, who walked the Long March as a twenty-year-old soldier, wrote an epic in which he refers to Mao 'making magic with military decisions' during this section of the Long March. Mao himself in later life referred proudly to his leadership around the Chishui period. But even if we assume Mao was solely responsible for strategy at this time, the Four Crossings only look magical from a respectful distance.

When the Reds first left Zunyi, their aim was to cross the Chishui, then the Yangtze, and finally hook up with the Fourth Front Army. Four crossings of the Chishui later, the Reds did ultimately find a way over the Yangtze and rendezvous with their northern comrades. Viewed from an overall perspective, therefore, you might argue this was a 100-per-cent successful campaign.

Up close, it's a different story. The 'Four Crossings of the Chishui' aren't a joined-up piece of strategy at all. The first crossing is dictated by defeat in a battle initiated by the Reds themselves. Instead of proceeding north, they flee west, cancel the plan to cross the Yangtze and concoct a new scheme to develop a base in Guizhou. The second crossing of the Chishui is part of this second plan – which also fails. The third crossing is determined by yet another defeat, once again in a battle the Reds themselves chose to fight. After the fourth crossing, they make a surprise move south that succeeds so well that Chiang Kai-shek winds up trapped in Guiyang fretting about his own escape while the Reds circle the city. But the evidence suggests the initiative for this manoeuvre came not from Mao, but from Peng Dehuai and Yang Shangkun, commanders of the 3rd Army Group.[2] The 'Four Crossings of the Chishui' are a neat trick: the failures bundled together with the successes and presented as one perfect package of propaganda.

In their book, *Mao: The Unknown Story*, Jung Chang and Jon Halliday argue that the Four Crossings were part of a deliberate effort by Mao to avoid going north, as he was afraid of uniting with the more powerful Fourth Front Army and losing influence to the Fourth's leader, Zhang Guotao. They say Chiang Kai-shek left the route over the Yangtze open and basically invited the Reds to cross. I think this is fantasy. Not only is there no positive evidence that Chiang did this, and abundant evidence to the contrary, but in proper Maoist fashion it also assumes that Mao was in total control of all decision-making and was perfectly informed of enemy troop strengths, movements and intentions. I am not aware of any evidence that Mao or any other Red commander believed the way north was open, nor that Red intelligence suggested this was the case.

The first thing you notice about Maotai is the smell. The stench of fermenting mash is suffocating; a sweet, sickly odour that sticks to skin and clothes. Sixty-eight years ago, soldiers were forbidden to enter the liquor shops, but the temptation was stronger than Red Army discipline.[3] 'We were just children, and we drank the half-fermented Moutai because it was sweet. We got drunk,' General Zeng had recalled in our interview back in Beijing.

By day, the town isn't as exciting as it first appears. It's like a much smaller, run-of-the-mill *zhen* blown up to giant size, without acquiring the refinements in terms of shops, restaurants and services of a county town. But at night, the south end of the riverside boulevard comes alive with sizzling food stalls that remain open until well after midnight, something I have never seen outside a county town before now. Andy's strength has faded once more and so we decide to stay an extra day in civilization before pushing west and back into Sichuan.

It's not a straightforward decision. I am anxious to get moving across the border. Andy definitely needs rest and care, but I'm afraid the authorities here might kill him with kindness. Of all the cultural clashes Andy and I experience on the Long March trail, our feelings about being 'welcomed' and 'helped' are perhaps hardest to explain to our hosts.

The leaders in Renhuai and Maotai can't do enough for us. From Changgang Zhen on, we are welcomed and aided every step of the way. On the road into Luban Chang, we are greeted by the Mayor of Renhuai and the Mayor of Luban Chang, and then in the town itself we find a twenty-strong crowd of officials, television reporters and newspaper journalists waiting for us at the Long March memorial.

Being honoured guests is very hard work indeed. We are shepherded to a restaurant where the boss showers us with cakes, fruits and all the finest things in his kitchen. It doesn't matter how many times we explain, please, we're tired and hungry, don't go to so much trouble, we just want some quick and simple stuff so we can go to bed early. This is interpreted as a stock refusal, as Chinese etiquette dictates that one must always make a show of refusing offers of generosity. How can we explain that, no, we're not being polite, we *really* don't want all this fine stuff? We can't.

No matter how many times we close the door and hope for two minutes' peace and quiet, within sixty seconds it bursts open again so that staff can give us more service. Please stop serving us so much, we beg, we'll pour our own drinks. Yes, yes, agree the staff. But they're back within a minute, ordered down by the boss to make sure we're being properly looked after. Our table is strewn with fancy fripperies that neither of us wants. We've asked for some basic vegetable dishes, but after an hour there's still no sign of them. Andy is slumped over the table making mournful jokes. 'I expect they're up there carving the potatoes into little aeroplanes,' he says. Actually, the carrots come first and they look more like helicopters.

Why do both of us feel so uncomfortable with all this service and generosity (the Mayor of Luban Chang also picks up the tab for dinner)? One reason is simple tiredness. Anybody might feel grouchy and unsociable after a day's march. Another reason may be a natural reticence. What makes me most uncomfortable is the feeling I can't do *anything* without reference to someone else. Being this mollycoddled is like being a child all over again.

Our friend Kath Naday has lived and worked in China for many years. When I complain to her about being mollycoddled, she recalls the time she first came to work as a tour guide.

'Some of my Chinese colleagues were incredibly nice to

me,' she says, 'They bent over backwards to help, and they wouldn't let me pay for anything, not even a can of Sprite. But this went on and on. I never stopped being looked after, never stopped being a guest. I was never allowed to just be one of them. After months of this, I got quite depressed. And then when my Chinese friends noticed I was feeling down and asked me why, and I tried to explain it to them, it just sounded like I was an ungrateful bitch.'

Some problems, however, are more to do with personal characteristics. Andy hates, just hates, people making a fuss over him. Being sick in China is his worst nightmare come true. It's torture for me, too. I don't want to be held responsible for a group of officials breaking into Andy's room, waking him up to ask him how he feels, and then hauling him off to hospital against his wishes. In Maotai, therefore, while Andy is safely tucked up in bed, next door I struggle against a roomful of well-meaning people desperate to take him to hospital, bring doctors round to see him, or at least give him a slug of Moutai, which every person in town swears is a kind of hard core cure-all. I start to explain that I don't think a dose of strong liquor is likely to help Andy's nausea, but then I realize it's a waste of time. What would Chairman Mao have done in this situation, I wonder?

'Thank you, that's a very good idea,' I say, and promise to take everyone's advice, just as soon as Andy has had a nice, long rest. When the enemy advances, I retreat, as Mao would say.

Spring returns as we push into Sichuan Province for the second time. We walk with birdsong under blue skies. Andy's health responds to the change and we are in good spirits as we catch sight of Dacun, which nestles in one corner of a wide, green valley, perhaps the broadest expanse of flat space we have seen since Hunan. We stop to photograph the scene and within five minutes a crowd of two or three dozen children gathers from the school directly below the road.

It's almost always girls who step forward when children gather in groups. Relatively speaking, Chinese boys seem to lack self-confidence in front of foreign men. This crowd is no exception. A short girl in a bright yellow top says in Chinese, 'Hello. Britain and America are attacking Iraq. What do you think about that?'

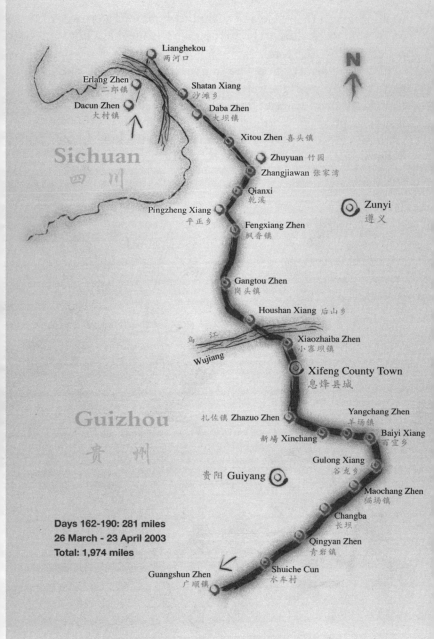

Lianghekou
两河口

Erlang Zhen
二郎镇

Shatan Xiang
沙滩乡

Dacun Zhen
大村镇

Daba Zhen
大坝镇

Xitou Zhen 喜头镇

Zhuyuan 竹园

Zhangjiawan 张家湾

Sichuan
四川

Qianxi
乾溪

Pingzheng Xiang
平正乡

Zunyi
遵义

Fengxiang Zhen
枫香镇

Gangtou Zhen
岗头镇

Houshan Xiang 后山乡

乌 江

Xiaozhaiba Zhen
小寨坝镇

Wujiang

Xifeng County Town
息烽县城

Yangchang Zhen
羊场镇

扎佐镇 Zhazuo Zhen

新场 Xinchang

Baiyi Xiang
百宜乡

Gulong Xiang
谷龙乡

贵阳 Guiyang

Maochang Zhen
猫场镇

Changba
长坝

Guizhou
贵州

Qingyan Zhen
青岩镇

Shuiche Cun
水车村

Guangshun Zhen
广顺镇

Days 162-190: 281 miles
26 March - 23 April 2003
Total: 1,974 miles

N

Chapter 8

Dark Country

We are weak. We need comforts and goals that are none too distant. All the way, we have the luxury of knowing where we are going. It doesn't matter if we get lost for a day or two, because the final destination is clear.

But the Reds had no way of knowing where or when their journey would end. And for them, getting lost could be a matter of life and death. When we visited him in his cosy Zunyi apartment, 1st Army Group veteran Wang Daojin cast his mind back sixty-eight years: 'Sometimes our guides made mistakes. After walking a whole night, we found we were still walking around the same mountain. Marching at night was very difficult. We didn't dare to use electric light because we were afraid to be found and bombed by [Guomindang] planes. We used straw ropes to keep the unit together while we marched.'[1]

Wang and his comrades couldn't look forward to a nice bed, a good meal and news from home every time they reached a larger town. Their future looked like struggle, confusion, doubt and death. Yet somehow they found the courage and optimism to carry on.

There is no record of when the Red Army leadership decided to abandon their plan to establish a new base in northern Guizhou, nor when they revived the aim of crossing the Yangtze and uniting with the Fourth Front Army somewhere in Sichuan (it was no longer clear exactly where this union might take place, because communications between the armies had been broken). The leaders probably came to an informal consensus that they had no choice. Chiang Kai-shek's forces were advancing from the north, west and east, and the Reds shifted this way and that in response to immediate circumstances, rather than in consideration of any overall plan.

The decision to cross the Yangtze and seek out the Fourth Front Army must have been taken almost immediately after the defeat at Luban Chang and the third crossing of the Chishui. But instead of going directly north to the Yangtze as Chiang Kai-shek expected, they upset their enemy's calculations by dashing in the opposite direction, where Chiang's forces were weakest. They raced due south, made a feint towards the capital of Guizhou, Guiyang, where Chiang Kai-shek himself was in residence, then veered west towards Yunnan Province and their new goal – a crossing far upstream where the Yangtze is known as the Jinsha Jiang, the River of Golden Sands (it becomes the Yangtze at Yibin, where the Jinsha meets the Min River). This great loop added hundreds of miles to the Long March, but at its end the Red Army finally found a safe route to the north.

We spend our last day in the company of the Chishui River following the highway along its east bank. The road barrier is decorated by cute concrete bollards in the shape of red-and-white liquor bottles, and at one point the cliff opposite reveals three enormous Chinese characters, which locals allege to be the biggest in the world. They read: '*Mei Jiu He,*' 'Beautiful Alcohol River,' or as Andy prefers, 'Beautiful River of Booze.' At Lianghekou, there is a high bridge with a wide gap in the east wall. A teenager named Chen Jiamei tells us that two days earlier, a truck smashed through and fell into the river. Driver and passenger were both killed.

A Beijing friend once told me about one of his driving

lessons. When he used his indicator to signal his intention to change lanes, the instructor yelled at him: 'What do you think you're doing? Never do that! If the car behind you knows what you're up to, he won't yield. He'll accelerate!' Road accidents are the leading cause of death for Chinese people between fifteen and forty-five. The World Health Organization estimates around 219,000 road deaths a year,[2] or almost the entire population of Plymouth, Andy's home city. Andy and I are often told our marching must be a lot easier with all the new roads, but it's with great relief that we turn east and get back into the mountain trails.

The wealth of the Beautiful River of Booze has not trickled down to these rural areas. The paths are so poor it takes all day to move 10 miles, a distance we would cover in one morning under normal circumstances. I have never seen so many children out of school. It's time to plant the next rice crop, and whole families are bent over green seedlings in fields of mud. With labour this intensive, it's no wonder peasants want more children than the state allows. Every available hand is put to work. I thought grass sandals belonged to Long March legend, but here peasants still wear them in the fields.

Our maps and Long March records are blank at this point. We reconstruct a route using local knowledge, going from peasant to peasant rather than point to point. Our research leads us across the county border to Zhuyuan and then, at sunset, to a village called Zhang-jiawan, where Wang Xiang invites us into his home.

If Wang told me he was 16, I would believe him immediately. He's actually 22 and has a wife and two children. A boy from the house above Wang's spends the whole evening hanging around, asking us about our homes and our journey, and defying repeated attempts by his mother to make him go home to bed. His name is Wang Guhua. He looks about 10.

'How old are you?' asks Andy.

'Fifteen,' says Wang.

'Are you still at school?' I ask.

'No, I left already.'

'What do you do, then?'

'I look after the cows. When I get old enough, I'll go and *da gong* like my older brothers and sisters.'

'How old do you have to be before you can *da gong*?'

'I think 16 is old enough.'

The Wangs embarrass us with their kindness. Wang Xiang vanishes into the night for almost an hour to find vegetable oil for Andy. In the meantime, we share sweets with various visiting children and show our maps to the adults. I never thought of a map as anything special before the Long March, but most villagers we meet have never seen one before. 'What are these blue lines?' one asks, pointing at the Beautiful River of Booze. They are especially fascinated by maps of their own area. Wang Xiang's father digs out a pair of spectacles and spends fifteen minutes poring over the map of Zunyi County, trying to make the picture in his head fit with the lines and names on the page.

Our most magical toy, however, is the video camera. Andy moans about carrying it, but when he sees the delight it gives to young and old, he never thinks of getting rid of it. He films the family for a while and then lets them watch themselves. It's the fastest way to break down barriers. Once people get a look at themselves on the video, the two of us are no longer strange beings from TV-land. Now we're all on TV. We're all equal.

Zhangjiawan got its electricity quite early by local standards – three years ago. There is no road to the outside world. But Wang Xiang is up to date on events.

'Why are you attacking Iraq?' he asks.

We stumble through another explanation of how we, personally, are not attacking Iraq, and that he shouldn't think that just because we're English, we necessarily support everything the British government does.

'I don't like your war,' says Wang. 'The Americans and British say they're liberating Iraq, but I don't understand that. You shouldn't use force to solve these problems. China is not like that. China is a peaceful country.'

'But what about Tibet?' asks Andy, 'What about Taiwan? What if China invaded Taiwan to "liberate" the Taiwanese people? Would that be wrong?'

'That's different. They are Chinese, like us. The Iraqis are not your people.'

I had never heard of Japanese singer Ayumi Hamasaki before the Long March, but now I carry her picture wherever we go. She is the face of 'The Fifth Season' range of fruit drinks, and when you are marching all day in blistering heat, you cannot overstate the importance of a sugary fruit drink – especially one featuring a lithe pop starlet with bleached-blonde hair and hip-hugging trousers that change colour according to the flavour (brown for orange, blue for lemon). Ayumi turns up in the most unlikely places. We might be in a remote village with one tiny shop that has never seen an international brand name product, yet Ayumi beams back at us from the shelf.

The strawberry blonde on a bottle of orange pop raises our morale whenever we see her, and our morale now needs all the help it can get. Andy is falling apart. As if his chest and stomach ailments aren't enough, a piece of tooth falls out of his mouth. We separate for a day while Andy invokes Long March medical emergency rules and takes the bus for Guiyang to see a dentist. I begin life in Xifeng County Town with a visit to the laundry.

'I'm not washing these,' says the laundry woman, 'They're too dirty.'

'Would you like me to bring my clean clothes next time?' I ask. She doesn't think I'm funny.

Back at my lodgings in the 'Minzheng District Service Centre', I'm greeted by an aggressive woman and two

men, one in uniform. After the usual interrogation and
form-filling, I'm left to my own devices, 'pay attention to
safety' ringing in my ears.

What's the most dangerous thing I can do here, I
wonder? The answer is waiting at the bottom of the street
– a motorcycle taxi with a leopardskin seat, operated by a
twenty-six-year-old gentleman named Yang Guining.

Andy and I have been in several towns where cars are
unaffordable or inconvenient, and fleets of motorcycles
therefore fill in as taxi services. There are no safety
helmets for passengers and, apparently, no road rules
either. It's a one-*yuan* thrill ride, great fun and very risky.

'What's the local speciality here?' I ask.

'Xifeng people like *laziji* [a highly spiced chicken dish],'
says Yang.

'Take me to the best *laziji* in town, then.'

Yang takes me out of town to a strip of restaurants by
the entrance to the Guiyang highway. Andy has been
absent less than twelve hours and my vegetarian inclina-
tion has already vanished. I order a chicken killed, eat its
boiled blood and relish the meat, cooked in a steel pot
with masses of garlic and hot pepper. Yang hangs around
while I eat. In between mouthfuls, I vent my bad temper
about the town's over-eager policing. Yang nods and says
it's all very simple – the insistence on filling in forms
comes from fear that if something happened to visitors
from outside, this would cause a lot of trouble.

'I'm the same,' says Yang. 'I should take you back after
you finish, because what if something happened to you?
The police would find out that I brought you here, and
then I would be in trouble.'

And I thought he was just sticking around to make
some more money. But actually he's also covering his
back, as a culture of buck-passing has made him temporarily responsible for my well-being. In the meantime,
the forces of law and order – having filled in all the correct

forms – can safely wash their hands of the troublesome visitor. The idea that I might be allowed to take responsibility for myself doesn't seem to occur to anyone. Whether I like it or not, I'm a guest – and the guest is the only person to whom the buck cannot be passed.

Andy returns without a miracle cure for his teeth. The dentist talks in terms of operations and treatment spread over months. Andy explains that this approach isn't very convenient right now. The dentist gives him a new toothbrush and a bottle of mouthwash and wishes him good luck.

North of Guiyang, the Long March trail follows a highway that passes through flourishing towns, but as soon as we strike east to circle the city, we enter a distressed region whose poverty is only emphasized by the excellence of the main road. Water buffalo are more common than vehicles. But this is an advanced area in one important respect – it has CCTV-5 and the most important match of the year is on tonight. Arsenal take on Manchester United in a probable title decider, and so we halt in Yangchang Zhen specifically to make sure we can see the game. It's scheduled to kick off at 2.30 a.m., Beijing time (despite the fact that the country theoretically stretches over five time zones, the whole of China is on Beijing time, which makes for very late sunsets in the far west).

Yangchang has only one guesthouse, a ramshackle wooden affair with 5-yuan beds. The landlady wants 20 yuan each.

'Can you absolutely guarantee we can watch a TV with CCTV-5 at 2.30 a.m.?' I ask.

'Yes,' says the landlady. She takes us into an adjoining room and demonstrates CCTV-5 on a small set. Twenty yuan it is, then.

'Right, we're going to bed now,' says Andy. 'Please make sure no one – and I mean "no one" – disturbs us.'

Andy has evolved a new strategy for ensuring rest. He

takes the spare bedstead in our room and jams it against the door. It's eight in the evening when we fall asleep.

Two hours later, the lights come on.

There's a commotion as someone tries to force the door, then a pair of eyes appears at the window, where a missing pane has enabled access to the string light switch.

'We're the police,' say the eyes. 'Let us in.'

Not this time. 'Go away and come back in the morning. What time do you call this?'

'*Mei shi*,' say the eyes.

Well, now he's said the magic words, we're definitely not getting up. After rattling the door for a couple more minutes, the public security representative concedes defeat and leaves. Andy crows and claims the 'Long Marcher of the Day' award. I object. 'Why didn't you take the bulb out of its socket, as well?'

Downstairs at 2.20 a.m., all is dark. When we wake the landlady up, she says we must have misunderstood. There's no TV. She doesn't know what we're talking about.

We've heard this 'misunderstanding' line dozens of times. Sometimes it's true, but generally it's a way for people to evade having to admit mistakes, or do things they don't feel like. It's the rural equivalent of pretending you've written someone an email and blaming a fault in the system when it doesn't arrive. Andy coolly sizes up the situation and devises a face-saving approach. He begins banging on doors and shouting at the top of his lungs, 'You've cheated us! You've cheated us!'

Lights go on along the street outside the guesthouse. Andy beats the walls while I berate the landlady.

'I'm calling the police,' says a man who emerges from a guestroom above us. 'GOOD!' yells Andy. More lights go on. And then suddenly I experience a moment of clarity. Somehow my sleep-deprived, stress-fractured mind recalls every detail of my earlier conversation with the landlady.

'What do you mean, "misunderstood"?' I say. 'You

said . . .' – and I repeat, word for word, the exact deal struck seven hours before.

Five minutes later, we are sat in front of a television set in the landlady's son's living room. Our fellow guest has made good on his promise, as well. A policeman joins us for kick-off. He looks familiar . . .

'Can I see your documents please?' he asks.

It's amazing how tolerant Chinese people can be. Back in England, surely the local constabulary would have thrown us in a cell for acting like a couple of hooligans. Here, Officer Cao copies down our details, discusses the merits of David Bei-ke-ha-mu ('handsome') and Michael Ou-wen ('good'), wishes us well and then says goodnight. Remarkable.

'Do you like football?' I ask the landlady.

Am I still a little crazy, or does she actually grin?

The match wraps up just before dawn (2–2) and we set off by the light of a full moon. Today is the halfway point of our journey, or would be if Andy's various ailments hadn't put us a fortnight behind the Red Army's schedule. We have walked 184 days and close to 2,000 miles.

We move so fast I have little sense of place. I experience China as a series of surface impressions. Friends all want to know, what's the Long March like? Today, it's moonlight on dying rape flowers. It's an argument over the price of vegetables. It's a cookery lesson that produces the first mushroom omelette in the history of Baiyi Xiang. It's a siesta in the shade of a pine forest on the slopes of the Nanming River valley. It's sunset on golden hay by a nameless river, where a young man named Zhou Guiquan floats on a rubber tyre and fishes with nets. Yes, the Red Army crossed here, he says, as we wait for the ferryman to pole his boat across to us.

'How many fish will you catch today?' I ask.

'If it's a good day, 5 kilos [11 pounds].'

'What are they worth?'

'Six yuan a kilo.'

The Long March is 30 yuan for a good day's work, for a man with one child who plans another, in a place where one semester of middle school costs at least 400 yuan. It's tasteless Rich Tea-style biscuits and young boys showing off with mock fights by Pingzhai's village pond. It's darkness and uncertainty, a giant dog and a teenager who finds us a place to sleep. It's tiredness so deep that we leave the door unblocked and the light-bulb in its socket.

For the last few days we have been hearing vague reports of a health scare in Hong Kong. Something called 'SARS' has killed a handful of people, and no one can figure out where it came from or what to do about it. Rumours have also reached us from Beijing. When Andy's coughing was especially bad, his doctor in Beijing went through a list of SARS symptoms with him over the phone. Teacher friends tell us expat parents are considering taking their children out of school; hospital doctors say they are being threatened not to talk to journalists about suspected SARS cases. We have hardly given this a moment's thought. It all seems a long way away and besides, SARS sounds just like a glorified flu bug. They come around most years and we don't worry about them, either. What's the big deal, we think? Everyone's always overreacting to this kind of stuff.

In the town of Qingyan on 20 April, we are obliged to reconsider. We don't usually pay much attention to the television – unless there's football or propaganda pageants, of course – but we notice there's a woman speaking English this morning. As we tune in to what's going on, we realize something fundamental has changed.

We are watching the State Information Council's first press conference on SARS. The English-speaking woman is interpreting for deputy health minister Gao Qiang, who is having to deal with blunt questions about the truth of the

SARS situation in Beijing. From his evasive reply to a query about the absence of his boss, Zhang Wenkang, it is clear the Minister for Health has either resigned or been fired. Gao is eating humble pie about the ministry's failure to give the public sufficient information and organize the medical response to SARS effectively. Instead of a handful of cases, as previously claimed, we learn there are hundreds.

I'm taken back to my student days in Minsk, which lies in the area affected by fallout from the Chernobyl nuclear disaster in 1985. The Soviet authorities initially lied about the accident. As radioactive fallout blew across the city, the government went ahead with an official parade – including schoolchildren – to assure people everything was fine. Within a few days, however, the scale of the disaster swept the official lies away. It prompted unprecedented openness in the Soviet media and government, and some analysts argue that this was a watershed in Soviet history. Discredited by their catastrophic incompetence and dishonesty, so the argument runs, the Communist authorities could never again exercise the same level of control over information.

I'm afraid this is wishful thinking. Governments everywhere get caught lying all the time (weapons of mass destruction, anyone?), and it never seems to stop them doing it again. Still, over a cup of tea in a Qingyan hotel room, it's tempting to think of SARS as China's 'Chernobyl moment'.

As far as we know, we're in the safest place possible. We're worried about friends in Beijing, but not in the least concerned about ourselves. We maintain a blasé optimism that SARS won't spread to the countryside and certainly won't bother us. Friends, family and supporters call to ask if we are going to carry on marching. Of course, we say. And after six months on the Long March trail, we know exactly how to reassure them: '*Mei shi*!' we say.

Once again, the route is uncertain. From Qingyan, the nearest point we can head for with confidence is Guang-shun Zhen, two days to the south-west. The first day yields no new clues. We camp in pouring rain in a disused paddy above the village of Shuiche. Andy snores while I study the map by the light of my head torch. Guangshun is in the county south of our position. There is no road, but the river below our paddy crosses the border. That river then runs all the way to the Guangshun highway. It runs in an almost straight line, and our rule of thumb for Red Army route-finding is: if in doubt, look for the shortest distance between two places. Experience suggests that in almost every case, the Reds went straight – straight over obstacles, rather than around them.

Andy salutes my plan because in this case, there should be no obstacles. Crossing borders usually means climbing mountains, and he recognizes that a river raises the strong possibility of a flat, easy trail.

Reality exceeds even this optimistic forecast. Just a couple of miles from our campsite, we find a bridge that leads to a new, sealed road on the south bank of the river. I stop a peasant: 'Does this road go to Guangshun?' I ask.

'Yes, just carry straight on,' says the man, bless him.

We step out confident we can reach Guangshun by early evening. It doesn't occur to either of us to wonder why there should be such a nice road in such a place, or why this road is not on the map.

Half a mile further on, we round a corner to find the road blocked by a gate with four large red characters painted on the right-hand pillar. I can only read three out of four. They add up to 'Military District'.

'But what's the fourth character?' asks Andy.

'I don't know, but it looks like that one you see in "No smoking" signs in Beijing taxis. I guess it means "for-bidden" or something like that.'

'Are you sure?'

'No.'

'Could it mean, "Military-district welcomes foreigners"'?

That's the spirit. We walk in to spread the word of international friendship. A young man in military fatigues dashes out of the gatehouse. He looks distinctly perturbed as he fastens his belt buckle.

'Where are you going?' he asks.

'Hello comrade!' I beam. 'We're going to Guangshun. This road goes there, doesn't it?'

'You can't come in here,' says the soldier. 'This is a military zone. You should get the bus the other way to Huishui, and then to Guangshun.'

'But we can't get the bus, you see. We're retracing the Long March, and we think the Red Army came this way. We only want to walk through. We won't bother anyone.'

'No, you can't come in, it's not allowed.'

The smiling approach hasn't worked. I try a Sad Face. I explain our Long March, appeal to the soldier's sense of Red Army history, and point out that it would take us at least two days to walk around this area, whereas we could be through the Military District and out the other side in little more than an hour.

The young man's resolve wobbles. 'I'll go and ask,' he says.

Just at this moment, an older soldier emerges from the gatehouse. He hears the explanation from his subordinate and then from me again. To our amazement, he nods his head.

'Just follow the road,' says the young soldier, waving us on our way.

It's a lovely spot for a morning march. The road cuts through thickly forested hills, the river to one side, lakes to another. A couple of soldiers push a barrow of vegetables past and smile a greeting. A Jeep drives by and gives a friendly honk. We wave back at it. As we take a five-minute picnic break, I enthuse, 'What a great country!

Can you possibly imagine this happening in England or America?'

Andy shakes his head. It's an absurd thought. Imagine if two Chinese people showed up at a military base in England, carrying an assortment of still and video cameras, and said, 'Excuse me, we're walking from Land's End to John O'Groats, can we walk through your secret military base?'. The reaction would surely be, well, probably something like what happens next.

A Jeep screeches to a halt beside us. Four soldiers pile out while a fifth, the driver, screams, 'GET IN THE CAR, GET IN THE CAR!' Andy and I are bundled into the Jeep, the driver spins the car around and we race back the way we came, siren wailing. We're the only vehicle on the road.

'What are you doing here?' yells the driver, wild-eyed.

I take a deep breath. 'Um, well, like we already explained to your comrades at the gate . . .'

I explain at least four more times to the soldiers in the Jeep, and then go through it all again three times for the benefit of an unpleasant officer outside the barracks we walked past twenty minutes earlier. The officer hasn't buttoned his uniform, although he is one step better off than his subordinate, who hasn't zipped his fly. It's hard to take them very seriously.

'This is a military district!' the officer scowls. 'Foreigners aren't allowed here.'

'Yes, well, we understand that,' I say. 'But we did discuss this with your men at the north gate and they gave us permission to come in. We didn't sneak in.'

'You can't be here taking pictures.'

'We're not taking pictures. We're walking straight through like we were told and like we promised. Didn't the men at the gate contact you?'

'You've gone the wrong way. The Red Army didn't come through here.'

Sigh. 'Look, if we'd been told not to come in at the gate,

we wouldn't have come in. Your men told us we could walk through. Whose fault is this?'

We all repeat the same points several times until the officer tires and steps away to make a phone call. We're surrounded by young soldiers trying to look serious, but every so often we catch an eye and flash a smile. They can't help themselves. They grin back, then hurriedly recompose their features before their superior notices this indiscipline.

My main worry is they might throw us back out the north gate, but after five minutes the officer returns and gestures south. He's not such a bad guy, after all. We are ordered back into the Jeep and driven out through the south gate. 'Don't come back,' says the driver.

Ten minutes' walk later, the river flows into a splendid, broad-bottomed valley below the village of Beisang. We sit on the edge of the road – now merely a dirt track – and enjoy the view while recapping recent events. Andy frets that we've veered off course again.

'Bollocks,' I say, 'That officer's got absolutely no idea.'

'But how can you be so sure?' says Andy. 'He's in the army, after all.'

'Let's find out,' I say. A forty-something peasant draws level, carrying buckets ready to be filled with fertilizer for the rice paddies.

'Excuse me comrade,' I say, 'Is this Beisang?'

'Yes,' says the man, 'Where have you come from?'

'England. What's your name?'

'My name is Luo.'

'Hello, Master Luo. The two of us are researching the Long March of the Red Army. May I ask you, do you know if the Red Army passed Beisang during the Long March?'

'Yes, they did.'

'Which way did they come?'

'From up there,' says Luo, as he turns to point north along the river valley, straight back into the military district.

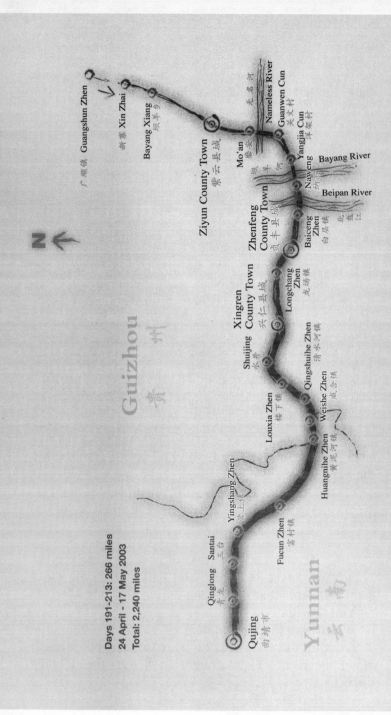

Days 191-213: 266 miles
24 April - 17 May 2003
Total: 2,240 miles

N

Guizhou 贵州

Yunnan 云南

广顺镇 Guangshun Zhen

新寨 Xin Zhai

Bayang Xiang 坝羊乡

Ziyun County Town 紫云县城

Mo'an 磨安

无名河 Nameless River

Guanwen Cun 关文村

Yangjia Cun 洋架村

Naweng 纳翁

Bayang River

Beipan River

Baiceng 白层镇

北盘江

Zhenfeng County Town 贞丰县城

坝羊河

Longchang Zhen 龙场镇

Xingren County Town 兴仁县城

Shuijing 水井

Qingshuihe Zhen 清水河镇

Weishe Zhen 威舍镇

Louxia Zhen 楼下镇

Huangnihe Zhen 黄泥河镇

Yingshang Zhen 当上镇

Santai 三台

Fucun Zhen 富村镇

Qinglong 青龙

Qujing 曲靖市

Chapter 9

SARS

South-west of Ziyun County Town, we follow a dirt road as far as the village of Mo'an, where we spend a night in the schoolhouse. Teachers are our natural allies. I often think of our Long March as an educational project, but not just for Andy and me. Children especially are excited to see us and talk to us, and I hope our brief appearance might leave some useful, lingering memories. I have this idealistic notion our journey might bring others behind it, connecting these places with the outside world in some more tangible fashion, broadening horizons and encouraging bigger dreams.

Teacher Lu Tianrong, thirty-three, also owns one of Mo'an's two shops. In the living area behind the store, we feed on rice and a collection of boiled runner beans and squash, which are dipped into a bowl of chilli sauce for flavour. Like almost everyone else in Mo'an, Lu is a member of the Bouyei minority, China's 11th-largest ethnic group, numbering around 3 million. His wife takes care of the cooking. She doesn't say a word all evening. Even educated people in this area rarely introduce their women to guests.

'This is the poorest county in Guizhou,' says Lu, who might have added that Guizhou is the poorest province in China.

'How much do peasants here earn?' asks Andy.

'A household of four might make 2,000 yuan a year, but many would average 300 yuan a person.'

'Do they have to pay for children to go to school?' I ask.

'The primary school where I work charges 60 yuan a semester. Only 10 per cent of girls go to school. We go to the parents to encourage them to send their girls to school, but they are simply too poor. If they do send a child to school, it's the boy.'

Not far before we reached Mo'an, we passed a curious collection of new brick homes, apparently well built and all of identical design. It looked like a housing estate in Milton Keynes. 'How did those buildings get there?' I ask Lu.

'Those were built with money from the central government to re-house people from very poor areas.'

'You mean people get relocated *here* from *poorer* places?' says Andy.

'There are other places in Ziyun where people might live on 100 yuan a year. They can barely get enough to eat and they dress in rags. Mo'an is much better than that.'

When Western journalists call for Long March updates on our satellite phone, they often ask about poverty. Up to now, I've always told them I have seen nothing too shocking. In fact, I've seen worse in the developed world, especially in aboriginal areas of rural Australia. Some of the housing estates around Bradford, where I went to college in the 1990s, were more depressed and depressing than most Chinese villages. Wherever we have been, the basics of food, clothing and shelter seem satisfied. Everywhere has at least limited access to electricity. Younger people are significantly taller and better nourished than their parents and, especially, their grandparents. School buildings are often new and failure to complete lower middle school seems very much the exception, despite the cost of study. Children often act as our interpreters, as they know standard Mandarin whereas their parents communicate more in local dialect. We have met children as young as eight who take care of business for their parents, for example calculating prices and dealing with money transactions in shops and restaurants.

But the Bouyei areas of Ziyun, Wangmo and Zhenfeng counties challenge these perceptions. Beyond Mo'an, there isn't any business for children to take care of, because there are no roads to move goods or people in and out. There is no distinctive style to Bouyei architecture, because homes are stitched together from whatever is available. One wall may be brick, another random rubble, a third wood and a fourth made of bamboo lattice. Just across the border in Wangmo, the village of Biedang is the first we see totally without access to electricity. None of the women here speaks more than a few words of Chinese, which they call '*han hua*', the language of the Han.

We pass through villages that are like museum recreations of the settlements of Neanderthal man; no electric power, mud and dried grass the main construction materials. I'm sure many villages in medieval England would have had more activity and wealth than these. We must ford river after river, because there are no bridges and the waters are swollen after a series of thunderous rainstorms during recent nights.

The river crossings especially take a psychological toll. Walking a clear path is only a physical challenge. The mind is free to roam. In the water, we have to concentrate every moment. The stones under our feet shift and slip, and one false step could be a leg-breaker. Progress slows to a crawl. Under a clear sky the thermometer hovers between 30 and 35°C. A full day's march moves us forward only about 10 miles. At dusk in the village of Guanwen, we slump in a field in view of a row of houses and hope for the best.

It takes less than five minutes. First one family invites us to sit with them and drink tea, then a rather pushy young man invites us to follow him. He leads us into quite the most unusual home I have ever seen.

It is large by Guanwen standards, and modern in that one wall is made from bricks – without mortar. It is a single hall divided into three sections. But what makes this place special is the row of benches that occupies the ground in the left wing. In front of the benches are a television set and VCD player. China never really had videotapes or videotape recorders. Instead, they jumped straight to video compact discs. DVDs have already taken over the cities, but the VCD still hangs on in the countryside. Wei Bin has constructed a home cinema, and later in the evening at least thirty people show up to watch Hong Kong movies.

'My elder brother is *da gong* in Guangzhou,' says Wei, who is twenty-four. 'He brought the TV and VCD player back and sends me films.'

'Do people come here every single night to watch?' I ask.

'Yes.'

'Don't you ever get fed up of having your house full of people every night?'

'No.'

Wei first struck me as a bit of a show-off, keen to act big in front of his fellow villagers. As the evening wears on, I realize this was an entirely false impression. He is a modest and generous young man, and nothing makes him happier than to have guests and look after them. He apologizes over and over for the poverty of his welcome to us. To start with, all he can produce to eat are some sweet, sticky rice balls and fried peanuts, plus a bowl of boiled noodles. He is stumped by Andy's refusal to eat meat, but then he has an inspiration. He disappears for a minute and returns with his pièce de résistance – a single egg. He cracks the egg into boiling water and then adds some hot pepper, and this is spooned over the noodles to complete the meal.

I'm moved by Wei's generosity – to us and to all the people who share his home for the evening. It's clear we are being treated with the greatest honour, yet a single egg is the only luxury Wei can provide. The video show lasts until 11.30 p.m., but we have long since laid out in sleeping bags in a space among the rice sacks upstairs.

Naturally, Wei refuses all attempts to give him any money in the morning. But there is one thing he wants that we can give him. He wants to call his brother on our satellite phone. And so on 1 May 2003, the village of Guanwen makes the first telephone call in its history. Wei's brother doesn't sound even a little bit surprised.

I've never experienced a feeling like this before. Perhaps because I usually pass in and out of poor areas very quickly, my selfish skin is thick enough to keep empathy at bay. But the relentless poverty of the Bouyei country grants no relief. This poverty is like a physical sensation, like the cold and damp of the Guizhou winter that seeped into my muscles and bones and woke me every morning full of miserable aches. I feel strongly for all the people I meet, but I also want to get out of here as quickly as possible.

Poverty is what drove peasants to join the Red Army. For the Long Marchers, deprivation and suffering were nothing new. Although veterans may begin by reminiscing about 'revolution' and overthrowing their exploiters, when they come to talk about life before joining up, they almost all say one thing: they were hungry. Rudolf Bosshardt, the Swiss priest captured and held by the 6th Army Group, witnessed many recruitment interviews. He wrote that when asked, 'Why do you want to join the Red Army?', peasants inevitably replied, 'I have nothing to eat.'

Something very odd happens in Luoyan, the last village of Bouyei country. It seems just like any other village on any other sun-baked afternoon, where we are about to run out of water once again. This shouldn't be a problem. I leave my rucksack in the shade with Andy while I look for a helpful local.

A group of women are digging on a hillside above the road. I hail them. They move further up the hill and then one shouts down, 'There's no water.'

'There must be water somewhere,' I call back. 'Where can I get some?'

'No water.'

I continue through the village and hear the sound of children and an adult coming from a brick shed (the local school, as it turns out). As I approach, a group of children walk out, see me, and run back inside. As I enter, I hear what sounds like another door being barricaded. No one answers my calls. I take my search into the courtyard of a house next to the shed, where I find a fifty-something man and a group of women. I relax, approach holding up two water bags, and am just starting to say, 'Hello, I was wondering . . .' when I'm interrupted by the sight of the man picking up a log. He immediately brandishes it in my direction and shouts at the same time. I don't speak Bouyei, but I get the message.

I run back to where Andy is napping. Andy has a rare talent for resting in uncomfortable places. He stirs at my arrival.

'Where's the water, then?'

'I don't know. I can't understand it. Everyone here is terrified of us.'

'So what are we supposed to do?'

I'm at a loss. Without the support of the peasants, the Long March is stymied. It's well over 30°C, so we can't go anywhere without water. We decide to let the day cool off and hope something turns up in the meantime. Andy lays out the camping mat and we try to sleep under a blanket of flies.

It's the man-with-the-log who finally approaches – minus the log, happily. He takes his time, edging closer until he summons up the courage to approach and speak, this time in Mandarin.

'You want some water, don't you?' he says.

'Yes, please,' I say.

'Give me your water bags. I'll get you some. I'm sorry about before, but the children were frightened.'

'Thank you very much,' I say, handing the water bags over. The man takes them, pauses, then looks at the two of us.

'You're not from Guizhou, are you?' he says.

At sunset, a man in a white coat chases us across the bridge over the Beipan River. We're too tired to pay any attention. According to our records, we should have reached this point three days after leaving Ziyun County Town. It has taken us six days. Previously, I always found the Red Army's feats of speed and endurance comprehensible, because Andy and I could match them. Not this time. I cannot begin to understand or imagine how the Red Army could have traversed Ziyun and Wangmo counties so fast, even with guides to help them.

Long March histories make little mention of this stage of the journey. The Guomindang could not pursue through such remote country, so the main danger came from above. As the Reds approached the border of Yunnan Province, the convalescent unit to which Mao's wife had been attached since giving birth was caught in the open. On its first pass, the Guomindang plane felled several bearers; as it came round for a second pass, He Zizhen threw herself over a wounded political commissar named Zhong Chibing. She took seventeen shrapnel wounds from the bomb that fell beside them. He Zizhen's Long March would continue on a stretcher.

The man in the white coat is still flapping and talking. I imagine he's just another young man seeking a free English lesson until he summons a man in a uniform to compel us to follow him to an office on the east side of the bridge. They point to a handwritten sign on the roadside and teach us two new characters: 非 (*fei*) and 典 (*dian*), the Chinese for Severe Acute Respiratory Syndrome, better known as SARS.

The central government has finally swung into action and, because the earliest symptom of SARS is a high temperature, all travellers are having their temperatures tested for signs of irregularity. Doctor Wang frowns at my thermometer.

'Yours is a bit high,' he says.

I don't have the strength to talk, let alone argue. Fortunately, Dr Wang can read faces. My face says, 'I've just walked 15 miles blazing heat carrying 45 pounds up and down a mountain. Of course my temperature's high, you idiot.'

'Yes, well, it's OK,' says Dr Wang. 'Carry on.'

I think back to the man with the log. Was that just a coincidence? The next time I get a chance to watch television, twenty-four hours later in Zhenfeng County Town, I decide it almost certainly was not. Rolling Iraq war news has been replaced by twenty-four-hour SARS coverage. The images from Beijing are apocalyptic – empty streets and men in white, bio-terror outfits screening buildings and public transport. Every other channel carries infection numbers and death counts.

On 5 May we receive an email from our friend Nicole in Beijing. She says people from the city have been attacked by stick-wielding peasants in Huairou County, north of the capital. Other friends tell us of peasants in suburban Beijing digging up roads to keep the plague away.

'It's madness here,' says Tom Spearman, who usually updates us on important football scores rather than plague statistics. Tom's wedding has been cancelled – his fiancée Liu Jianya is Chinese, and SARS has closed the office where foreigners and Chinese must register to marry.

We're supposed to be in a SARS-free area, but as we pass a crowd outside Zhenfeng, instead of overhearing 'attack Iraq', we hear, 'foreigners . . . *fei dian*'. It seems any outsider is suspect, and no one stands out as outsiders quite like us. As we approach a river crossing below the village of Tudipo in Yunnan, a group of labourers is about halfway through building a new bridge. A supervisor yells and waves us back. This is not unusual. We are sometimes stopped at roadworks while blasting takes place. We halt and wait for the explosion – but nobody else moves away.

We call across: 'What are you yelling at us for? What's up?' More hand gestures. We repeat our question three times. Finally, the man comes over, together with a group of tall lieutenants. 'It's about SARS,' he says.

'Oh, you've got SARS, have you?' says Andy.

Black humour is lost on these people. 'We're not allowing strangers into the village,' says the man.

'We don't want to go into your village,' I say, 'We just want to walk along the road.'

The men confer and allow us to pass. Half an hour later, however, another group intercepts us.

'No outsiders allowed in our area,' says their leader.

'Who told you that?' I demand.

Silence. I resist an urge to cough on them.

'Come on, who says we shouldn't be here? We've been tested enough times. What about you?'

'There was an announcement,' is all the explanation we receive.

There's not much we can do about this situation. We

can't say, OK, let's drop our bags and make camp until SARS is over. Nor does it make any sense to turn around – the people behind were just as scared and unwelcoming, so maybe we would be stuck on this stretch of dirt road, looking for a way past peasant barricades in either direction. Our only choice is to face our opponents down. We make ourselves as tall and intimidating as possible and walk on.

Nobody tries to stop us this time, but we are both aware this is a risky strategy. Before SARS, we could count on people in the countryside for support – directions, food, sometimes lodging. Now I feel nervous every time we enter a new village. If the peasants are scared enough, it seems quite possible they may use force to keep us away.

Lü Sitao chooses this moment of low morale to make the longest pizza delivery in Chinese history. From a Pizza Hut in Guangzhou to our lonely campsite in north-east Yunnan comes to around 2,000 miles. The trip takes Sitao thirty-six hours and, by rights, he should never have got to us at all. At least, that's what news from Beijing led us to believe. We were told the SARS epidemic had blocked travel across China, especially from infected areas such as Guangzhou. Jia Ji has already cancelled plans to meet us up ahead in Qujing.

Sitao finds us at dusk. We have just emerged from a hastily built shelter after the day's second heavy thunderstorm. The rain has scuppered efforts to reach safe harbour, but already the sky is clearing and a full moon lights our work as we pitch camp. We hug our friend in delight.

'How on earth did you get here?' I ask.

'No problem,' says Sitao.

The men in white coats checked his temperature twice en route, took his phone number and let him pass. Sitao is not your average young man. He knows that just because absolutely everyone says you can't do something is no reason not to try – especially in China.

The next morning, the three of us push over the mountain to Zhujie for lunch. A minivan with darkened windows pulls up at the edge of the village. Dr Lei Yusu emerges and barks at us to, 'STOP RIGHT THERE!'

'All right, calm down,' says Andy. 'What do you want?'

'WE'RE FIGHTING FEI DIAN.'

'There's nothing wrong with our ears, you know,' I say.

Dr Lei glares. 'FOLLOW ME.'

With the mysterious minivan guarding our rear, we are led to the village clinic. Once inside, we are shut in the 'Fever Observation Room'. Qinglong has two thermometers. Foreigners are tested first. Dr Lei checks our temperatures.

'So, everything OK then?' asks Andy. 'Can we go now?'

Dr Lei ignores him, walks out and shuts the door.

I wish it didn't have to be like this. I wish it were possible just to have an open and polite discussion and come to a reasonable solution. Maybe six months ago, when we were fresh and cheerful young marchers just stepping out on a great adventure, maybe then. But not any more. We open the door and walk out. We shout at the doctor. He shouts at us. We denounce our treatment and the filthy condition of the health centre. He protests that nothing is his fault. He says we must wait for 'higher leaders' to arrive from Qujing.

'When will these "leaders' arrive?" I demand.

'Soon.'

'Who were those people in the minivan with you?'

'The local leaders.'

'Tell them to come down and talk to us.'

No one shows up from the local government. We're all in favour of fighting SARS, but this is ridiculous. Do the 'higher leaders' have some SARS test especially for foreigners? Qujing to Qinglong is about an hour's drive. After two hours of mutual abuse, no food and no additional information, we decide to take our chances. We put on our rucksacks and walk out of the compound.

Dr Lei's lungpower is exhausted. He sulks by the gate. The local leaders, in the meantime, are skulking in their government building up the hill. We pop in to give them a fright. I half-expect to find them barricaded in like the children in Luoyan, or like the last human survivors in a Chinese horror movie, where zombie *laowai* ravage the country. Actually, it turns out they're getting ready for lunch.

'Just wait a minute,' says Party Secretary Li. 'Have something to eat with us.'

'Thank you, Party Secretary Li, but we've had enough of your hospitality already,' I say (although I fear I may also have inserted a few rude words; like Long March veterans' reminiscences, my diary is chaste). As we walk out of the government compound to start the climb over to Zhujie, Sitao wants to know why we didn't just walk out earlier.

'Because we didn't know what might happen,' I say. 'SARS has got everyone so scared, you can't predict any more what people are going to do. They had no right to keep us there once we passed the temperature test, but who knew what they might do if we walked out. They might quarantine us for months, arrest us, beat us up, who knows?'

'So what makes it OK to leave now?'

'Hm . . . well, I want to get to Qujing before dark.'

An hour down the road, the 'higher leaders' finally arrive in a Jeep and a black sedan. Mr Fang of the Foreign Affairs Office greets us effusively.

'Terribly sorry,' he says. 'It's all a mistake. These locals don't understand the situation.'

A lower official proffers three bottles of Lancang Jiang beer and a bag of sticky buns, then they all drive off saying they want to have a word with the Qinglong leadership. We plod on for a very late lunch, impressed by the beer but still wondering why they couldn't have phoned instructions to free us three hours ago.

Andy's sense of humour has turned morbid since we left the Bouyei people. His persistent health problems seemed to diminish for a while, but in Zhenfeng he started to sicken once again. I didn't think too much of it at the time. The strain of exhaustion, dehydration and poor diet had hurt me, too. I needed to sit down and recover after tackling a single flight of stairs. Dehydration made my fingers cramp so badly I couldn't hold a pair of chopsticks.

But Andy weakened progressively. He felt especially poor after eating oily food or hot peppers. The latter was particularly distressing, because he reckoned a dash of chilli was about all that made his diet tolerable. He tried switching to tins of Chinese rice porridge as he searched for nutrition his stomach could handle. It didn't last long: he soon suffered a fresh round of nausea attacks, stomach cramps and diarrhoea.

Reaching the outskirts of Qujing, we plan to veer slightly off the Red Army's trail. The Reds never entered the city and made little effort to take it. Instead, they skirted it to north and south and rushed on towards the Jinsha Jiang, the River of Golden Sands. As we go one better than the Reds and penetrate the suburban area, Andy's not rushing on anywhere except the toilet. He is almost overwhelmed by pain and nausea, but drags himself to the Qujing Hotel, where Jia Ji has sent supplies ahead.

The staff at reception want to take our temperatures before we check in. I don't fancy Andy's chances of passing the SARS test, so I persuade them to 'wait a while' as we're 'overheated from the journey'. Sitao hustles his sick friend upstairs and into bed. It's FA Cup Final day and, courtesy of Sichuan TV, the three of us suffer one of the dullest games in memory. Sitao leaves in a sombre mood the next day. He had hoped to walk with us, but Andy is bedridden.

I'm still optimistic. I don't think it's a pathological condition; I've just got used to seeing Andy look like death warmed up. He collapsed for ten days in Zunyi, a week in Renhuai, another week in Guiyang, and every time he eventually got up and got going again. I expect a few days' rest here will be enough to refuel for the next leg, which surely cannot be as tough as the last. I can't help feeling we must be over the worst, despite the mountains, dogs and swamps to come.

'Don't you ever feel like giving up?' ask friends and strangers alike. Andy freely admits he thinks about it every day. I know he won't, though. It's easy to talk about giving up, but to actually chuck it in when the back of the journey is already broken? As long as he can put one foot in front of the other, I know Andy will carry on. He's a vegetarian.

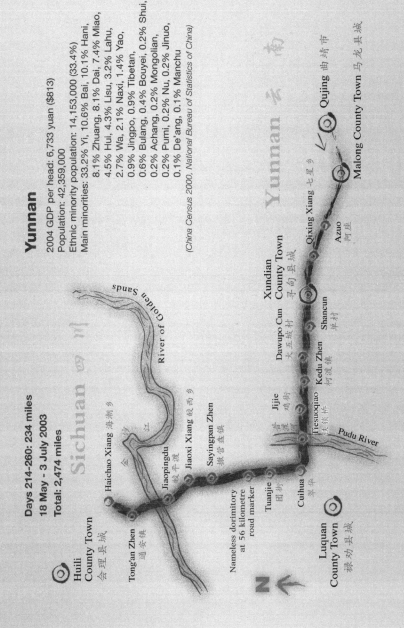

Days 214–260: 234 miles
18 May – 3 July 2003
Total: 2,474 miles

Yunnan

2004 GDP per head: 6,733 yuan ($813)
Population: 42,359,000
Ethnic minority population: 14,153,000 (33.4%)
Main minorities: 33.2% Yi, 10.6% Bai, 10.1% Hani,
8.1% Zhuang, 8.1% Dai, 7.4% Miao,
4.5% Hui, 4.3% Lisu, 3.2% Lahu,
2.7% Wa, 2.1% Naxi, 1.4% Yao,
0.9% Jingpo, 0.9% Tibetan,
0.6% Bulang, 0.4% Bouyei, 0.2% Shui,
0.2% Achang, 0.2% Mongolian,
0.2% Pumi, 0.2% Nu, 0.2% Jinuo,
0.1% De'ang, 0.1% Manchu

(China Census 2000, National Bureau of Statistics of China)

Sichuan 四川

River of Golden Sands

金沙江

Yunnan 云南

Huili County Town 会理县城
Tong'an Zhen 通安镇
Haichao Xiang 海潮乡
Jiaopingdu 姣平渡
Jiaoxi Xiang 姣西乡
Sayingpan Zhen 撒营盘镇
Tuanjie 团街
Cuihua 翠华
Nameless dormitory at 56 kilometre road marker
Jijie 鸡街
Tiesuoqiao 法锁怀
Kedu Zhen 柯渡镇
Dawupo Cun 大五坡村
Shancun 单村
Xundian County Town 寻甸县城
Qixing Xiang 七星乡
Azuo 阿座
Malong County Town 马龙县城
Qujing 曲靖市
Luquan County Town 禄劝县城
Pudu River

N

Chapter 10

End of the Road, Part 1

The doctor's latest theory is that Andy has giardia, a parasite common in western China that causes serious bowel dysfunction. The drugs don't work. Andy's muscles are wasted and every detail of his ribcage can be traced against his skin. I suggest he tries the 'Yao minority herb bath' included among the soaps and shampoos in the hotel bathroom. The packet claims this potion fixes everything from muscle tiredness to skin problems and stomach disorders. Women who bathe in it return to the fields only seven days after childbirth with 'no gynaecological problems'. It clears my eczema almost immediately, but after ten days in Qujing, Andy is worse than ever.

'I can't diagnose this by phone,' says the doctor. 'You need to go to a real hospital.'

In the spirit of the Red Army, Andy and I confer to decide strategy. The Qujing Meeting resolves to declare a state of medical emergency and withdraw to Kunming, capital of Yunnan Province, where Andy will be placed in the care of the No.1 People's Hospital.

Kunming should be a bustling tourist centre at this time of year. Yunnan trades off an extremely diverse climate and population. Twenty-six of China's fifty-five official ethnic minorities live in the province. From Kunming, visitors head south-west to the subtropical Xishuangbanna region on the border with Myanmar and Laos, or north-west to the ancient Bai minority capital of Dali – one of the most popular backpacker towns in the country. Beyond Dali lies the beginning of the Tibetan Plateau, whose snow-capped peaks are alleged to have inspired James Hilton's *Lost Horizon* (via articles in the *National Geographic*; Hilton himself never set eyes on a Tibetan mountain). By decree of the State Council, the county of Zhongdian was shamelessly renamed 'Shangri-la' in May 2002.

We find Kunming practically deserted, its economy crippled because of the SARS outbreak. The provincial government has stopped all tour groups to the region, although the province is officially SARS-free. Cabbies tell of incomes slashed by up to 80 per cent. Our hotel, the Baiyun Dajiudian, has closed three of five floors and laid off most of its staff. I run into one of its former managers touting as a prostitute in the bar of the Holiday Inn. She said she resigned after her salary was cut from 2,000 to 700 yuan a month. The Yunnan Flavour restaurant down the street, a nightly sell-out in normal times for its 'minority culture' minstrel shows, has closed its doors completely.

While Andy is poked and prodded in hospital, I read an English-language copy of *The Woman in White* I find in the Xinhua Bookstore, drink coffee alone in the In City Cafe, and tell myself that everything is going to be fine. In the mornings I shop at the Carrefour supermarket (Kunming is a very pleasant, middle-class city), then take my purchases to the No.1 People's Hospital and cook Andy sickbed food.

After ultrasound tests, the doctors declare Andy has small gallstones and a probable infected liver. They give him glucose drips and medication and schedule further tests. After several days without improvement, they change their minds and prescribe different drugs. They don't work either. When the doctor makes his morning call, Andy pins him down:

'You don't know what to do, do you?'

'Certainly I do,' says the doctor. 'I need to do more tests. But I can't do them here. We don't have the equipment.'

Whenever we face a choice between two trails, one that goes up and one that goes down, the upward path always seems to be the one we have to take. Andy already knows the answer to his next question.

'Where can I get those tests done?'

'There's only one place – Beijing.'

It's no exaggeration to say I'm scared of carrying on by myself. Who knows when I could do with an extra stick to fight the dogs? And what if I get sick? Who, then, carries me? With no one around to debate options with, isn't it more likely I'll make the wrong choices? I ponder the possible impact of the loneliness, the disappointment of the end of all Andy's efforts, the weight of having to finish this thing alone. But I can't wait any longer. The great Snow Mountains still lie ahead. If winter sets in before I cross them, the passes will close. I calculate that I have to leave within three days, by Sunday 15 June at the latest, or risk losing any chance of completing what is left of the Long March.

On the morning of 13 June, Andy is about to order his ticket back to Beijing when a successful trip to the toilet persuades him otherwise.

'I'm not leaving,' Andy says, encouraged by this sudden improvement. 'You said we've got 'til Sunday. I'm going to stay and try and carry on marching.'

I have been dispirited and listless for the last fortnight, but packing up and hitting the road again fills me with energy and unreasonable optimism. As we walk out of Qujing, four weeks after first arriving there, it actually feels normal, like ordinary daily life, to be walking along once more watching the peasants at work. The rice has grown high during our hiatus, the paddies now a lush emerald green.

Although Andy has been better since his bowel movements improved, he still isn't what you'd call 'well'. Last night, he didn't eat anything but granola bars and went to bed complaining of a stomach ache. The road from Qujing to Malong is a straight, flat 20 miles. In normal times we would swing along it in seven hours and feel almost like we'd had a day off. Now, Andy trudges ahead like an old man. I bring up the rear because I'm afraid that if I set the pace, I will turn around after a while and find he isn't there any more.

Three miles outside Malong, I see Andy trip and only just steady himself. He tells me later he considered whether it would be preferable just to fall flat on his face rather than carry on. Bile periodically surges from his stomach into his throat, so that he literally 'eats bitterness'. Along Malong's main street, I walk just a few paces behind, ready to catch my friend, who stumbles, but does not fall.

For the fit and healthy, it's a beautiful time to be marching. We are more than 6,500 feet above sea level and there is no more of the enervating heat that oppressed us in south-west Guizhou. It's the height of the growing season for tobacco and rice, the economic staples for every one of the ethnic groups who inhabit this area. North-west of Malong, Xundian County is a Hui and Yi minority autonomous county, although our Hui host in Qixing, Ma Qinglun, tells us there are actually five times as many Han as the minorities put together. Beyond Jinsuo, north-west of Xundian County Town, a stream of horse-drawn carts pass us, carrying people and goods back home from market. Many are filled with women in coloured head-scarves, who shout and wave. 'Come with us,' they cry. They are Miao, of course.

Not only is this area multi-ethnic, it is also multi-religious. The Hui's heritage is mixed, to say the least. Some hark back to Muslim traders travelling along the Silk Road who settled and intermarried with Chinese women. Others are said to descend from Mongol, Turkic or other Central Asian settlers who once formed the dominant social stratum during the Mongol Yuan Dynasty. They are less an ethnic than a religious group, defined by their historical attachment to the Muslim faith. Shops and restaurants here feature pictures of Mecca rather than portraits of Chairman Mao. Arabic script is all around, though I don't meet anyone who can read it. Mosques are discreet – the only one I see is a large, modern building in Xundian County Town. Ma Yaocong, who runs the Hui Jinxuan Restaurant near Jinsuo, tells us religious observance is mostly a matter for the elderly.

That is emphatically not the case with the thriving Christian congregations beyond Xundian in Luquan County. I find it both strange and comforting to see a church in every village on the road. Each has a new, white-tiled facade on a white concrete building. Inside, the only decoration is the cross on the wall behind a table that serves as both altar and pulpit. The pews are wooden benches. The congregations are multi-ethnic, Yi, Han and Miao, and so preaching is mostly done in Mandarin so everyone can understand.

The unmistakable sound of a church choir greets us in Zhenjinwan Cun. The church hall is crammed with men and women of all ages, practising hymns in the Yi tongue. As an atheist, I find it especially curious that I should feel so much at home here. An old lady in sober, traditional Yi costume breaks away from choir practice and asks me, 'Do you believe in the Lord?'

'I'm afraid not,' I say.

The lady looks downcast. She returns to her singing. The church elders invite us to join them next door, where they are preparing a small celebration to mark the completion of a new building attached to the church. The main preacher, Li Guolin, says the congregation numbers 340 to 350, mainly Yi like himself, but with some Han, as well.

'Basically, every big village has a church,' says Li. 'There are over 200 churches in our county, 40,000–50,000 believers.'

'Where did you learn about Christianity?' asks Andy.

'From Britain. The congregation in Sayingpan was also converted by [the same] British priest. He died here 100 years ago.'

There are three men present who are old enough to remember 1935, but none of them has any memory of the Red Army. One says they definitely did not come through this village at all, though some soldiers were known to have foraged for food nearby. No one knew if they were Reds or Guomindang, as the locals fled at the sight of Han soldiers of any description.

The relationship of these old men with communism is complicated by their faith. The Zhenjinwan congregation was destroyed by the intolerant fervour of New China after 1949, and these men were punished for their beliefs.

'Believers in Jesus were all criticized, some were arrested,' says Li. 'Some were investigated. They suffered a great deal. Congregations stopped. That was from 1950 to 1979. After 1979, we could breathe again. Before 1979, you couldn't believe in Jesus. We couldn't even believe in Jesus in our own homes.'

Those dark days seem distant as we listen to hymns while chewing on sunflower seeds and sweet home-made biscuits. A fleshy eight year old circles the room wearing an Inter Milan soccer strip, while his equally prosperous-looking father tells me the government now supports Christianity because of its positive moral teachings.

Chen Jie, 80, joined the Reds at the age of 11. He accompanied them on the Long March as far as northern Sichuan Province, where he was injured and left behind. (Youshan Zhen, Jiangxi Province, 28 October 2002)

Chen Yingchun, 89, joined the Red Army when it passed through his village at the outset of the Long March. Chen's unit was cut off from the main force during the battle for Xinfeng County Town one week later. Unable to cross the Xinfeng River, Chen returned home to peasant life. (Licun Xiang, Jiangxi Province, 17 October 2002)

The Red Army vanguard made the first crossing of the Xiang River at this point. (Pingshan Ferry, Guangxi Zhuang Autonomous Region, 2 December 2002)

This pontoon was originally built by the Red Army to cross into Dao County Town. (Hunan Province, 11 November 2002)

This slogan was left in the home of a Miao minority family whose head, Long Qianchen, was a Communist sympathizer. Half is missing; the full original read: 'Unite with the Miao to defeat the landlords and evil rich'. (Shuangjing Xiang, Guizhou Province, 31 December 2002)

'Growing oranges is better than raising children', reads the slogan. Lü Sitao displays the precious produce. (Xinfeng County, Jiangxi Province, 27 October 2002)

Workers' playtime at an open-face coal mine above Guandian Xiang.
(Guizhou Province, 24 January 2003)

Xiong Huazhi, who may be the long-lost daughter of Mao Zedong and He
Zizhen, with her three daughters: Yang Tingyan, Yang Tinghua and Yang
Tingyu. (Tianchi Cun, Yunnan Province, 17 February 2003)

Andy's health began to give way as we approached Zunyi for the second time. (Rongguang Xiang, Guizhou Province, 28 February 2003)

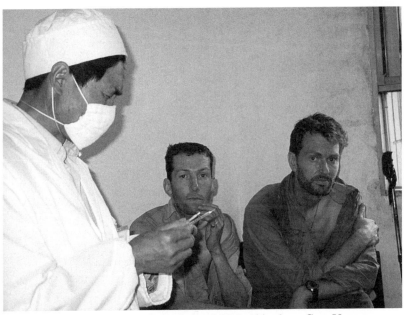

Dr Lei Yusu makes sure we haven't got SARS. (Qinglong Cun, Yunnan Province, 17 May 2003)

Gear Guy rides to the rescue. (Huili County, Sichuan Province, 8 July 2003)

Schoolteacher Xiong Li dressed up in her traditional Lisu minority garb at Yang Xiao's request. (Jinsha Xiang, Sichuan Province, 12 July 2003)

Memorial to the 'Yihai Union'. (Yihai, Sichuan Province, 23 July 2003)

Standing on Luding Bridge, Li Guoxiu describes the battle she witnessed as a teenager. (Luding County Town, Sichuan Province, 10 August 2003)

These women were living and working without any male company near the pass over Dagushan, the highest mountain of the Long March. (Heishui County, Sichuan Province, 18 September 2003)

Baozuo Muchang, the first village on the northern edge of the Swamps. (Ruo'ergai County, Sichuan Province, 26 September 2003)

Memorials to the Red Army's passage abound on the road to the Jinsha Jiang, the River of Golden Sands, and they crop up in unusual places. Outside Jinsuo, we happen on one in the car park of a Hui restaurant. Usually, memorial stones record the local government and Communist Party's role in erecting the monument, but this one notes only the Jinxingyue Restaurant as its patron. We find another half a mile beyond Jijie, well hidden at the back of a compound where Li Yunquan and his family are building a catch-your-own fish barbecue restaurant. At Tiesuoqiao, the iron-chain bridge built in 1928 still stands across the rushing Pudu River. On the north end, a plaque records how Mao and the Red Army crossed here towards the end of April 1935. The bridge has been closed for ten years, its boards removed and its gates locked, but that doesn't put off the local children. Before we can stop her, nine-year-old Dai Rouxiang, whose big brother runs the restaurant that stands at the south end of the modern stone bridge, climbs around the barriers and shows how the bridge can still be crossed along the bare chains.

From Tiesuoqiao, the main force of Mao's First Front Army continued almost due north to the ferry across the River of Golden Sands at Jiaopingdu. In the meantime, the young commander of the 1st Army Group, Lin Biao, led a feint south against Kunming that took his troops to within sight of the Yunnan capital on 29 April 1935. Panic gripped many foreign residents, who evacuated themselves on a special getaway train south to Tonkin.[1] In response to Chiang Kai-shek's call for help, Yunnan warlord Long Yun had sent the best of his forces into Guizhou when the Reds feinted towards Guiyang; now he scrambled for defences as Lin Biao played the same trick again. Once the crossing at Jiaopingdu was secured on 3 May, Lin pulled his men away and ran for the river.

It's as easy as ABC, then. Mao orders a diversionary

move against Kunming; Long Yun panics and orders his troops to the defence of the provincial capital, clearing the way for the Red Army to march unmolested to the River of Golden Sands and cross safely into Sichuan at last. Mao's a genius, QED.

But are cause and effect really so simply and conveniently related? An eccentric American botanist and anthropologist named Joseph Rock was in Yunnan as the Reds approached Kunming. Rock wrote in his diary: 'If I were Long I would let them [the Communists] go and to hell with [the Guomindang] . . . Chiang is forcing the Communists to the south into Yunnan, closing their way to the north, but Long undoubtedly will play him the trick and let them slip west . . . and Chiang will be in the lurch and it will serve him right.''[2] An official at the Yunnan Provincial Museum told Harrison Salisbury that Long Yun received a telegram from the representative of 'some influential people' in Hong Kong two days before Lin Biao appeared at the gates of Kunming. The telegram said: 'I have talked with people in Guizhou and Hunan. My impression is that they just want to see the Red Army out of this area and the Red Army wants to go through Yunnan into Sichuan, so better let them do that without having to fight.' Long Yun noted on the telegram: 'This is a statement based upon the interest of the South-west.'[3]

Could it be that the Red Army would have marched unmolested through Yunnan even without the masterful tactical feint against Kunming? This diversion forced the 1st Army Group on one of the toughest forced marches in its history, leading to non-combat losses as weaker troops simply fell away. Less than a week after crossing the River of Golden Sands, Mao faced stiff criticism from Lin Biao, who called on him to turn over the military command to Peng Dehuai. Mao's myth-makers don't pause to ponder the reasons for Lin's attack; they only celebrate the

Chairman's put-down: 'You're a baby.' Lin was twenty-seven, Mao forty-one.

Ever since I started taking history seriously, I've been drawn to Tolstoy's portrayal of Napoleon in *War and Peace* as fundamentally impotent, issuing orders that never even reach the battlefield, yet taking credit for every victory. More important than the exalted leader is the man who, seeing the standard bearer fall, picks up the standard, rallies the men around him and charges the enemy. Victories are won through individual acts of courage, most of which are never recognized.

Shangpingzi is not the kind of place where you expect to find such a Hero of the Revolution. The closest shop is a mile-and-a-half away, the nearest telephone 20 miles. The village itself is a shambolic cluster of mud-brick homes clinging to the northern edge of Yunnan. Below rushes the River of Golden Sands; above is a climb of more than 3,000 feet to the nearest pass out of the valley.

Zhang Chaoman is easy to track down. Everyone for 20 miles either side of the border seems to know about him. Neither he nor his grandson, Pei Xinfu, seems at all fazed by our sudden appearance. They welcome us into their two-storey courtyard home, a fine one by local standards (it has real bricks), and Zhang immediately settles on to the sofa and into his tale.

Zhang was twenty-two when he met a vanguard unit of the Red Army. The soldiers said they needed boats and men who could row them across the fierce current of the Golden Sands.

'A Red Army propaganda unit came here first. They said, "Don't be afraid, we are the Red Army, proletarian soldiers, children of poor people. We kill rich people and save poor people; we kill officials and protect the people; we beat bad rich people and give the fields to the farmers. We defeat the government and save poor people, don't be afraid. We don't steal food. If you have meat, you can sell it to us. We have to pay." '

Zhang and his four brothers were won over by the Reds' propaganda.

'The Reds got here at 11 p.m. I took them to find boats. We found one boat by the bank of the Golden Sands. The Reds found four more. The big boats could carry sixty people . . . There were two companies of Guomindang on the far bank. After they were defeated and ran away, the chief commander said, "*Laoxiang*, you must row quickly. Take our army across." We rowed until dawn and took more than a regiment over.'

The Reds could find only two further boats. Thirty-six local men, including the Zhang brothers, ferried around 30,000 soldiers to the Sichuan side of the river. It took seven days and seven nights, working around the clock at the Jiaopingdu crossing, less than 2 miles from where Zhang now lives in Shangpingzi. Not a man had been lost as the last units crossed into Sichuan on 9 May.[4]

'Every Red soldier carried a rice bag,' says Zhang. '[When it was over] they put a big pot by the bank and gave each of us a cup of rice. They also killed a pig for us to eat. Liu Bocheng [who commanded the crossing operation] said, "*Laoxiang*, they have dragon meat in heaven, on earth donkey meat is delicious." '

At this point, I no longer have any idea what Zhang is talking about. That's the problem with oral history. I change the subject.

'What happened to you after the Reds left?'

'Later, the Guomindang "cleaned the village". Before the Guomindang got here, we damaged all the boats so they couldn't chase the Reds. I was arrested for seven days. Bao Zhang [a local leader] shouted that I'd pay for his boat, "You've got some nerve. How dare you steal my boat, help the Red Army cross the river and then destroy my boat?" We had to lie to him: "No, no, not us. The Reds forced us to do it."

'We had to pay two boats given to us as reward by the Red Army, and several pigs, sheep, cows and some money borrowed from our relatives. An investigation followed. Bao Zhang led a gang of people to my house, hunting for bullets and opium. They dug a big hole in the floor but found nothing. They stole my wife's clothes, bedding and blankets. After I returned home, I consoled her: "It doesn't matter. At least we're alive." '

Zhang's family had to pay 280 taels to win his freedom. According to the tale as Zhang recounted it to William Lindesay a decade before, he and all his brothers were arrested. He said, 'I was strung up for twelve hours before they cut me down to be taken to Luquan for execution. Luckily, though, Bao Zhang believed the many villagers who told him we were forced under threat of our lives to help the Reds.'[5]

Zhang is almost deaf, but still lively at ninety. His contribution to the Revolution was ignored before Harrison Salisbury interviewed him in 1984, after which the government granted him a pension. I say, 'If it wasn't for you and your brothers, there might be no New China. Did you think of this before?'

'I didn't think of it at the time. I found out from history books afterwards.'

Our first sight of the River of Golden Sands on 29 June is one of the most emotional moments of our Long March. For five days after leaving Qujing, it was touch-and-go whether Andy could continue. Each night he was at the end of his rope, yet each morning he somehow found it in himself to carry on. Fortunately, as the roads turned into footpaths that began to climb ever higher and steeper, Andy's strength began to seep back.

The path to the Golden Sands is the longest and hardest

of all, 20 miles that take us from a cool, high plateau into a baking subtropical valley. At lunch in Shaleshu, it is around 25°C; by late afternoon the thermometer is at 40 and we are sheltering in the shade of banana trees. I am first round the corner that brings us within sight of the Golden Sands. Andy sees my grin, then the river, then drops to the ground in relief. A month, even a week earlier, neither of us thought he would ever reach this point.

Even at night the temperature in Jiaopingdu never falls below 30°C. Our room swarms with bugs, the guesthouse toilet has rats in the shitholes and cockroaches for wallpaper. I opt to use the cabbage patch next door. I'm not the first person to have this idea. The only road out of Jiaopingdu leads straight up the mountain, Zhongwushan, on the north side of the river. Although we rise at 5 a.m. to beat the heat, this is the longest, highest, hardest ascent of the entire journey. At times we slow to a crawl, resting every twenty minutes, even every fifteen. It is only just past 2 p.m. when we start the descent into Tong'an Zhen, but both of us are wrecked – a bad moment to encounter a SARS checking station.

The day before, I clocked 40°C at the SARS station on the Jiaopingdu bridge. The doctor looked at the sun, looked at my crimson face, and let me off. This time, just to be on the safe side, I make sure the thermometer exits my armpit before things get too hot. Andy passes the temperature test easily, but it's the only health test he will pass for a long time. Already his stomach is cramping. He staggers the last 3 miles to Tong'an and is in bed even before the police show up to welcome us back to Sichuan.

Andy manages only 5 miles the next day. All his former ills have returned in force. We beg a bed from the local government in Haichao, hoping a rest will allow him to finish the 30 miles between here and the county town of Huili, but there is no miracle this time. That night Andy takes a trip to the toilet, which is at the bottom of a gentle slope at the back of the compound. Only the thought of being discovered laid out on the ground by a government worker forces him through the 20-yard crawl back to privacy.

In the morning, we admit defeat and pack ourselves on to a bus for Huili. Andy's next stop is Beijing Xiehe Hospital. We are nearly two months behind schedule and there's no more time to play with. Today I have lied by omission to Jia Ji, but tomorrow I will have to admit the truth. Andy cannot go on like this. His Long March ends on 3 July 2003, after 261 days and 2,488 miles. This disaster is only mitigated by one thing . . .

4 July. A pedicab pulls up in front of the Huili Hotel and a Chinese man in perfectly pressed grey hiking clothes jumps out. He waves a fist in the air. 'The Red Army fears not the trials of the Long March!' he cries.

Yang Xiao – Gear Guy – to the rescue.

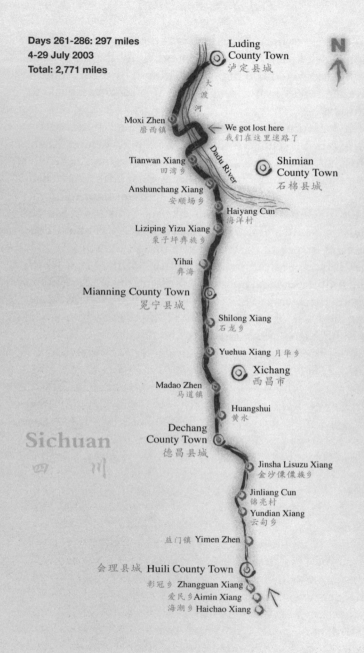

Days 261-286: 297 miles
4-29 July 2003
Total: 2,771 miles

N

Luding
County Town
泸定县城

大渡河

Moxi Zhen
磨西镇

We got lost here
我们在这里迷路了

Shimian
County Town
石棉县城

Tianwan Xiang
田湾乡

Dadu River

Anshunchang Xiang
安顺场乡

Haiyang Cun
海洋村

Liziping Yizu Xiang
栗子坪彝族乡

Yihai
彝海

Mianning County Town
冕宁县城

Shilong Xiang
石龙乡

Yuehua Xiang 月华乡

Xichang
西昌市

Madao Zhen
马道镇

Huangshui
黄水

Dechang
County Town
德昌县城

Jinsha Lisuzu Xiang
金沙傈僳族乡

Jinliang Cun
锦亮村

Yundian Xiang
云甸乡

Sichuan
四　川

益门镇 Yimen Zhen

会理县城 Huili County Town

彰冠乡 Zhangguan Xiang
爱民乡 Aimin Xiang
海潮乡 Haichao Xiang

Chapter 11

Blood Brothers

The Red Army's trek west ended at the River of Golden Sands, the greatest of the tributaries to the Yangtze River. From there, they marched almost due north 250 miles to the south bank of another fearsome river, the Dadu, where they would fight the most celebrated battle of the Long March. In between, they had to cross the country of the Yi people in Liangshan.

While approximately 7 million people are now designated as Yi minority, the 2 million who belong to the Liangshan group have a unique historical and cultural identity. In 1935, these Yi were quite unlike the peaceable Christians of northern Yunnan. They were warriors who cared nothing for Han people – Communist or Guomindang. They ruled themselves, as they had for thousands of years. Yet although they were feared and loathed as barbarians by other ethnic groups who lived close by, the Yi of this area had also evolved a complex and sophisticated society.

They were one of the few Chinese minorities to have developed their own form of writing and had produced texts on astronomy, created their own ten-month solar calendar and written books of scripture and history. Liangshan was the only Yi area to preserve a caste system into modern times (it was abolished in 1956). Society was based on a hierarchy of five castes, at the bottom of which was the Gaxi slave caste.[1] The Gaxi were mostly slaves taken from other ethnic groups, and this practice no doubt accounted for much of the fear and loathing the Yi inspired. The folk memory of barbarous times still breeds prejudice. To reach the Yi lands, we must cross the counties of Huili, Dechang and Xichang, and all the way people purse their lips and warn us to be careful. There are robbers and violent men ahead, they say.

Andy and I part at Huili bus station with promises of a swift reunion, but I don't expect to see him return. He is too weak even to pack his own bag. I never imagined I'd be grateful for SARS, but Yang Xiao is only here because his usual work with tourists in Beijing has been eliminated by global panic over the disease.

'I can go with you this month,' he says. 'After that, I just don't know. I want to cross the Snow Mountains with you, but if business recovers I'll have to go back to Beijing.'

Huili sits in a broad, fertile river valley on the route of the ancient Southern Silk Road that led from the Chinese capital Chang'an (modern-day Xi'an) into Persia. Locals call it a 'Spring City' like Kunming, because its mild climate is similar to that of the Yunnan capital, which also sits at around 6,500 feet above sea level. Today, Huili retains more flavour than most county towns. The modern Highway 108 cuts through carrying traffic from Yunnan north to Xichang and on to Chengdu, but the life of the town still feels focused on the old main street that runs parallel about 100 yards to the west. This bustles with small trade, while the narrow streets to its east and west are alive with peasants selling produce from their fields. A few wear Yi and Miao garb, but this is a Han town, as it has always been. Many low, old buildings share space with new concrete blocks in the centre, but the city wall is gone. Only one gate still straddles the main street, marking the point where the Reds' assault failed.

The town was defended by Guomindang forces under the command of Liu Yuantang, who employed medieval methods to great success. As the Reds tried to scale the walls, vats of boiling rice porridge were emptied on to their heads. The attackers tried digging mines under the walls; these had water poured into them. The assault lasted five days before it was called off.

'Yes, I saw the Red Army,' says Wang Zhugui, seventy-seven, who minds a metal goods shop a few dozen metres north of the gate. Wooden panelling above the shop front bears a faded slogan in white paint wishing 'Ten Thousand Years' to the Communist Party.

Wang points to the gate. 'They were right here, where we are now, but they couldn't get past the wall into the rest of the town.'

'Did Red soldiers paint that slogan on your shop?' asks Yang Xiao.

Wang laughs, 'No, it was Red Guards that did that.'

The Red Guards were teenage hooligans unleashed by Mao's Cultural Revolution in 1966. Mao began the campaign to bring down the Party leaders he blamed for betraying his socialist revolution – 'taking the capitalist road', as he put it. Towards the end of his life, Mao became increasingly concerned about 'revisionism'. He believed the gains of the revolution were threatened by the emergence of a 'bourgeois' class within the Communist Party itself. This class was satisfied with its privileged position and content to apply a managerial approach to politics, focusing on incremental development rather than revolutionary progress. Mao saw the influence of revisionists in the opposition to his Great Leap Forward, and in the pragmatic recovery programme led in the early 1960s by Liu Shaoqi, Zhou Enlai, Deng Xiaoping and Chen Yun (all of them Long March veterans). He also nursed a sense of grievance at personal slights and perceived betrayals – such as Peng Dehuai's criticism of the Great Leap Forward at Lushan in 1959. After the failure of the Great Leap Forward, Mao retreated from day-to-day involvement in policy-making. Although he still made proposals, he often felt they were amended or ignored – in particular by Liu Shaoqi and Deng Xiaoping. In a speech to provincial officials in October 1966, he whined, 'From 1959 to the present, Deng Xiaoping has not consulted me about anything . . . It's not so bad that I am not allowed to complete my work. But I do object to being treated like a dead ancestor.'[2]

As his doubts about the Party leadership grew, Mao began to look beyond the Party – back to the masses. At the 'Seven Thousand Cadres' conference in 1962, he attacked Party bureaucrats: 'Those of you who . . . do not allow people to speak, who think you are tigers, and that nobody will dare to touch your arse . . . will fail . . . You think that nobody will really dare to touch the arse of tigers like you? They damn well will!'[3]

The Red Guards were Mao's arse kickers. They began as radical 'anti-revisionist' student groups in Beijing's universities and middle schools, where they emerged in summer 1966 against a background of escalating political conflict. The name itself was first used by students at Tsinghua University Middle School and it was acknowledged by Mao in an enthusiastic letter of support on 1 August, the same day he convened a meeting of the Party Central Committee to discuss the political and ideological basis of the Cultural Revolution. When this meeting failed to kowtow immediately, Mao called together the Standing Committee of the Politburo and told them, 'There are monsters and demons among those present here.' On 5 August, Mao issued one of his most famous statements. Under the headline, 'Bombard the Headquarters', he wrote that certain 'central leading comrades' had opposed the Cultural Revolution and enforced a 'bourgeois dictatorship'. Mao continued: 'They have encircled and suppressed revolutionaries, and stifled opinions different from their own. They have practised White terror, glorifying capitalism and denigrating the proletariat. How venomous!'[4]

Thoroughly intimidated, on 8 August the Central Committee unanimously agreed to a document known as the 'Sixteen Points'. This stated that the objective of the Cultural Revolution was, 'to struggle against and overthrow those persons in authority who are taking the capitalist road, to criticize and repudiate the reactionary bourgeois academic "authorities" and the ideology of the bourgeoisie and all other exploiting classes and to transform education, literature and art and all other parts of the superstructure . . . so as to facilitate the consolidation and development of the socialist system.'[5]

With Mao's encouragement, the Red Guard movement caught fire. At dawn on 18 August, up to a million schoolchildren and university students gathered on Tian'anmen Square to see Mao greet them and accept a red armband from one of their number. During the next three months, more than 10 million Red Guards travelled to Beijing for further mass rallies. But these were not peaceful carnivals of happy children; they were the inspiration for mass violence and destruction. The Red Guards were Mao's tool to terrorize, subjugate and, in some cases, kill his opponents. Their model, the Tsinghua Middle School group, wrote, 'We will be brutal! . . . We will strike [Mao's enemies] to the ground and trample [them].'[6] The national police chief told subordinates, 'If people are killed, they are killed; it's no business of ours.'[7] Freed from normal social and legal constraints, some students gave free reign to their ugliest fantasies. Teachers and other authority figures were tortured and murdered, while children were tormented and beaten for belonging to 'reactionary' families. Gangs ransacked homes searching for evidence of bourgeois tendencies. Temples and other monuments to Chinese culture and civilization were smashed up and burnt down. By the time Mao brought their activities under control two years later, Red Guard groups had ravaged the whole country to demonstrate their loyalty to the Chairman and their enthusiasm for the call to 'Destroy the Four Olds': old thought, old culture, old customs and old practices.

On the other side of the Huili town gate, Yang Xiao and I take a rest in an old teahouse. Yang Xiao looks askance at his teacup. The boss explains its saucer was taken away in the Cultural Revolution, along with the mahjong and chess sets.

I've heard so many horror stories from the Cultural Revolution, but I'm almost equally impressed by this vision of children taking the adults' toys away. This is living history, too – thirty-five years later, a roomful of old men still deprived of their saucers and chess sets.

In another old teahouse on a southern extension of the main street, Yang Xiao and I become something of an attraction for the children of the local No.2 Primary School. They crowd in and treat us to song and dance routines. The adults smile indulgently, until the kids recite a poem they have invented on the basis of a Tang Dynasty classic by Li Bai, a poet also celebrated for his love of liquor and for allegedly drowning in AD 762 after getting drunk and trying to embrace the moon's reflection in the Yangtze River. The original poem expresses a longing for home inspired by moonlight; in the children's contemporary version, Li Bai awaits his wife by moonlight, but when she doesn't show up the enraged poet tears his trousers in frustration. Yang Xiao resists the adults' attempts to shut the children up and shepherd them away. 'Let's have that one again,' he says.

People on the Chinese mainland aren't allowed to read that last paragraph. This book was first published in a Chinese translation in January 2005. You could probably make a fair guess at some of the sections that were censored: stories that show the authorities in a poor light, such as the Tongdao Incident; disrespectful comments about Chairman Mao; tales of inter-ethnic conflict in the Tibetan regions (read on!). I could understand the logic of censorship like that – and even sometimes argue against it. The story of Mao's daughter was originally scheduled for deletion, but finally appeared in a reduced form. I convinced the Chinese publisher to include other historical revelations that initially made them nervous. But there are other aspects of censorship that are totally illogical – and the Li Bai poem fell victim to one of these.

'Chinese people won't like it,' said the editor, Chen Xi.

'What do you mean, "Chinese people" I asked. 'Yang Xiao's Chinese and he thought it was funny. Those children were Chinese.'

'Li Bai is a very respected figure. Chinese people will find this hard to accept.'

What Chen Xi meant, of course, was that *she* found it hard to accept. It made *her* feel uncomfortable, so while Andy and I were allowed to tell stories about police harassment, official incompetence and historical cover-ups, we were strictly forbidden to make fun of a poet who had been dead for well over a thousand years.

What you have to understand is that, for most publications, there is no official censor. Only books that touch on officially sensitive topics such as, for example, Chinese foreign policy, must be reviewed and authorized by the censors. In all other cases, it is up to editors and their immediate bosses to make their own guesses as to what is acceptable and what isn't. The boundaries of acceptability are deliberately vague. When editors get it wrong and higher authorities are displeased, punishments are meted out. Fear of getting it wrong keeps the Chinese media in check. It's a self-censorship system. And because editors effectively have to make the rules up for themselves, they also get to smuggle in their own prejudices. Sex is a particularly troublesome topic. At Chinese New Year, Andy sent an innocuous monthly column to the English-language *Beijing Today* in which he mentioned the word 'tomboy'. The paper's chief censor, a cultured and genial middle-aged fellow, looked the word up in his dictionary and decided this was a coded message about lesbian love. The article was spiked.

From Huili, the Long March trail basically follows Highway 108 for 150 miles to Mianning County Town. We find few footpaths to ease the pain of walking on hard road. Yang Xiao is anxious to get away from the highway and camp. '108 depresses my spirit,' he says. 'There's nothing to see, too many cars.' The tarmac also ruins his feet. Within five days they are blistered and bleeding. To make matters worse, once over the mountain above Yimen Zhen we descend deep into the valley of the Anning River, where the humidity rises as the thermometer goes back up into the low 30s. Banana trees reappear among the paddies for the first time since Jiaopingdu. Yang Xiao hobbles far behind, but to me it's a restful interlude. Although the mountains tower to our east and west, the valley broadens until it is at least a mile across around Dechang County Town. I've become oppressed by the narrow horizons of mountain trails, but now that feeling of claustrophobia lifts and for once the beauty of the landscape is a cause for joy rather than gloom.

Above Yimen we meet an unkempt man boiling a pot

on a patch of waste ground. It's impossible to tell if his lank hair has been braided or has simply knotted itself. He looks the image of the village idiot. He greets us with a broad smile. His name, he says, is Chen Zhengao, and he is fifty-four years old.

'What's in the pot?' asks Yang Xiao. Chen Zhengao lifts the lid to reveal nothing but boiling water.

'Haven't you got anything to put in that?' I ask. Chen shakes his head. I reach into my bag and produce a bag of instant noodles. Chen is delighted. He doesn't bother with ritual refusals. Yang Xiao asks what he's doing. Chen explains that he lives on the road, moving from place to place. He points to a bicycle parked a few metres away.

'That's my home, there,' he says. The bike is loaded with canvas and plastic, the materials we see erected into shelters for itinerant labourers every time we follow a road.

'What do you do?' I ask.

'I believe in the Lord,' says Chen.

I've never considered this as a job before. 'How do you earn money like that?'

'I sing songs, and people sometimes give me money. When I recognized the Lord, he gave me the gift of song. I didn't have it before.'

'Sing us a song, then,' says Yang Xiao.

Chen stands up and obliges. It's true, he does have a gift, though it could do with polishing. Several peasants have stopped on their way to market by this time. Between the sight of me and the performance of Chen Zhengao, this must be Yimen's best show of 2003.

'The people in the church won't let me join their congregation,' says Chen. 'They say I'm crazy.' His smile widens even further.

The congregation is probably also confused as to which church Chen should be in. He announces he doesn't eat pork and expresses satisfaction with Allah. The Lord is the Lord, as far as Chen is concerned. And with his personal God to ride beside him, Chen is the happiest, friendliest soul I have met on the Long March.

About 15 miles past Chen Zhengao's campsite, Yang Xiao and I are delayed in Yundian Xiang by the invitations and protestations of the local government, which has occupied the restaurant where we try to buy supplies. When we finally convince the officials that we really can't stay and share their feast, the Party Secretary orders the restaurant boss to give us all the foodstuffs we ask for, and no amount of appealing to Red Army spirit can stop this extravagance being added to the people's bill. It's close to sunset by the time we get out of Yundian, and the prospects for camping are poor.

This valley is one place where the mantra that 'China has too many people' rings true. The fertile land has attracted people to plant every available space. At dusk we climb into Jinliang Cun, which rises on a series of terraces above the east side of the river. The only flat space large enough for a tent is on a path that leads to a farmhouse. Outside the front door, a peasant is dealing with waste stalks from a recent harvest. We unload our rucksacks, squat down with him, and Yang Xiao launches William Lindesay's favourite gambit for striking up a rapport in rural China.

'Do you have any boiled water?' he asks.

Gu Xianhai sends the elder of his two sons to fetch a bottle and two cups. We discuss the name of the village, Gu's crops, the weather, who we are and where we are going. Yang Xiao winks at me. '*Man man lai*,' he says – 'Slowly does it.' His mind is already at countryside speed.

Once we have our cups of hot water and the basic topics of conversation are exhausted, Yang Xiao says, 'We're looking for a place to sleep. Would you mind if we put our tent up on your path?

Gu doesn't mind at all. In fact, he'd rather we came into

his house and slept there. But the view over the Anning River is so magnificent, the prospect of sunrise so appealing, and the ham provided by the Yundian government smells so good that we persuade him not to insist.

Gu is a quiet man. He brings us seats and hot water for washing, then leaves us to the attention of other villagers. Once they have left after dinner, he returns with his two sons to sit for a while. I ask Gu how much land he has. 'Only one *mu* for rice,' he says. There are six *mu* to an acre. 'It's not enough to feed my family,' he continues. 'Sometimes I go to Dechang to *da gong*. I can earn 15 yuan a day there.'

'Do you have any other way to earn money?'

'My wife will go to market tomorrow to buy eggs. We will hatch them into chicks to sell. The eggs cost five *mao* each [there are 10 *mao* to the yuan], and we can sell the chicks for five yuan, but since we have to feed the chicks for a month before we sell them, the profit is only one yuan each.'

Yang Xiao tells the boys Long March stories before bedtime. He describes the crossing of the Yi country and the battle at the Dadu River. After the children leave, he shakes his head at the poverty of the peasants and the munificent government banquet we witnessed in Yundian. 'You didn't object to eating their ham, though, did you,' I say. My new marching partner grins. Nobody's perfect.

In preparation for our march into Sichuan, Yang Xiao, whose family moved to Chengdu, the capital of Sichuan Province, when he was eleven years old, makes a suggestion.

'You know what?' he says. 'You need to learn some Sichuan dialect.'

'Why?' I ask.

'It's very important. Sichuan people like to insult people and you have to be able to argue with them properly. I very rarely argue when I'm in Beijing, but I do it all the time in Sichuan. People won't listen to you unless you abuse them in Sichuan dialect. When I was on the bus coming to meet you, there was a man standing next to me who kept spitting on the floor by my feet. It was disgusting. I asked him several times to stop, but he didn't pay any attention to me, so finally I lost my temper and called him a "*gui erzi*". He was really taken aback, and he stopped after that.'

Gui erzi, Yang Xiao explains, is a Sichuanese insult that literally means 'son of a tortoise'. (Tortoises and turtles get a raw deal in China. Not only do people like to put them in soup, but a 'turtle's egg' is a severe insult in the northern provinces.) Personally, however, I've found sheer weight of words is the most effective way to get what I want. It's exhausting, but when it comes to solving problems it's no good just being right – you have to prove you are right ten times over in ten different ways to hold back the tide of excuses. Chinese people talk a lot (our mutual friend, Kath Naday, who guides foreign tourists around China, compares them to Italians) and I find the best way to get past obstructive characters is simply to talk more than they do. They are lost for a response as long as you keep the initiative, and it's especially confusing for them to be out-talked by a foreigner. The clincher is physical contact. Grasp a hand and shake it vigorously, give a big smile and a heartfelt, 'thank you, thank you,' and then wrap it up by announcing how happy you are and that, 'we're friends.' It's amazing how often this works.

Of course, on the Long March we don't always have the patience for such time-consuming rituals. Yang Xiao introduces me to an alternative method of problem solving. In the town of Yonglang, faced with a bill of 15 yuan for a plate of *ji zong* wild mushrooms that cost 7 yuan in Huili, he simply explodes: 'Bullshit!'

He demands the authorities be summoned. He quotes

regulations that say restaurants must have menus with prices. The boss calls the police and then pulls out his menu as if to say, 'A-ha!'. He doesn't look so smug after he discovers the menu doesn't list any of the dishes we have eaten. Two cops arrive on a motorcycle. Although the boss knows both of them, this *guanxi* is no defence against such a strident assertion of rights – especially in the presence of a foreigner. The cops take the boss out back and return with a bill slashed by more than 50 per cent. The boss looks very glum. I shake hands all around, 'Thank you, thank you!'

'Do you think they would have paid any attention to you if I hadn't been here?' I ask Yang Xiao afterwards.

'Hard to say. But they should. There are rules and you need to know them and try to make people obey them. You know, there's a regulation now that policemen should salute before they address you. I went to Shanghai and I noticed they were all doing it. They're very polite. But as soon as I got back to Beijing, I got harassed by a policeman outside the train station. "Why don't you salute?" I asked. "I don't need to," he said. Some of my more daring friends in Beijing have started having fun with this. If they get any trouble from a policeman, they say, "Don't talk crap! First salute!" It's right. They should treat you with courtesy, at least.'

I'd salute the man who introduced that law. In some ways, Chinese society is already more advanced than England.

This area has attracted migrants from other parts of China, drawn by the temperate climate, low prices and relatively high standard of living. A railway line runs all the way through the valley south of Lugu Zhen, which is almost the size of a small county town, and a brand new highway runs from Huanglian Zhen through Xichang to Mianning, where the Yi lands begin. Another will soon connect Xichang to Chengdu. The airport at Xichang completes a network of communications like none I've seen since Qujing.

Six miles north of Xichang, Anning is a town dedicated to pleasure. There is none of the range of goods and services I associate with the average *zhen* – just a vast array of shiny 'entertainment city' clubs full of karaoke, mahjong and pretty girls. There is a street in Xichang known as 'corruption street' for its array of pleasure services, both legal and illegal. Anning is like that street multiplied by ten. To its south, Xixiang is much the same, only its entertainment centres are lower class, serving the local factories rather than the middle-class trade. Other forms of business seem almost superfluous here. We arrive hungry for lunch, but it's easier to buy a prostitute than a meal. Six miles to the north, Lizhou has all this and more. It hums with the life of a real town, with a thriving market, shops and even the kind of shiny hotel generally reserved for county towns.

The chaos, thrill, problems and potential of China's dash for development are all here. Xichang and its surrounding area have a greater sense of energy than anywhere else on the Long March trail. I like it very much. I'm especially excited by the prospect of seeing the Satellite Launch Centre outside Manshuiwan Zhen, just across the border of Mianning County. China's own-brand 'Long March' rockets are fired from here. This is one place our Long March surely cannot miss.

A billboard at the gate announces that the Satellite Launch Centre is a 'patriotic education base'. I head for the ticket office, but a guard intercepts me.

'No foreigners,' says the guard. He notices Yang Xiao and adds, 'No Hong Kong or Macao people, either.'

'That's a funny way to teach patriotism,' I say, but the guard is unmoved.

Denied the boyish thrill of rockets and spaceships, we trudge north. At Lugu, the railway turns east towards

Chengdu and the level of development and activity starts to fall away. The centre of Shilong Xiang, where we plan to spend the night, is so small we walk right through it without noticing. A middle-aged woman leads us back to an incongruous, three-storey residence covered in fresh white tiles. The Wu family apparently does a fine trade in pigs to Xichang, and their clean, bright new home is open to lodgers.

We feed on donkey meat fried with green pepper, fried egg, a bowl of egg and tomato soup and rice. The main room where we eat is large and pleasantly furnished. A television set occupies one corner, where the son of the house, twenty-year-old Wu Tao, home on holiday from university in Chongqing, watches CCTV-1 with three friends. Wu's grandmother sits quietly on a sofa opposite our small table. She looks old enough . . .

'Grandma,' says Yang Xiao, 'Do you remember the Red Army?'

The old lady is delighted with this invitation to reminisce. 'I remember,' she says. 'I was sixteen. My family were landlords and we all ran away to Houshan. All the local landlords were scared. When we came back, most of our food and clothes had been taken.'

'If you were landlords, were any of your family hurt by the peasants or the soldiers?'

'My aunt was taken away, but she was old and they let her go at Daqiao. They took another landlord from here, as well. He was taken to Luding, but then they let him go and he came back.'

It seems the Reds didn't only kill landlords. Sometimes they took them along for a kind of propaganda show-and-tell, to prove to the peasants that the Red Army was their army, the army of the poor.

When we describe our plan to follow the Reds' trail into the mountains to Yihai, Wu Tao and his family repeat the familiar warnings about the dangers that lie ahead.

'It's very dangerous up there,' says Wu. 'The Yi people are wild. They rob people. And they're dirty.'

All this prejudice has affected Jia Ji, who has been calling up local authorities to seek assurances about safety. The authorities have fuelled her fears, confirming that yes, indeed, those Yi are not to be trusted. In Mianning County Town, however, we lunch with the tourism bureau and the county Party Secretary, all of whom dismiss the danger stories. They're not worried at all. Quite the opposite: they're delighted to have tourists visit, and hope many more will come in our wake.

Secretary Kang is one of those Communists who could give the Party a good name. He is a short, quiet, sober man who does not like drinking Moutai and is happy for us to take only a sip of wine for form's sake. He arrives direct from the scene of a mudslide, his trousers spattered. There have been no deaths in this accident, but the danger is on everyone's mind. Last week a mudslide in the Tibetan area of Ganzi killed fifty-one people. The ground in this part of the world is unstable. Each day we walk around, over or through the aftermath of landslips. Further down the road, the side of a hill collapses right in front of us, bringing part of a farmer's cabbage patch down with it.

'There won't be any *Huoba* festival for me this year,' says Kang, who returns to work immediately after finishing his meal. Today is the second day of the three-day Yi festival of *Huobajie* – a public holiday in the Liangshan Yi Minority Autonomous Region.

After all the wealth and development we've seen recently, I want to know how things are going in Mianning. Kang says the county is among the four poorest in Liangshan, along with Huili, Dechang and Xichang – the Long March trail, in other words. Beyond the flourishing river valley and the city of Xichang itself, the fruits of development have not trickled down to the masses.

'The local government is in financial trouble, too,' says Kang. 'We used to levy a "special agricultural tax" of 20 per cent, but the central government abolished it. Obviously, that made the peasants better off, but we haven't found a way to make up the gap in government finances.'

'So what's the future of development in Mianning?'

'In the long term, it will be exploitation of mineral resources. We have the second-largest reserve of rare earths in the country after Baotou in Inner Mongolia.'

It's a grim vision. Baotou is a hideous industrial conurbation; Mianning is beautiful. The county town enjoys a spectacular setting, cupped by high mountains on its northern and western edges. The river flows clear. The air is pristine. And from here the Long March trail enters one of its loveliest stretches – across one low pass that leads into the valley where the Daqiao Reservoir stretches at least a mile to the far shore, over the water that drowns the scene of the Reds' first struggles with the Yi, and then back up into forested hills to Yihai Lake. Pepper trees surround the trail, and a light mist descends as the day darkens.

The story of the Red Army's journey here is one of the strangest and, says Yang Xiao, most beautiful of the Long March. The Reds were racing north to reach the Dadu River before the Guomindang. They could ill afford delays. The Reds had enough enemies already and throughout the march the leadership had pursued a hands-off approach to the minorities to encourage trust and support for the Communist cause. Mostly, minority peoples ran at the sight of Han soldiers. Not the Yi.

Their lands begin about 10 miles north of Mianning County Town and stretch for 40 miles further north towards the Dadu. When the Red Army's advance units reached the border between Han and Yi settlements, they were confronted by armed tribesmen demanding money. The Yi were more concerned with robbery than murder. They took the money the Reds offered, then came back for more. They stole equipment from other units and even stripped one group of their clothes.[8]

The poet Xiao Hua was a young soldier with the advance party that first entered the Yi area. Many years later, he wrote the story of what happened next:

'We asked the interpreter to explain to them that the Red Army was totally different from [the Guomindang], and that its sole purpose was to pass through the Yi area on a northward march. It would not rob or kill the Yis, nor would it even stay one night in their area. In spite of all the explanations, the Yis waved their hands and weapons and continued to protest, "No passing!" In the midst of this confusion, we saw a cloud of dust rising at the mouth of the narrow valley before us. A tall, middle-aged Yi on a black mule was galloping towards us at the head of a group of people . . . The noisy crowd calmed down a little as he drew nearer. I was told that the man was the fourth uncle of [Xiao Yedan], chief of the local Yi tribe.

'I asked the interpreter to tell him that the commander of the Red Army wished to speak to him. The Yi readily agreed to talk . . . Knowing that the Yis had a high regard for brotherhood, I told him that Commander [Liu Bocheng], who was personally leading a big army in a northern expedition, was passing through, and would like to become a sworn brother of the Yi chief.'

The chief's uncle 'was all smiles' at the thought that the commander of a big army wanted an alliance with the Yi chief. According to Xiao Hua, Chief Xiao Yedan was head of the Kuchi clan, which was constantly at war with another clan, the Lohung. By allying with the Red Army, Xiao Yedan hoped to defeat the Lohung.

The Reds weren't interested in taking sides in the Yi's internal affairs, but they didn't stress this point at the time. Commander Liu Bocheng rode to meet Xiao Yedan and his uncle that same day, 22 May 1935, and the three men went together to the west shore of Yihai Lake. Two bowls of water were drawn from the lake. A cockerel was brought and slashed above the beak, then its blood was sprinkled into the water. The three men knelt side by side before the two bowls. First, Liu Bocheng swore brotherhood and drained his bowl at one gulp; then Xiao Yedan and his uncle took the other bowl, made their own oath, and drained the bowl between them.

This oath, the 'Yihai Alliance', is celebrated for allowing the Reds to continue their drive north to escape Chiang Kai-shek. The next day, Xiao Yedan's uncle rode as escort to Liu Bocheng all the way to the northern border of the Yi lands. Xiao Hua wrote: 'Instead of being suspicious and blocking our way as they had done the day before, [the Yi] now flanked the mountain path, watching the long columns of the Red Army march away to the north.'[9]

We pitch camp at sunset at the exact spot where Liu Bocheng and Xiao Yedan met. The lake is a jewel, about 500 acres in area. From the west shore, I can see the full expanse of its clear waters. It is almost unspoilt. A small pavilion and hall above the north bank are the only constructions in view. But it's hard to imagine tourism developers will resist the lure of this place forever. The only blots on the landscape are a few broken bottles and other items of rubbish left by previous campers. Yang Xiao mutters about the attitude of his compatriots towards the environment, takes a plastic bag and a pair of chopsticks, and does his best to clean the site up. My night by Yihai is disturbed by a bad dream of future restaurants, hotels and karaoke bars. It might be better if people do stay frightened of the Yi.

Despite the blood oath, Red detachments that followed Liu Bocheng didn't all get the red-carpet treatment. Long March stragglers were robbed and stripped, while snipers shot from the hills.

'My father was attacked and injured by Yi tribesmen near Yihai,' says Chen Zhifu. 'He was brought as far as Yanru, where the villagers took him in.'

Yang Xiao and I are having a cup of tea in Yanru, high on Songlinggpo Mountain above Chaluo Xiang, which Xiao Hua remembered as the first Han village out of the Yi area. The ethnic map in this area, about 30 miles north of Yihai, is a patchwork of Han, Yi and Tibetan. Yanru is a Han village that sees few outsiders. The first man I meet asks me what province I am from, completely oblivious to the possibility I might be from another country.

Chen Zhifu is the village head and the sixth son of Chen Liaojin, who joined the Red Army in Jiangxi in 1931. He shows us a photograph of his father, who died in 1991 after spending the rest of his life in Yanru, leaving seven sons. I'm captivated by the image of a young man walking thousands of kilometres from his home, being injured and rescued by strangers, and making a new life in a remote place, forgotten by the history he had helped to forge. I also think back to a brief meeting in Xichang with the prefect of Liangshan. It would be fair to say that the prefect, Qumu Shiha, owed his position directly to the Long March. His father, Qumu, joined a diversionary force of the Red Army as it crossed the Yi country around Yuexi, and was one of thirty-six Yi soldiers to survive all the way to the end of the Long March. I also remember what Sitao said about the first Long March veteran we met. Chen Yingchun had not made it across the river at Xinfeng and so sixty-eight years later he and his family were still peasants. If he had reached Wuqi, said Sitao, he might be a retired general living in a Beijing courtyard. His family might be part of China's elite. Chen Liaojin was also left behind, and his family has never left the mountain village where Chen lived out the rest of his long life. But there in Xichang, occupying the highest post in the land of his father, was the son of a man who did make it to Wuqi.

For a fortunate few, the Long March would be a ticket right to the top.

The Dadu is a ferocious and frightening river. It rushes past with the noise and churning impatience of a mountain stream, although it's almost as wide as the River of Golden Sands at the point I first see it. Three miles upstream, Anshunchang Xiang is one of the only places where the river broadens and slows sufficiently to make it possible to put a boat across.

Seventy years before the Red Army arrived, another rebel force came here. Where the Reds preached the gospel of communism, the last army of the Taiping Heavenly Kingdom preached Christianity with Chinese characteristics. It's a bizarre story. The Taiping Rebellion was inspired by a man who believed he was the son of God and younger brother to Jesus Christ. Hong Xiuquan gathered an army of fellow believers and together they conquered Nanjing in 1853 and established it as their Heavenly Capital. They then marched north to overthrow the Qing Dynasty itself. In some ways, they were the revolutionary forerunners of the Red Army: unbinding women's feet and redistributing the land.

Despite its initial successes, the northern expedition failed and Hong Xiuquan fell out with other leaders of the rebellion. One of these, Shi Dakai, took his army and marched west, where they were finally hunted down by Qing troops. In early June 1863, they halted at the Dadu to celebrate the birth of Shi's son. There was no time to get across as the imperial troops closed in. The story goes that Shi Dakai gave himself up and pleaded for the lives of his men, but the Qing commander showed no mercy. The Taiping were slaughtered and the Dadu ran crimson with their blood.[10]

If anyone in the Red Army didn't already know this story, the Guomindang did its best to educate them. Planes dropped leaflets announcing that Zhu De and

Mao Zedong were the 'new Shi Dakai', and therefore anyone who didn't want to be chopped up and dumped in the Dadu had better surrender, quick.

Anshunchang today is a curious mixture of old and new. Its main street preserves buildings from Long March times in a way I haven't seen since Jieshou on the Xiang River. The pleasant memorial museum is housed in a building that the army used as lodgings in 1935, though this is soon to be replaced by a large new construction by the river. At the other end of the village is a group of modern brick buildings with swimming pool, restaurants, karaoke and crowds of young women – entertainment for the wealthy class of nearby Shimian County Town. One of the boats used by the Red Army to cross the Dadu stands outside this complex. A shoddy, handwritten sign saying 'Red Army Boat' hangs from the prow. Partygoers use it as a litter bin, perhaps on their way to the outside toilet that stands behind it. The dustbin of history, indeed.

When the Red Army vanguard took Anshunchang, they found only one boat, big enough for about a dozen men plus six more to man the oars. It must have been a tremendous task to row across the Dadu even here. Such is the strength of the river, the landing site on the east bank is 200-300 yards downstream from where the advance party set off. Above this launching point, where steps lead down to the riverbank from the forecourt of the new museum building, Yang Xiao and I meet Yu Fengying, seventy-eight. She says she saw the whole thing.

'I lived on the other bank,' says Yu. 'We came out to watch the Red Army try and cross.'

'What did the Guomindang do?' I ask.

'They fired at the boat, but then they ran away. They came back after the Red Army had left.'

From the Communist point of view, it's another tremendous story of daring heroism and triumph. For the Guomindang, it's another extraordinary example of incompetence and cowardice. One wooden boatload of Red soldiers, struggling across a rampaging torrent, somehow manages to rout the defence and take control of the crossing. It's as if the Germans had allowed the Allies to take the Normandy beaches in the Second World War with a dozen men in a rubber dinghy.

Mao's idea had been to put the whole army, between 20,000 and 30,000 men, across the Dadu at Anshunch-ang, but the Reds found only two more boats. With seven boats and a much easier river, it had taken a week to cross the Golden Sands. Chiang Kai-shek could march from Chengdu to Anshunchang and back again before the Red Army could cross the Dadu in three boats. Mao instead turned to Plan B, an improbable scheme that led to the most celebrated and thrilling event of the Long March.

The only other place where the Dadu could be crossed was 75 miles away to the north – the iron-chain bridge at Luding, built in 1705 to connect the trade route from Chengdu to Tibet. There was no road to Luding on Mao's side of the river. A vanguard battalion of the 1st Army Group, commanded by Yang Chengwu and Wang Kaix-iang, was ordered to find a path, defeat the bridge's defenders, and rescue the Red Army. They were given three days.

The Reds' schedule went like this:
Day 1 (27 May): leave Anshunchang early morning, camp near Tianwan.
Day 2 (28 May): reach Moxi 2 p.m., push on overnight;
Day 3 (29 May): reach Shangtianba, 3 miles south of Luding, at dawn. Begin battle for Luding bridge at 4 p.m.

Yang Xiao doesn't hesitate: Of course we should try and get to Luding as fast as Yang Chengwu.

To make the attempt we change policy. Yang Chengwu and his men travelled as light as possible, throwing away superfluous items en route. We arrange for our heavy equipment to be sent on to Luding, and pack nothing but food, water and cameras. If we have to sleep outside in the rain, then so be it. For the one and only time on our Long March, we add a little bit of re-creation to our retracing.

We set off exactly two months late, on 27 July. It's raining, but we're in good spirits because the doctors have finally nailed Andy's problem. He calls to give me the good news.

'I've got "erosive gastritis and reflux oesophagitis," ' he says.

'What does that mean?'

'Basically, I think it means my stomach and throat are gradually dissolving in acid. Remember all that coughing? It was bile. The doctor says I should rest for six months.'

'What are you going to do, then?'

'I'll see you in Luding in six days.'

The locals tell us our plan is impossible. The old paths have washed away, they say, and the peasants don't use them anymore. But I've been hearing things like that ever since Jiangxi. During the course of route-finding throughout the journey, I hear the face-losing words 'I don't know' exactly twice. I can see on the map there are no roads to connect the villages that dot the route along the west bank of the Dadu. 'That means there must be paths of some sort,' I assure Yang Xiao.

We reach the top of Wangang Mountain above Tianwan near dusk on the first day. Unlike the Red vanguard, we have fought no battles, built no impromptu bridges and carry no rifles, bullets or hand grenades, but we are exhausted. We struggle down the mountain just after dark to find Tianwan in the grip of a two-day power cut. There is nothing to eat but noodles and a boiled egg. 'The Reds would have savoured such luxury,' says Yang Xiao, but I'm not in the mood for English-style ironic humour, especially not from someone Chinese.

From Tianwan to Shangtianba is another 49 miles. The

Red vanguard did it in one shot with no rest. Halfway there, at Moxi on Day 2, we are four hours behind schedule and the sun is setting. I ask a local man about the path to Luding. 'The Red Army path?' he marvels. 'That's all washed away. No one uses that any more. You have to follow the road along the other side of the river.'

I seek a second opinion from the boss of the Friendship Guesthouse. 'No problem,' he says, and points to a scar running diagonally up Mogangling Mountain, which divides Moxi from the Dadu valley. 'The Reds went that way. You can follow the path all the way to Luding.'

Yang Xiao and I stare at the darkening trail over Mogangling. Who is telling the truth? We lean towards the guesthouse boss, but could we really find the path in the dark? A terrific thunderstorm settles the question. We have dinner and go to bed. We'll never be as tough as the Red Army.

The guesthouse boss is quite right. From the top of Mogangling to Luding is no problem at all, if you think of walking 25 miles plus, as no problem. We reach Shang-tianba at 9 p.m., about thirteen hours late.

'Now I know,' says Yang Xiao, 'The "*fei duo luding qi*" [dash to seize Luding Bridge] is no joke. It's no boast.'

Yet the history books do exaggerate. The official Chinese version is based on Yang Chengwu's account,[11] which estimates the distance from Anshunchang to Luding at about 160 kilometres (100 miles); our own measurement comes to 75 miles – and that includes a major diversion when we go the wrong way on Day 2. Maybe Yang made an honest mistake (after all, peasants have told us towns 15 miles distant were '100 kilometres away'), but there's no need to go on inflating the figures as if the truth is not impressive enough. During the forced march from Tianwan to Shangtianba, I reckon Yang Chengwu and his men covered between 46 and 49 miles in 25 hours – that's almost the equivalent of two mara-

thons, back to back. At least half of that was on treacherous mountain paths; a third of that time they marched in
the dark. You try it.

But getting to Luding was the easy part. What's most
remarkable about this story is what happened next.

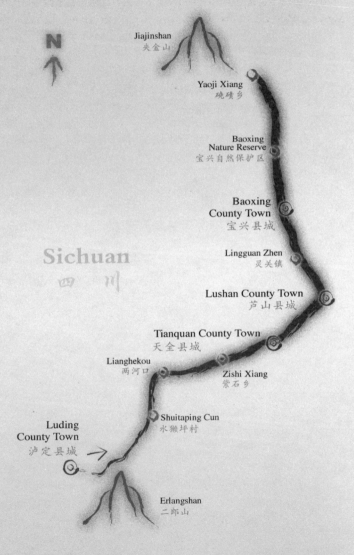

Days 287-311: 162 miles
30 July - 22 August 2003
Total: 2,933 miles

Jiajinshan
夹金山

Yaoji Xiang
硗碛乡

Baoxing
Nature Reserve
宝兴自然保护区

Baoxing
County Town
宝兴县城

Sichuan
四川

Lingguan Zhen
灵关镇

Lushan County Town
芦山县城

Tianquan County Town
天全县城

Lianghekou
两河口

Zishi Xiang
紫石乡

Luding
County Town
泸定县城

Shuitaping Cun
水獭坪村

Erlangshan
二郎山

Chapter 12

Luding Bridge

Andy arrives in Luding just in time to wave goodbye to Gear Guy. As I feared, Yang Xiao has been summoned back to work. His replacement is a half-man. Andy has put on 9 pounds during his four-week absence, bringing him up close to 10 stone (140 pounds) – at least 3 stone below his normal weight. His stomach illness has been diagnosed as chronic, dating back to long before the Long March began. The only treatment is long-term rest and recuperation. I don't think he should even be here, but he announces a way he can conquer the Snow Mountains.

'The doctor says a controlled diet is critical. I have to eat six regular, small meals a day.'

'And how do you plan to do that?' I wonder.

'I eat rice porridge for breakfast, lunch and dinner, and carry hard-boiled eggs in my pocket.'

Nobody – and I suspect that includes Andy himself – believes this plan will work.

The first time I see Luding Bridge in daylight, I can't escape a sense of disappointment. I pictured it swaying precariously over a gaping chasm, nearly 200 yards above the surging, swirling Dadu. This is Red Army Commander-in-Chief Zhu De's fault – when he was interviewed by American journalist Agnes Smedley in Yan'an in 1937, he told her the bridge was made up of 'about 20 heavy iron chains ... swaying over the roaring torrent 500 feet below' and stretching about 300 yards across the river.[1]

The roaring torrent is actually less than 10 yards below. Locals say when the river is in flood, it's even possible to dangle your feet in it. This seems a foolhardy idea – so powerful and capricious is the current, it's easy to imagine foot-washers being tugged off. The iron chains span 108 yards between two ornate, wooden gatehouses. There are thirteen thick chains, each link about 4 inches across. Nine chains lie under wooden planks; two form an airy barrier and hand-hold on either side. There is a central walkway about 1 yard wide fully covered in wooden planks, but either side of this, planks are laid about 3 inches apart. The gaps provide a fine view of the swirling waters beneath your feet. I grip the top chain as peasants bearing heavy loads on carrying poles bounce past, bound for market. William Lindesay saw a woman stumble and fall to her death when he walked this section of the Long March ten years before us.[2]

When the Red vanguard reached Luding, they found the bridge had been reduced to a skeleton. Its defenders had torn up at least half the wooden planks, leaving nothing but bare iron chains.[3] The enemy occupied the bridgehead on the opposite bank. Twenty-two volunteers were chosen to lead the assault.

Yang Chengwu's version of the assault on Luding Bridge goes like this:

'The attack began at four in the afternoon. The battalion commander [Wang Kaixiang] and I directed it from the west end of the bridge. The buglers of the battalion gathered together to sound the charge, and we opened up with every weapon we had ... The twenty-two heroes, led by Commander Liao [Dazhu], climbed across the swaying bridge chains, in the teeth of intense enemy fire. Each man carried a tommy gun, a broad sword and twelve hand grenades. Behind them came the officers and men of Third Company, each carrying a plank in addition to full battle gear. They fought and laid planks at the same time.

'Just as the assault squad reached the bridgehead on the opposite side, huge flames sprang into the sky . . . The enemy was trying to throw a fire barrier across our path . . . Our assault squad hesitated for a few seconds and then plunged boldly into the flames. Commander Liao's cap caught fire. He threw it away and fought on . . . Our gallant twenty-two fought until all their bullets and grenades were gone. There was a critical pause as the Third Company came charging to their rescue . . . In two hours, we destroyed more than half of the two enemy battalions, and the remainder broke ranks and scattered.'[4]

In Yang's description, every one of the twenty-two survives the suicidal charge. The official version, as inscribed into the plaque on the bridge itself, says eighteen survived.

That's impossible, you say. Chairman Mao's bodyguard, Chen Changfeng, wrote that he walked with Mao over Luding Bridge. 'Chairman,' he said when they reached the end, 'With one squad we could hold a bridge like that indefinitely.'[5] How could the Guomindang possibly fail to defend such a point? How could they inflict only three casualties?

In their recent biography of Chairman Mao, Jung Chang and her husband Jon Halliday answer this question very simply: the Guomindang didn't fail to defend Luding Bridge because the battle never happened. 'This is a complete invention,' they write. 'There were no Nationalist troops at the bridge.' The Battle of Luding is a piece of Maoist propaganda first sold to a gullible Edgar Snow, the first journalist to interview Mao in Bao'an in 1936, and polished tirelessly ever since.

Chang and Halliday cite one key source for their 'scoop'. In 1997, they interviewed a 'sprightly 93-year-old' woman who said her family was running a beancurd shop right by the end of the bridge held by the Reds. 'She remembered the Communists firing . . . "Only Yin a shell, and Yang a shot" – a Chinese expression for sporadic. She did not remember her side of the river being fired on at all.'[6]

Leaving aside the obvious question of who the Communists were firing at if 'there were no Nationalist troops at the bridge', Chang and Halliday place a lot of faith in a single witness, especially one whose testimony consists mainly of what she didn't see.

After ten days in Luding, Andy and I also track down a woman who lived by the bridge on 29 May 1935. She remembers events quite differently.

'I was fourteen years old,' says Li Guoxiu. 'The Red soldiers came at eight in the morning. I ran up on to the hill behind.' Li gestures upwards from where the three of us are standing close to the west end of the bridge.

'Did you see the battle?' I ask. 'Did you actually see the Red soldiers cross the bridge?'

'Yes. Local people led the way. The locals were in front, Reds behind. The Reds didn't know how to cross the bridge. There was no wood, just iron chains hanging there. The locals at the front were all shot and killed.'

Li still lives in the same place, just a few steps north of the bridge along the west bank of the Dadu. Her house is brick and concrete today. In 1935, it was all wood, and the boards were torn down by the Reds to make new planks for the bridge. I ask Li what life was like in those days. She is overwhelmed by emotion recalling her youth.

She cries with a mixture of sorrow and anger when she talks about the '*huai dan*', the bastards, as she calls the local Guomindang leaders.

'Life was very bitter then. Now it's good, but I'm old. Before there was nothing to eat, we could only eat very little at every meal. And there were people on our backs oppressing us. The Guomindang put us in prison and only provided us with a very small bowl of food. They held people as security and forced the peasants to [work] for them.'

Chang and Halliday say Luding Bridge is the 'centre of the Long March myth'.[7] They are anxious to debunk it because their overall thesis is that the Long March itself is a propaganda trick, rather than a (basically) true story exploited for propaganda purposes (as I would say). Their claims about Luding Bridge have been widely reported and accepted as fact, and so I think it's important to dwell on this because their version of events and presentation of the 'myth' in my view is wrong on almost every count.

Chang and Halliday write: 'The Communists claim that the bridge was defended by a Nationalist regiment under one Li Quan-shan.' No, they don't. Even the most boastful of the Communist accounts, that of Yang Chengwu, says the bridge was defended by two battalions of enemy troops (judging by Otto Braun's description, a Red Army battalion at the start of the Long March comprised around 270 men).[8] There is a complete consensus that these were not regular Guomindang/Nationalist forces, but belonged to the 38th Regiment of the Sichuan Provincial Army. This was indeed headed by Li Quanshan, but 'the Communists' say his headquarters were 24 kilometres (15 miles) south of Luding in Lengji. According to the Guomindang's own contemporary report, Li directed two battalions to run to Luding on the evening of 28 May, the day before the battle.[9] So in one sense, Chang and Halliday are right – there were no Nationalist troops at the bridge. What they mean, however, is that there were no enemy troops at all. This is not true.

'Central to the myth,' write Chang and Halliday, 'is the claim that part of the bridge was set on fire and soldiers had to crawl across on incandescent chains.' Those incandescent chains are a nice touch, but the only place you will find them is in Chang and Halliday's book. The only part of the bridge to burn in either Yang Chengwu's account or the most famous Long March propaganda movie, *Ten Thousand Rivers, One Thousand Mountains* (made in 1959), is the gatehouse. There are no glowing chains in any Communist version of the battle of Luding Bridge.

'The strongest evidence debunking the myth of "heroic" fighting is that there were no battle casualties,' write Chang and Halliday. Whatever you think of their overall thesis, Chang and Halliday's account of the Long March is distinguished throughout by distortion and factual error. In this case, their 'strongest evidence' is indeed a complete invention. With the exception of Yang Chengwu, no source even suggests that there were no casualties on Luding Bridge. The very first description of the battle, given by Edgar Snow in *Red Star Over China* in 1937, cited three deaths. The official number, inscribed on the bridge itself, is now four. Chinese moviegoers as long ago as 1959 could watch Red soldiers die on Luding Bridge. The Guomindang report of the battle speaks only of 'casualties on both sides'. Because the official number is so unbelievably low, I lean towards Li Guoxiu's version of events. With local peasants to shield them, it makes more sense that the soldiers could advance under fire and suffer relatively few casualties.

To deny that a battle took place at Luding Bridge, it's necessary to call Li Guoxiu a liar. I don't believe she lied –

especially as her account differs so strikingly from the official version. Still, she is only one witness, recalling a battle she watched as a child nearly seventy years ago. But abundant other evidence supports the fact of the battle and also suggests that Red losses were greater than the official version admits. Zhu Taibing, the curator of the Long March memorial in Luding, told us there were different versions of what happened. Some old locals who watched the battle from the hillside told him only five soldiers initially made it across; the rest all fell to their deaths in the river. If all these people are lying in the service of Maoist propaganda, it's odd that they can't get their story straight after having nearly seventy years to practise.

There is one more reason the Reds could overcome apparently impossible odds and cross Luding Bridge, the same reason they were able to capture the river crossing at Anshunchang – they were not faced with Chiang Kai-shek's regular Guomindang forces, but with poorly armed provincial units. Neither these men nor their leaders were especially eager to fight the Red Army; they certainly had no cause for which they wanted to martyr themselves. When they failed to win an easy victory, they gave up and ran away. Had Chiang's own troops occupied Anshunchang and Luding, there is no way the Reds could have crossed. I don't believe they would even have tried. During the Long March, the Red Army avoided set-piece battles wherever possible. The only times they had initiated major engagements, at Tucheng before the first crossing of the Chishui and at Luban Chang before the third, they had fled in defeat.

This does beg an important question: why weren't Chiang's troops at Anshunchang and Luding? Jung Chang and her husband claim it's because Chiang didn't want to block Mao. According to their version, Chiang deliberately let the Red Army go, even facilitated its progress at times.

There are legitimate questions about how much energy Chiang devoted to exterminating the Red Army. US Army colonel Joseph Stilwell, who as General Stilwell later commanded Chiang's forces during the Second World War, wrote in January 1936, 'The accusation has been made that Chiang simply herded the bandits [Reds] through Hunan, [Guizhou] and [Sichuan] as an excuse to follow with his own troops and thus establish himself in areas which previously were only nominally under [Nanjing] control. Whatever the plan, such was the result.'[10] I think this accusation both understates Chiang's efforts and gives him far too much credit. Like Tolstoy's Napoleon, Chiang was never in control of events. When he issued the orders to surround and destroy the Red Army before they made the third crossing of the Chishui, the result was that he 'herded' them straight towards Guiyang, where Chiang himself was sitting almost undefended. This doesn't look like a strategy to let the Reds go; it looks like a mistake.

Whenever there's a choice in history between a conspiracy and a cock-up, I lean towards the latter every time. To argue that Chiang deliberately arranged matters to let the Red Army squeak through to the north-west with less than 10 per cent of the forces with which it started assumes Chiang was something of a genius. He was not. In Stilwell's words, he was 'a stubborn, ignorant, prejudiced, conceited despot'.[11] Chiang didn't fail to garrison Anshunchang and Luding because he planned to let the Reds cross the Dadu. He just screwed things up.

The Red Army wasn't looking for a fight on the Long March. It was running away. But it fought when it had to, and at Luding Bridge the enemy quailed before the courage and determination of the Red soldiers. I don't doubt that this is true. The 'legendary' version of this battle owes its origin almost entirely to Yang Chengwu. Edgar Snow doesn't record who told him the story in Bao'an, but I'm willing to bet it was Yang, who wasn't one to be backward about putting himself forward. With the exception of Liao Dazhu, Yang recorded none of the names of the 'twenty-two heroes'. If Li Guoxiu's memory is accurate and locals did sacrifice themselves for the sake of the Red assault squad, it makes sense that Yang should leave them out, as they don't fit with his personal mythologizing of the event. But I don't think we'll ever know for sure. Yang Chengwu died in 2004, three months after the end of our Long March. I never got a chance to speak to him. If I do him an injustice with these words, I am very sorry.

Luding is a town on the edge, where the Sichuan Basin meets the Qinghai–Tibet Plateau. From here, the road rises swiftly west into the Tibetan Kham region. Each day, convoys of military vehicles rumble through, heading for what locals say is a spot of trouble in Mankeng, just over the Sichuan provincial border in the Tibet Autonomous Region. The 69,000 residents of Luding County are 91 per cent Han. Those few Tibetans who live here appear fairly well integrated into Han society, speaking Mandarin and often intermarrying. Yet even they are far from completely assimilated. On our last night in Luding, we dine with a group that includes some of the people who helped us locate Li Guoxiu. Some of those around the table are strangers to one another, and it takes almost an hour before everyone realizes there is not a single Han present. We've already chatted about minority cultures, but suddenly there's a palpable sense of relaxation. No one has anything bad to say about the Han, but it's clear the absence of any representatives of the majority makes them feel more comfortable asserting their own identity and discussing how it feels to be a member of an ethnic minority. Every Chinese citizen must carry an identity card which includes information on 'ethnic group', a category assigned at birth by the state. One of those at our table is the child of a mixed marriage: Tibetan father, Han mother. 'On my identity card I'm Tibetan,' she says. 'But if I go to Chengdu, I'll say I'm Han because of the way people there treat Tibetans. On the other hand, if I'm in Dege (one of the great centres of Tibetan culture in western Sichuan), I'll say I'm Tibetan.'

It's a depressing thing to cover up your identity. I recall our own unwillingness to admit to being from England during the Iraq war – though that was more from a sense of shame than fear of others' backward attitudes.

Andy has timed his return perfectly. Straight out of Luding, we must climb over Erlangshan, the highest mountain yet. Luding is 4,000 feet above sea level; the pass over Erlangshan is nearly 10,000 feet high. This should sort out whether or not he's in shape to continue the march.

Above Tuanjie Cun, it's a lonely road. Below Tuanjie, a tunnel has been cut through the mountain, rendering our Long March trail redundant. We see a grand total of two vehicles on the old highway all day. It has been raining for nearly a week and the road lower down is interrupted by half a dozen minor landslips. We walk as far from the mountainside as we can. The road winds in great, looping switchbacks that vanish around the mountain before reappearing 50 yards further up. On the first loop out of Tuanjie, I ask a group of workers for directions to the footpath.

'You won't find it,' says one of the three. I knew he'd say that. Life on the Long March has become one endless pantomime performance.

'Yes, you're right – if you don't tell me where it is, I won't find it,' I reply.

'No, even if I tell you where it is, you won't find it,' says the man.

'Oh yes I will,' I insist.

'Oh no you won't,' says he.

This routine goes on until one of the other two men can't stand it any longer. He admits the footpath starts beside the road works office. Andy and I walk about 200 yards to the office and instantly locate the footpath. You can see it from 30 yards away. It's so obvious I need never have asked.

Close to the pass, we meet a solitary herder and go through the same performance. We take the obvious path without hesitation. But after five minutes, it begins to vanish into undergrowth. We crash on. Five more minutes and we have to climb over a tree that has collapsed on to the trail. I fall off the trunk when a dead branch breaks off in my hand. Finally, the 'undergrowth' becomes taller than us and we slash a way through with our hiking sticks. Covered in twigs, scratches and mud, we stagger out on to the main road where it makes the first of many switchbacks. The next section of footpath goes straight off a sheer cliff.

So when should you heed local wisdom? After walking for more than nine months and 2,500 miles across China, I can say with complete confidence that I still have absolutely no idea.

Andy confounds us all. Although his taste buds may die of boredom, a regime of rice porridge, egg whites plus a tin of protein powder seems to be doing the trick. Once Erlangshan is behind us, Andy grows visibly stronger during a week of relatively kind trails. From the Dadu River we have walked almost due east back into a Han Chinese region. The temperature begins to cool as we turn north towards Jiajinshan, the first and most notorious of the great Snow Mountains, on the border of the Tibetan

Autonomous Prefecture of Aba. The path begins to rise along the Lushan River valley, where it's now harvest time. Almost all the way to the centre of Lushan County Town, families are busy with mounds of corn, tearing away the husks and hanging the cobs up to dry, or stripping the corn from the cobs for the final drying stage – laid out on mats or directly on the road.

North of here, we pass into the valley of the Baoxing River, and as we gradually climb upstream agriculture gives way to industry. This is marble country. We spend one night in Lingguan Zhen, where even the hole-in-the-wall restaurant tables are made of marble. The main street is lined with factory shops selling marble items ranging from ashtrays to a full-scale Venus de Milo. But the most popular objets d'art are white marble pandas with painted black eyes, because Baoxing County is mostly famous as the scene of the 'discovery' of the Giant Panda. The panda was unknown in the West until 1869, when native hunters in Baoxing showed a dead specimen to French missionary Armand David.

The pandas have fared little better since David sent his historic pelt to the Museum of Natural History in Paris. There are probably more panda-shaped dustbins in the tiny county town than actual live pandas in the Baoxing Nature Reserve, which begins a further 16 miles to the north. The workers on the reserve say the last census found 119.

'There are 100-plus now,' says Yang Min, a Tibetan woman who oversees a controlled feeding programme for the wild animals. 'Some have been taken away to zoos. The pandas here are particularly good looking, you know.'

I didn't know. I thought pandas were like *laowai* – they all look the same. But Yang Min insists pandas from different places have different characteristics, and that you can't beat a Baoxing panda.

While Andy forces down his regulation gruel, I share the workers' dinner of rice, boiled beans and squash, pure fat that they optimistically call *la rou* (a form of bacon), potato strips, hot peppers and pickled cabbage. They tell us that plans are afoot to create a tourism 'loop' that will run from Chengdu to Sichuan's most famous mountain, Siguniangshan, then across Jiajinshan and through Baoxing on its way back to Chengdu. Today, however, there are no visitors but us two, and the tourism industry comprises a couple of local families who have opened guesthouses at three times the normal price – which is why we are staying down the street with the hospitable workers.

'Could we see a wild panda here?' asks Andy.

'We have one tame male panda for tourists,' says Ye Yinzhi. 'The last time I saw a panda in the mountains was last year. Japanese people like to go looking for them and we'll take them if they want, although you can only go looking in pairs. Any more than two people and the pandas will certainly hear you coming and run away.'

Neither of us wants to see the lonely tame panda. After a night made sleepless by the workers' karaoke session, we push on to the last stop before Jiajinshan.

Yaoji Xiang is the closest Tibetan town to Chengdu. It's a thriving boomtown on the edge of destruction. Hundreds of workers have come here to build a hydroelectric power station to take advantage of the waters rushing off the Jiajin range. When the dam is complete in around two years, the valley will be flooded and Yaoji will cease to exist. Xia Rui, the likeable boss of the Daziran Restaurant where we spend the night, tells us the population must move to a new settlement further up in the mountains to the north-east. Even the Long March memorial, an obelisk that dominates the town from its highest point, will be moved. Future seekers of the

Long March will have to don snorkel and flippers to see the point where Mao's armies prepared for their climb of the first Snow Mountain.

For the first time, I feel real apprehension about the challenge ahead. Long March histories speak of deep snow, frostbite, deaths at the peak from altitude sickness and further casualties as soldiers slipped and plunged over cliffs on the descent. In Xichang, Yang Xiao and I met an eighty-four-year-old veteran named Peng Shuquan who told us, 'On the Snow Mountains, the soldiers were so weak they couldn't stand up after they squatted to go to the toilet.' Second Front Army veteran He Wendai told Andy and I, 'We couldn't rest at the top of the mountain. After we walked up we needed to slowly go down. Some people didn't know this. After they climbed up the mountain, they rested; later, they couldn't stand up. The snow was very deep. If you walked the wrong way into a snow hollow and couldn't get out, you would die.'

Neither of us has ever crossed a mountain high enough to cause altitude sickness. We prepare a bag of powerful drugs in case lack of oxygen makes our brains swell or our lungs fill with fluid. We pack extra food and, for only the fourth time, seek out a local guide to lead us on the trek.

Yang Xuequan, thirty-five, joins us in the courtyard of the Daziran Restaurant. Short, overweight and sucking on an after-dinner cigarette, he doesn't seem at all cut out for such an arduous journey. My confidence soars.

'I've been across many times,'' he says. 'There's no snow on the mountain now. We'll be over in two days, no problem.'

Yang bids us an early goodnight and leaves us to the attentions of the local English teacher, who hurried round the minute he heard of our arrival. Liu Jiantao is a Han exiled to this outpost from his home in Hanyuan, more than 120 miles to the south. He is a very unhappy man.

'Maybe one in one thousand people here read a book,' says Liu. 'For twenty, thirty years people do not pick up a book, but they are not ashamed. They just want to play mahjong. They can play mahjong from the first day of January to the last day of December, and they are not ashamed.'

Liu is alienated culturally. This sense of being a square peg in a round hole is what has brought him rushing over to talk to us. He is in search of fellow feeling.

'They do not want to know about international affairs, and they laugh at me when I tell them how things are done in America.'

Liu admires Americans deeply and seems disappointed to discover we are only English. He cheers up when Andy tells him he lived near New York for six years. But Liu isn't really a racist. His suffering is not caused by the fact he is a Han living amongst Tibetans. It's because he's a middle-class intellectual amongst peasants. The class divide seems greater than any national sentiment.

Whenever a friend from Beijing has walked with us, it seems the modern, urban Chinese has as little in common with his peasant compatriot as we do – perhaps even less. On one occasion much further down the road in Gansu Province, we are chatting with a middle-aged woman not far from Lüjing Xiang. Jia Ji is with us, but has fallen behind. When she catches up, Andy mischievously suggests she should practise her Long March route-finding.

'Ask this woman which way we need to go and how far it is,' he says. Jia Ji does so, using her finest Beijing Mandarin, the Chinese equivalent of BBC English.

The woman laughs. 'I can't understand what you're saying,' she says, and looks at the two of us for enlightenment. After all, she knows she can understand us, because we've been talking to her for five minutes. Jia Ji is furious.

'Impossible!' she splutters, 'I'm talking Chinese!'

'I can't understand what you're saying,' says the woman. 'Impossible!'

We're trying not to giggle too openly. 'Shall I interpret for you?' says Andy, 'She said . . .' Jia Ji doesn't think he's funny. She thinks the woman is just plain stupid. But it's really just a cultural problem – an outsider is an outsider. We were greeted the same way, but after a little persistence the woman accepted that she could, after all, talk to these strange beings. Temporarily, Andy and I have become part of the peasant world. We're used to the pace of life, the daily concerns, the way people speak and even the way they think. Even if we don't always understand this final aspect, we're used to operating in a fog of incomprehension. We expect to misunderstand, whereas Jia Ji, for example, gets exasperated by her inability to communicate with people she had previously considered as, essentially, the same as herself.

Jia Ji gets her directions in the end. '*Man man lai*,' as Gear Guy would say.

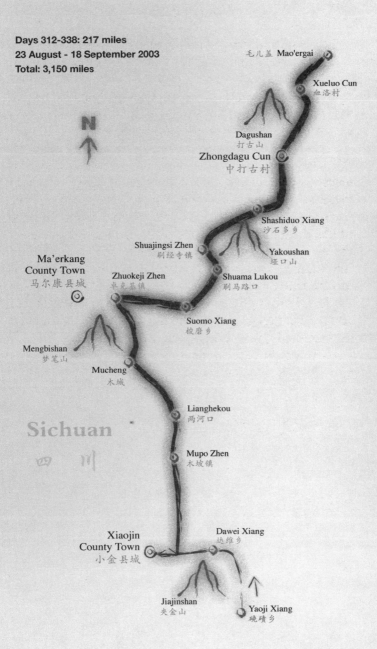

Days 312-338: 217 miles
23 August - 18 September 2003
Total: 3,150 miles

N

毛儿盖 Mao'ergai

Xueluo Cun
血洛村

Dagushan
打古山
Zhongdagu Cun
中打古村

Shashiduo Xiang
沙石多乡

Shuajingsi Zhen
刷经寺镇
Yakoushan
垭口山

Ma'erkang
County Town
马尔康县城

Zhuokeji Zhen
卓克基镇

Shuama Lukou
刷马路口

Suomo Xiang
梭磨乡

Mengbishan
梦笔山

Mucheng
木城

Lianghekou
两河口

Sichuan
四川

Mupo Zhen
木坡镇

Xiaojin
County Town
小金县城

Dawei Xiang
达维乡

Jiajinshan
夹金山

Yaoji Xiang
硗碛乡

Chapter 13

The Snow Mountains

There is no snow on the first Snow Mountain when we arrive on 23 August, but even if we had been on time, the mountain is not what it was. As the Reds began to climb Jiajinshan around 16 June 1935, the high ground was buried in snow and ice. Older residents of Yaoji recalled that in those days, the snow in June could be waist high. 'In June these days there is a thin layer of snow, but for six months the mountain is snowless,' says our guide Yang Xuequan. 'If you want to cross it in winter, you must take a team of people, otherwise it's too dangerous. It's easy to fall into a drift, and without enough people to help there's no way out. People do get lost up here and sometimes they die.'

Today, the great Snow Mountain of bitter Red Army folklore is verdant and warm, bathed in glorious sunshine. Clouds drift the occasional chill shadow across our path up the valley above Yaoji. Yang stops frequently to chat with curious passers-by. While in the town, most people used Chinese to communicate, Yang now speaks Tibetan to almost everyone he meets. He tells us Yang Xuequan is his Chinese name; he is Zangbo in Tibetan. A stream leads us gently up to 8,000 feet above sea level. The climb proper begins after lunch, which we eat at the foot of the mountain in a combined forestry station, guesthouse and karaoke bar. The staff says tourists come almost every day to climb the mountain, though no more than a handful at any one time. There is a road across now, built in 1987, but it would take at least one extra day to follow its switchbacks rather than the old footpath, which is kept in use by forestry workers and herders as well as tourists.

We climb drenched in sweat and rest every twenty minutes at most, even though the slope is not steep. During breaks, leeches crawl on to our boots and backpacks. Yang burns them off with his cigarette. We share snacks and Yang throws the wrappers on to the ground. Andy discusses the Chinese litter problem and the beauty of Jiajinshan. Yang quietly picks his wrappers up.

Sunset sees us cross the tree line, leaving the leeches behind. At 11,000 feet, there is only grass, grazed short by herds of cows, yaks and goats. Before us and to both sides the mountain describes a great arc, but Yang says the ridge above us is not the peak. We will not see that until morning.

We make camp among the animals, our sleep disturbed by the bulls bellowing across the valley. The night is pitch black when a gun-toting Tibetan herdsman stops by our camp. He shouts to an unseen friend on the mountainside, summoning him to join us. To our relief, his friend never comes. It's too dark even for a local to find the way. Yang offers cigarettes and biscuits in the courteous countryside manner, but he also seems anxious. He doesn't use Tibetan himself and says that we can't speak anything but English. Andy and I play dumb. The stranger playfully points his gun at Andy, who motions he is going to bed. Finally, the unwelcome guest takes himself and his rifle away.

Yang has brought no camping gear. He squeezes into the tent between the two of us, and borrows Andy's extra jacket for warmth. He sleeps heavily, snores loudest and is last up in the morning. I have to wake him to borrow his lighter to fire up the stove for breakfast. My own high-tech *Extreme II* lighter has developed altitude sickness, whereas Yang's 1-yuan red plastic lighter is fine – a valuable lesson for the road ahead.

We reach the pass three hours after breaking camp. The grassy peak of Jiajinshan rises to the east of the pass; it's only another 300 to 400 yards to the top, but this is as high as we go.

I have had this mountain in mind ever since I first read about the Long March. It's a touchstone of modern Chinese history, one of the most important symbols of the Red Army's suffering and sacrifice. Every Chinese person I have ever spoken to associates the danger and 'bitterness' of the Long March with two particular places: the Swamps of northern Sichuan and the Snow Mountains.

'The peak of Jiajinshan pierced the sky like a sword point glittering in the sunlight,' wrote Mao's bodyguard Chen Changfeng. 'Its whole mass sparkled as if decorated with a myriad glittering mirrors. Its brightness dazzled your eyes . . . At the start the snow was not so deep and we could walk on it fairly easily. But after twenty minutes or so the drifts became deeper and deeper. A single careless step could throw you into a crevasse and then it might take hours to extricate you. If you walked where the mantle of snow was lighter, it was slippery; for every step you took, you slid back three! Chairman Mao was walking ahead of us, his shoulders hunched, climbing with difficulty. Sometimes he would slip back several steps. Then we gave him a hand; but we too had difficulty in keeping our foothold and then it was he who caught our arms in a firm grip and pulled us up. He wore no padded clothes. Soon his thin grey trousers were wet through and his black cotton shoes were shiny with frost . . .

'As we went up higher, the going grew more difficult. When we were still at the foot of the mountain, the local people had told us: "When you get to the top of the mountain, don't talk nor laugh, otherwise the god of the mountain will choke you to death." We weren't superstitious, but there was some harsh truth in what they said. Now I could hardly breathe. It seemed as if my chest was being pressed between two millstones. My heartbeats were fast and I had difficulty in talking, let alone laughing. I felt as if my heart would pop out of my mouth if I opened it. Then I looked at Chairman Mao again. He was walking ahead, stepping firmly against the wind and snow.'[1]

The peak is still very pretty, but I'm sorry to report that climbing Jiajinshan in summer is quite easy. That does nothing to diminish our sense of achievement, however – especially in Andy's case. He orders that we linger at the pass, in flagrant violation of Red Army instructions. Army doctors had ordered no rest at the top, but cooks from the 3rd Army Group also defied instructions. Harrison Salisbury records that after carrying up 55 pounds of pots and food, they halted on the heights to prepare hot pepper soup. 'But while they were passing out soup, two cooks collapsed and could not be revived.'[2]

A wooden sign marks the spot where the Reds slid down the north side of the mountain in June 1935. Snow covered the paths and so the soldiers simply sat down and hoped for the best. Salisbury writes that some were lost – 'catapulted off the cliffs'. Neither of us feels any symptoms of altitude sickness and it's hard to imagine how anyone could have careered off cliffs to their doom. Jiajinshan slopes gently from here and we stroll down to a stream for a lunch of instant noodles. Semi-wild horses share the stream with us. In the afternoon, we meander 12 miles through meadows and pine forest to the town of Dawei, where the advance guard of the First Front Army met soldiers of the Fourth Front Army for the first time.

Zhang Guotao's Fourth Front Army was not settled in a strong soviet base area as Mao and his comrades had hoped. With around 100,000 men and women under arms, it was a much larger and better equipped force than the First Front Army, but pressure from Guomindang attacks kept it in motion, and the area under Zhang Guotao's control shifted continually. In spring 1935, he had abandoned a short-lived Northern Sichuan Soviet and moved further west into areas dominated by ethnic minorities, principally Tibetans. In his autobiography, Zhang says he moved west to support the First Front Army in its efforts to march north.

The first solid reports of the First's movements appear to have come through sometime at the end of May or beginning of June 1935, when Zhang says he heard that Mao's men had crossed the River of Golden Sands.[3] He guessed they would head for the Dadu and ordered a force under Xu Xiangqian to march south to help them. These were the men who welcomed the First Front Army vanguard at Dawei. For the veterans we meet from both armies, it was a joyous occasion.

Fourth Front Army veteran Yang Jin told us: 'We hugged! Class friendship, blood brothers. The [First Front Army] Reds carried paper umbrellas. The Sichuan Reds used large bamboo hats soaked in tung oil that kept the rain off. The [First Front Army] Reds liked these the most, so we presented hats to them. The hats had four characters written on them: "Death to Liu Xiang" [Liu was the general of the Sichuan Provincial Army who had defeated the Reds at Tucheng]. The First Front Army's clothes were very poor. Their long trousers had worn down to short trousers. The cloth was poor and very thin. Their legs were covered with streaks of blood. Joining the [First Front Army] Reds was the happiest thing. I was too excited to sleep.'[4]

For the leaders, the union of the Red Armies created a difficult situation. Both Zhang Guotao and Mao Zedong were founder members of the Communist Party and both had obvious ambition. Zhang was in a much stronger position in military terms, but Mao had politics on his side. The bulk of the Party leadership had marched with Mao from Jiangxi and they had accepted his pre-eminence at the Zunyi Meeting. Zhang had no supporters on the Politburo, although he was a member of that body himself. The rivals met for the first time since 1923 just outside Lianghekou, about 80 kilometres (50 miles) north-west of Dawei.

Zhang was dissatisfied with the meeting. 'As the wave of warm-hearted rejoicing passed away,' he wrote, 'there came the internal strife of the Party.'[5] He felt the achievements and cadres of the Fourth Front Army were not given sufficient respect. He faced criticism for his political conduct in northern Sichuan, where he had failed to carry out land reform. He had also abandoned the policy of establishing 'Soviet' administration in favour of declaring a 'North-west Federation' that recognized the high proportion of ethnic minorities in the area. Although Zhang was made a vice-chairman of the Military Affairs Committee of a 'united command', he was unhappy at the results of the Lianghekou Meeting. The combined armies were ordered to move north across three more snow mountains to a place called Mao'ergai, in preparation for a further move into Gansu Province, from where they would either continue north or shift westward towards Xinjiang.

The specifics of future movements would be discussed at Mao'ergai. As to what Zhang termed the 'political problems within the Party', nothing was resolved at all.[6] Zhang also writes of tensions between the cadres of the First and Fourth armies. The veterans we meet, however, were all ordinary soldiers. They say they knew nothing at all of any political intriguing. They had united with new comrades and they were happy.

Jiajinshan guards the border of Aba Tibetan and Qiang Autonomous Region, an area about the size of Scotland with a diverse population of 790,000. As we move west from Dawei towards Xiaojin along the Wori River, the land becomes arid, the hillsides bare. At around 8,000 feet above sea level, the climate feels quite different. The air is dry and hot and we walk under pale blue skies. There will be stars tonight for the first time in weeks. Apple and pear orchards draw life from the river and wildflowers splash the roadside in purple, red, orange and white. Houses have turned to stone. People have turned into Tibetans, though they speak the Sichuan dialect of Chinese.

Andy and I have heard how the Red Army was greeted with hostility and violence in Tibetan areas. Yang Jin told us, 'The Tibetan upper classes, like the important Lamas, led their "*wazi*" (bondsmen) to attack us everywhere. To avoid the enemy's main forces, the Red Army on the Long March kept to footpaths with mountains and forest to either side. But Tibetans and bandits attacked us. They came from the mountains blowing horns and howling and whistling. They also had foreign rifles bought from Britain that shot very straight.'

In a minor fashion, our Long March also experiences a shift in local attitudes.

'No foreigners,' says the agitated guesthouse boss in Xiaojin County Town. 'It's not safe here. Go see the local government.'

Next door, I hear a variation – 'Not safe, go to the Telecom Hotel.' I have already been to the Telecom Hotel, which wanted 100 yuan a night. Our usual budget tops out at 20 yuan, so Andy and I scour the town for alternatives. There aren't any. No guesthouse will admit us, so I accost a policeman.

'Xiaojin must be a very dangerous place,' I say.

'Oh, no,' he says, 'There are no problems here. Why don't you stay at the Telecom Hotel?'

Dangers supposedly surround us throughout our journey, yet somehow they are always just beyond the horizon. We're continually asked, 'Aren't you afraid of meeting "*huai ren*" [bad people]?' To which we respond, are there lots of *huai ren* around here, then?

'Oh, no, not here, but there's lots in [insert local prejudice].'

Lucky us – the *huai ren* always live somewhere else. Except for the next couple of days, when Andy and I suffer from a growing feeling that they have all actually moved to Xiaojin County.

Never before on the Long March have we met so many discourteous, mean and calculating people. The 'zoo effect' of our presence in the county town is worse than ever. We run a gauntlet of shouting, laughing and pointing all the way along the main street. While he was on the Long March, Yang Xiao put such behaviour down to boredom – 'like dogs barking', he described it. I'm accustomed to the running public commentary on our every move, but it's unusual to hear people openly discuss how much they should overcharge us. My temper-control problems flare back up, while Andy conceives an instant prejudice against Tibetans.

On the first day out of the county town, we reach Mupo Zhen after dark and could easily walk right through without noticing. My first thought is that the town is suffering a power cut, but it turns out locals rely on hydroelectric power from the small river, and electricity is used only for essentials – such as the large TV/karaoke/music centre belonging to Zhang Mingang, our moustachioed host at Mupo's only guest-house.

Zhang and his wife are enjoying a VCD of a 'Dwarf Review' when we arrive. Dwarves sing, dance, stage mock boxing bouts and perform various unfunny vaudeville routines. I haven't seen anything as exploitative and demeaning since my childhood. Zhang giggles and points at the TV.

'They're dwarves,' he says. 'Huh-huh-huh.'

Tiring of tiny people, Zhang instructs us on Tibetan culture. 'Tibetans here have always been very good fighters,' he says. 'They fought the Emperor Qianlong for fourteen years. After they were defeated, many were taken to Beijing and then exiled to Heilongjiang.'

'Did they fight the Red Army?' I ask.

'Yes, but others joined the Red Army as well. Later on, near the end of the civil war, remnants of the Guomindang fled here and the Tibetans did a deal with the [Red] Army. For one silver dollar each, they helped mop up the Guomindang.'

'What kind of Tibetans joined the Red Army?' I ask. 'Was it just the poor?'

Zhang looks dismissive. 'Tibetans are very direct people,' he says. 'If you are a good person, they will be your friend. If you do bad things, they will not forget. We hate Hui people. They are not honest in business. Some Hui wanted to move in here, but we told them we would kill them and they stayed away.'

Zhang beams. He swills from a bottle of beer. 'I can drink twelve bottles,' he says. 'How many can you drink?'

At length, Zhang takes us upstairs to a dirty room with six dirty beds. We've stayed in hundreds of places like this. They cost five yuan or less.

'That'll be 25 yuan a bed,' says Zhang.

There's a difference between taking a negotiating position and attempting a barefaced swindle. We pick up our bags and head for the door.

'Where else will you stay?' asks Zhang.

It's 11.30 p.m. and pitch black outside. Mupo Zhen is asleep for the night.

'We'll go and find some Hui people to stay with, thanks

very much,' I say. We pitch our tent by torchlight in a field a couple of hundred metres north of the town.

Without the kindness of strangers, the Long March would be impossible. After Mupo Zhen, spirits sag. Our confidence in the warmth and honesty of local people is badly shaken.

The last village in Xiaojin County is Mucheng. The pass over the second Snow Mountain, Mengbishan, is only 4 or 5 miles to the north, and already we are more than 11,000 feet above sea level. Two stupas and a spectacular triangle of white flags decorate the hillside above the village: a cluster of stone Tibetan houses below the new road. After dark, a few lights burn dimly, powered by the stream that flows off the mountain. The buildings along the road have no electricity at all.

One of those buildings belongs to the road workers. We head straight for it. Andy and I have come to place great faith in anyone wearing an orange outfit bearing the road ministry logo. Something about the road workers' lifestyle seems to give them an affinity with us. They often come from other places and know what it means to live far from home, moving frequently. Their horizons are broader than the average peasant's, and their knowledge of distances is peerless. They are the most reliable source of information on the route of the Long March.

A young man named Liu Peijun invites us in and gives us a bucket of hot water to wash our feet. More workers drift in – Han, Tibetan and Hui Muslims, drawn from Mucheng and as far away as the county town. They sit around the fire, eat, drink and joke together. Candles are lit as the daylight fades.

'What's it like crossing Mengbishan?' I ask.

Very easy, they all say. There's no snow at all and the path isn't steep. We eat our fill and I even drink a couple of toasts to our hosts – the only time on the Long March I allow *bai jiu* past my lips. Finally, we retire to the double bed they have found for us. We've heard friends joke we're becoming like an old married couple; now we've got the bed to prove it – complete with a 'double happiness' marriage quilt.

In the morning, Cheng Shulan cooks breakfast. 'You've been so kind, let us give you some money,' I say.

Cheng's husband protests, 'Oh, no, we don't want any money.'

I secretly write a 'thank you' in childish Chinese characters, wrap it around 30 yuan and leave it under the pillow. Normal service has been resumed.

The Tibetan homes north of Mengbishan are a fine sight. The basic structure is a three-storey building of solid stone, with a shallow, sloped roof cut away at one corner such that about a quarter of the third storey is open patio. The stones around window frames are often whitewashed. The frames themselves are painted and embellished with simple geometric designs and swastikas in red, yellow and blue. Cultivated flowers round off the impression of a higher level of culture and sophistication than in other rural areas on the Long March trail.

The road from Mengbishan intersects with the Chengdu-Ma'erkang highway at Zhuokeji Zhen. This is by far the most splendid *zhen* of the journey. Its winding narrow stone streets and multicoloured stone mosaics survive fully intact. Lattice windows and their frames are painted brightly and flowers crowd the windowsills. In much of the town, only the electricity wires supply any hint of modernity. Because it is relatively easy to reach by road, Chinese film crews come here in search of Tibetan flavour, yet there is still barely a hint of tourism.

Zhuokeji's most celebrated landmark is the '*guan zhai*', the enormous former residence of the local chieftain, which dominates the town from the hillside at its eastern edge. Harrison Salisbury describes it in breathless terms: 'In their reminiscences Long Marchers wrote with awe of the seven-storey atrium, lined with wooden columns, lacquered in red and black and green, tiers of balconies, carved in wood and decorated with precious stones set into the pediments. Tapestries hung from the walls, living quarters were fitted with silken couches and carved stools, tables and cabinets. Tibetan scrolls filled the walls and there was a library of Tibetan and Chinese classics. One floor was devoted to shrines of Buddha framed in jade and gold and silver. There were sparkling windows of glass.'[7]

Today, the residence is empty but for a handful of workers renovating the building. The foreman says it will be reopened as a museum. He points out the bare rooms where he claims Zhou Enlai and Mao Zedong stayed briefly in 1935.

The old people of Zhuokeji can't speak Chinese. We can't find any witnesses of events in 1935, but towards dark we meet Jamjarjiu, a Tibetan trader who was educated in Shanghai and speaks fluent Mandarin. His mother lived in Zhuokeji when the Reds approached and he was raised on her stories.

'Zhuokeji was opium country in those days,' says Jamjarjiu. 'The Tibetans didn't use it much. Most was sold to Han people, and my father also traded it up to Xinjiang. When the Red Army marched into Zhuokeji, some people ran all the way to Aba, but others ran up into the hills above the town. They could see the Red soldiers coming and going from there. Only one man stayed behind. They could hear him shooting at the Red Army. He was killed of course.

'The *guan zhai* was much bigger then. The one you can see now isn't the same – it was built in 1936. It's not true that Mao stayed there. He couldn't have, because it had already been stripped and burned down by Zhang Guotao's soldiers before Mao got here. Mao must have camped in the field above the *guan zhai*, or maybe he lived in the temple below.'

This small temple is still standing just a few steps up an alley by the river that flows off Mengbishan, but Jamjar-jiu's local lore raises more questions than answers. As far as I can tell, Zhang Guotao's Fourth Army forces did not pass Zhuokeji until well *after* Mao had left. I've heard elsewhere that Mao met the master of the *guan zhai* in Beijing in the 1950s and thanked him for the use of his library.

Wherever he spent the night, from Zhuokeji Mao walked along the south bank of the Suomo River for 40 miles before turning north to cross the third Snow Mountain, Changbanshan (or Yakoushan, as locals now call it). The highway now runs north of the river and all but the first couple of miles of the old footpath have fallen away from the hillside. Jamjarjiu takes us along this section to see a group of stones that still bear inscriptions left by the Red soldiers. There used to be many more, he says, but the others have been taken away or have simply tumbled into the river along with the path. The surviving characters are insults directed at Guomindang comman-der Hu Zongnan, whose troops had harassed the Reds south of Mengbishan. Hu is a 'taxing bandit', according to one stone, while another complains, 'Hu Zongnan steals from the Hui people of the north-west, he is a running dog of imperialism' and is next to a line written in Arabic script – the first indication I have ever come across that there were Muslims in the Red Army.

We are standing about 50 yards above the river. From here, the footpath commands a view back over Zhuokeji. Closest to us is an open field where a handful of colourful tents have been erected in preparation for festivities marking the 50th anniversary of the Aba Tibetan and Qiang Autonomous Prefecture. Beyond the tents is the *guan zhai*, and below that the town squeezes in between the hills and the river. Jamjarjiu gestures towards the field.

'Mao didn't stay here long before he moved on to Mao'ergai. Because of the contradiction between Mao and Zhang Guotao, Mao might have been afraid Zhang would try to capture him.'

'I've heard that Mao was supposed to have worried Zhang would try and use force against him, but I've never seen any evidence,' I say. 'What makes you think Mao was really afraid?'

'Zhang's army had a battle here with Mao's front army. In our village, there was a field where they fought a lot. My father had a house there. When he came back home, there was so much blood in his house he had to use a ladle to scoop it out.

'The locals all ran to the top of the hill and only heard the shooting. After they came back, there were many dead bodies. They either buried them in the field or threw them in the river. There were corpses piled as high as a small hill. Zhang Guotao's army had good weapons. Mao Zedong was afraid and ran away.'

'Who told you about all this?' I ask. Jamjarjiu laughs. I'm not sure if he's entertained or rather embarrassed by this memory.

'When I was young, we children dug many bones up from that place. We sold them to a factory that made fertilizer.'

'You sold the Red Army's bones for fertilizer?' says Andy.

Jamjarjiu laughs again. 'We were just children. We didn't think about what we were doing.'

'How much did you get paid?' I ask.

'Three *mao* a *jin*.' (There are two *jin* to a kilo.)

None of us can resist the incongruous black humour of this story. The Red Army's celebrated discipline sometimes broke down in the Tibetan areas. The locals feared the Reds and mostly ran from them. Some attacked them. Only a very few helped them. Food was scarce and starving soldiers took whatever they could find. They even ate the yak butter icons in the Zhuokeji temple. Mao later told Edgar Snow that the Red Army owed its only 'foreign debt' to the Tibetans.[8] He never imagined the Reds would repay some of that debt with their dry bones at three *mao* a *jin*.

Jamjarjiu is the most enthusiastic local historian we have met. He continues: 'You know, in 1995 many journalists and television crews came to Zhuokeji because of the 60th anniversary of the Long March. One woman came to interview my mother. She said, "I heard that when the Reds came here, they helped you harvest the barley. Were they good to you?" My mum said, "Good, good, they stole our possessions and burned our houses. Good!" Even me and my family were surprised when Mum said that. Twenty years ago, you would have been shot for sure. But now we have freedom of speech!' (Not entirely, of course – this story was cut from the Chinese edition of this book.)

'Where are you from?' bellows a very large Tibetan man, the first person we meet in a town called Shuajingsi at the foot of the third Snow Mountain, Yakoushan. This is a thriving little waystation on the highway that leads across the Swamps to the towns of Hongyuan and Aba, and beyond to Gansu and Qinghai provinces. There is an imposing petrol station and a number of shops and restaurants. The community is a mixture of Han, Hui and Tibetan. Andy and I are in the Hui restaurant at the south end of town. The Hui appear to have a more consistent culture of cleanliness and they use vegetable fat for cooking, which makes ordering food easier for Andy. The Tibetan man has paused from slurping noodles through his moustache to pose his question.

'Ah, England is good! England and America are good!' he says.

I expect he's going to say something about being friends with the Dalai Lama next, but instead he booms: 'You beat Saddam! You kill Muslims. Tibetans like England. We don't like Muslims. They are terrorists.' I cringe. The Muslim restaurant boss brings us a pot of tea. He doesn't seem put out at all. In fact, he's laughing.

'How are relations with the Tibetans, then?' I ask.

'Fine,' says the boss.

'Not fine! Not fine!' shouts the Moustache, quivering with droplets of beef noodle soup.

I never imagined these remote peoples would have mastered ironic postmodern humour. I try to get into the spirit. 'I heard Han people say you Tibetans are terrorists, too,' I say.

But that's not funny. 'No, no, Muslims. Muslims are terrorists, not Tibetans,' says the Moustache, who lumbers out. The boss continues to insist everything is fine, but I can't help feeling there's many a true word spoken in jest.

Local wisdom says we can be over Yakoushan and safely down the other side in the village of Maheba in less than a day. There is a Long March martyrs' memorial at the pass and the path is 'easy' to find.

Shuajingsi is already 11,000 feet above sea level. The air is thin even as we begin to climb. It is very, very slow going. We rest fifteen minutes for every twenty we climb. It's all too easy to be distracted by the landscape. Below, the morning sunshine glitters in the river that flows south from Shuajingsi through a valley of tiny wooden houses – the grand stone structures of the Zhuokeji area disappeared the moment we turned north. In the far distance, there are snowfields on a great mountain range. As we approach the summit, both of us grow confused. How long have we been walking? Is it break time yet? Why are there three paths all of a sudden?

We don't have multiple vision. I reason that since we're crossing from west to east in order to walk north along a river valley, we should take the path that tends north. From a clear-minded, sea-level point of view, that would probably be the left path. It's 4.30 p.m. and we need to get down this mountain before dark. Andy is persuaded. We take the middle path.

The pass clocks in at 14,000 feet, nearly 1,000 feet higher than Mengbishan. The view is magnificent, the finest I have seen. It's a great rush to go from looking no further than a grassy slope in front of your nose to gazing across a deep valley to snow-capped peaks. There are vast ranges to the east and south-east. The highest peak dwarfs anything on our side of the valley. There is only time to descend a few hundred yards before darkness obliges us to camp. This is a lonely place. We have seen no people all day, and there is no sign of life in the valley below us. More worryingly, there doesn't appear to be much of a path, either.

We try to follow the main stream down the next morning, but it's impossible. Trees crowd around the water and there is no evidence anyone else has ever been this way. We are forced back out of the forest and up on to the coarse grass of the north slope, which is set at an ankle-breaking angle. This is strictly goats-only territory. But this left slope is interrupted by a fresh fold of hill, with its own mini-valley and stream in the middle. And where there's water, there's thick forest. Only this time, there's no way around. We simply crash, slide and fall through it. The branches grasp at our bags.

I reassure Andy. Since we were supposed to be able to get to Maheba yesterday, I predict we have crossed further to the north, missing the main trail. 'We won't have lost any time in the end, because we'll come down into the valley well beyond Maheba.'

Andy quietly busies himself with the leaves and branches attached to his hair, stuck to his clothes, jammed down his neck and even lodged under his watchstrap. He doesn't know that there's no point cleaning himself up just yet, because there is another of these mini-jungles only ten minutes away. And then another. And another. It's 2 p.m. before we find a path fit for humans. At last, just after 5 p.m., we come to the bottom of the valley and find a village. We are greeted by a group of young Tibetan men.

'What's the name of this village?' I ask.

'Maheba.'

'Where did you come from?' asks one of the young men.

'England . . . I mean, Shuajingsi,' I say.

'You've come the long way,' says the Tibetan.

Three down, two to go. From Maheba, we can look north to the Dagushan range and for the first time there is snow on the peak ahead. According to the diary of Luo Kaifu, the Chinese journalist who retraced the Long March in 1984–5, we should cross two mountains in two days: first is Dagushan itself, then Tuoluogang. The map then promises a 15-mile stretch of nothingness before Xueluo, the first settlement across the mountains in Songpan County.

The schoolmaster in the village at the foot of Dagushan gives us a bed for the night. Andy interrogates him about the availability of guides over the mountain. The schoolmaster, whose name is Ergede, assures him that the local Party Secretary will be happy to help in the morning. But next morning we can't find the Party Secretary. We can't find anyone at all, except one woman in a shop by the empty government compound up the road from the school. She promises we can follow a clear path up the mountain that leads to the home of an old woman who can speak the language of the Han. The old woman will be able to show us the way from there. Directions courtesy of Hans Christian Andersen: 'Stay on the path and ask the old lady who lives on the mountain.'

There is a clear path up the mountain – the wrong mountain. Only by good fortune are we spotted by an old lady who does, indeed, speak the Sichuan dialect of Chinese. Qiuzuo's husband is a Han from southern Sichuan. She calls to us from far below, 'Where you going?'

Qiuzuo carries an enormous load of twigs. Her adult son walks alongside carrying nothing, while her two-year-old grandson plays in the dirt. We explain our mission and Qiuzuo abandons twigs, scoops up tot, pops him into a papoose and leads us to the right path. As she walks, she picks wildflowers and hands them over her left shoulder to the fascinated boy. After about half a mile, we reach a point where the path divides. Qiuzuo indicates the left-hand trail.

'Follow this down to the river, cross the bridge, then follow the valley around to your left. Keep going until the river branches, then follow the right hand valley. That path will take you all the way to the pass. If you walk quickly, you can reach a place called Sanjiaoba before dark. There are herders and houses there where you can stay. There's nobody on the other side of the mountain.'

We don't walk quickly, but at 5.30 p.m. we find three log huts we assume are Sanjiaoba. Although nobody's home, the door of one small hut is unlocked. As it has just started to rain, we invite ourselves in.

The hut is a *niu peng*, a shelter built by the Tibetan herders for use whenever they happen to be in the area. There is nothing inside but a pile of firewood, a broom handle and a large fireplace. A length of strong wire is strung from a beam above our fireplace, allowing pots to be hung over the flames. As our fire settles down, the storm bursts outside. Lightning flashes through gaps in the cabin's log wall. I hang a pot of water over the fire and bless the herders.

The storm blows itself out by morning and we set off again. Two hours after breakfast, the valley widens into boggy pastures grazed by yak herds. I'm expecting to see the summit, but instead I see log houses and fluttering prayer flags. Qiuzuo was quite right – we needed to walk fast to reach Sanjiaoba last night.

We trudge through deepening bog to the nearest home, where a middle-aged Tibetan woman greets us from the porch and invites us in. A younger woman pours us yak butter tea and as we sit, numbers swell. They are all women. The youngest are nervous of us and peep in from the door for several minutes before being convinced it is safe to enter. Judging by their vivid, pristine clothes, two of the teenagers have dressed for the occasion.

'Where are the men?' I ask. There is a smattering of Chinese even here.

'Down the mountain,' says Kangzangcu. 'We are all women here. Nine of us.'

No men. No wonder they seem pleased to see us.

'How long have you lived here?' asks Andy.

'We're from Shang Dagu. We came up here a few days ago to tend the yak herds. We will take them down the mountain for the winter in four days.'

Tibetan music plays softly from a battery radio/ cassette machine. The room fills with stage whispers and giggles while Bangmuo prepares what she calls *momo* for lunch. She mixes maize flour and water into dough, then kneads and knocks it into circles about 8 inches across and cooks the dough on a hot plate briefly on both sides, then finishes them in the hot coals of the fire.

The bread is cut open and filled with yak butter. It's

exactly like an Australian outback damper. Andy adds salt and a decadent touch of honey. The Tibetan women are thrilled with Andy's gold foil-wrapped honey sachets. Andy is thrilled with the taste of freshly baked bread.

'How far is it to the pass to Mao'ergai?' I ask.

'Very close,' says Kangzangcu. 'Just follow the river. There are herders' tents on the other side.'

Sometimes I think it's just a waste of time asking for information and advice at all. Every person on the approach to Dagushan has assured us with the utmost confidence that we will find nobody, absolutely nobody on the far side of the mountain. But wait a minute, never mind the people – shouldn't there be another mountain over there?

'Where is Tuoluogang?' I ask. The women look puzzled. 'Tuoluogang, the next Snow Mountain,' I insist.

'I've never heard of it,' says Kangzangcu.

The others also shrug. 'You cross here and go straight down to Mao'ergai,' says Ciyingcuo.

'This is Dagushan, right? The Red Army crossed here, didn't they?' asks Andy.

'Yes, that's right.'

The fifth Snow Mountain has vanished! I'd jump for joy if I wasn't afraid of altitude sickness.

With hindsight, I think several generations of Chinese schoolchildren have been slightly misled. The vanguard of the Red Army crossed Dagushan three weeks before Mao and the other Party leaders. After climbing over a first pass they faced a second rise in the Dagushan range, which they called Tuoluogang and the history books claimed as the 'Fifth Snow Mountain'. Since the first pass didn't actually get them over the range, it doesn't really qualify as a 'pass' and I think it's a bit of a stretch to count two separate mountains. By the time Mao reached this point, the Red scouts had worked out a better route that took the leaders straight up and down – the same route that Andy and I have followed.

Andy and I have eight women for company over fresh-baked bread buns. We meet the ninth as we leave the settlement. Nineteen-year-old Remencu emerges from the last house holding a lead that connects to an enormous, shaggy and very angry dog. It's our first sight of the dreaded *zang ao*, the Tibetan wolfhound. Gear Guy warned us these things are nothing like other dogs. When he was a child on the Tibetan grasslands of Qinghai, even the horses were afraid of them. They are not cowardly curs, but vicious killers. Tibetan nomads keep them to guard their camps.

Remencu waves to us. 'Come and have tea . . . ooh!' She drops the lead and the dog races straight for me (maybe he hasn't noticed Andy). Remencu picks up her skirt and chases after. I've got a can of Mace in my pocket for occasions just such as these, but panic brings out the Prehistoric Man in me. I grab the nearest rock – and as I straighten up to launch my missile, the dog halts and allows Remencu to catch its lead. Yang Xiao is wrong.

Alone, at least, this hellhound is unwilling to risk a rock in the face.

Remencu is a beautiful, vivacious young woman who lives alone on top of a mountain with a killer dog. I wave to her and smile through ten days' worth of grime and stubble.

'No tea, thanks,' I say.

Gansu

2004 GDP per head 5,970 yuan ($721)
Population: 25,615,137
Ethnic minority population: 2,184,233 (8.7%)
Main minorities: "more than one million" Hui,
            "nearly 400,000" Tibetans,
            20.7% Dongxiang,
            0.7% Bao'an, 0.6% Yugu.
Other: Tu, Manchu, Hasake.
(China Census 2000, National Bureau of Statistics of China)

Gansu 甘肃

Days 339-346: 110 miles
19-26 September 2003
Total: 3,260 miles

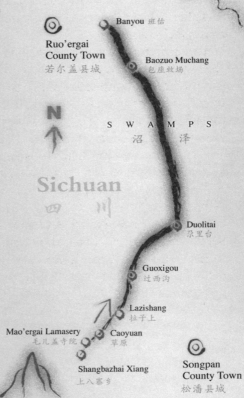

Banyou 班佑

Ruo'ergai
County Town
若尔盖县城

Baozuo Muchang
包座牧场

N

SWAMPS
沼　泽

Sichuan
四　川

Duolitai
朵里台

Guoxigou
过西沟

Lazishang
拉子上

Mao'ergai Lamasery
毛儿盖寺院

Caoyuan
草原

Shangbazhai Xiang
上八寨乡

Songpan
County Town
松潘县城

Dagushan
打古山

Chapter 14

The Swamps

It's a liberation to enter the valley of the Mao'ergai River. After weeks of towering peaks and narrow skies, it feels like the land itself has breathed a sigh of relief and settled into a more relaxed posture. The hills are low, the road is flat and the soil is fertile. Behind us, Dagushan is dusted with white – the first snow fell the night after we crossed the pass. North of the Mao'ergai valley lie the great swamplands, the *caodi*. In 1935, the Reds could only guess at the road ahead. No one lived in the Swamps. No trees grew in the poisonous bogs. From Mao'ergai to the northern edge of the Swamps was at least 60 miles; with no road, no landmarks, no shelter and no food.

'In Mao'ergai, I cried for the first time on the Long March,' veteran Ren Rong told a reporter for the '*My Long March*' project. 'I cried for my stable hand Old Liu . . . One day, some horses ate the Tibetan barley when they were very hungry, but the horses' stomachs couldn't digest it and they all died. Liu was sentenced to death and executed . . . He just didn't know the difference between grass and barley . . . I didn't even know his full name so after [1949] I couldn't even tell the local government to look after his children. It's the great sorrow of my life.'[1]

The Red Army stayed in the Mao'ergai area for about six weeks, while disagreements persisted among its leaders. A series of meetings to discuss the next move ended up in the Mao'ergai lamasery. Today, this is a rambling establishment that staggers down the north slope of the valley, surrounded by a pilgrims' prayer-wheel route. It is nearly 800 years old and home to more than 300 lamas, although we're told there were 500 or more before the Cultural Revolution, when the lamasery was closed and the lamas sent back to their families. It is like a small, self-contained village – there is even a shop within the compound, where lamas tell us they have never seen a foreign visitor before.

Zhang Guotao hoped to convene a larger meeting of senior cadres of the First and Fourth Front armies to thrash out serious political questions. He wanted to bring new people into the discussions of the Party Central Committee, where he currently had no backing. He perhaps wanted to put his own supporters on the Central Committee to strengthen his hand.[2] Zhang's plan was to pin some of the blame for the defeat of the Central Soviet Area in Jiangxi on the policy promoted by the Central Committee. It didn't work. Politically, Zhang was isolated. Mao and his supporters rejected Zhang's criticisms and suggestions. Militarily, however, Zhang was stronger than ever. He had an army of 100,000 troops, probably around 10 times as many as Mao, so he couldn't just be brushed off.

It was agreed to create a 'unified command' in which Zhang was Chief Political Commissar and Zhu De Commander-in-Chief. The Red Army would continue north across the Swamps, marching in two columns. Zhang Guotao and command headquarters were assigned to the Left Column, which was to move north along the western edge of the Swamps to Aba. From Aba, they would cross into Gansu, where they would ultimately reunite with the Right Column. The Right Column would take a more direct route towards Gansu, crossing the Swamps northeast of Mao'ergai to a village called Baxi. Mao and the

Central Committee leaders marched with the Right Column, commanded by two of Zhang Guotao's men – his senior military commander Xu Xiangqian and political commissar Chen Changhao. When the two columns set out in late August 1935, therefore, Zhang Guotao might not have got his way with the Party, but he appeared to be in control of the entire Red Army.

'Are there any old lamas alive who might have been here in 1935, when the Red Army stayed?' I ask. The lamas look doubtful. I press the question and they concede there might be one or two such old men.

'Could you introduce us?'

'They can't speak Chinese.'

'Yes, but you could interpret.' All the younger lamas seem able to converse reasonably well in Mandarin.

'No, no. I can't interpret.' It's the same answer from everyone. They will not take us to see any old monks, and they won't tell us why. Otherwise, however, they couldn't be more obliging. We accept an invitation to eat from Qu Qiu, a twenty-two year old who has been in the lamasery since he was fourteen. Qu lights a fire in the stove that occupies the centre of his wood-panelled room, boils a pot of tea and steams bread made from white flour. He pours the tea into a bowl and, before Andy can stop him, adds a generous dollop of prime yak butter. We're still over 10,000 feet above sea level, so a pure-fat diet is no doubt just what a doctor would order – except that Andy's doctor has ordered him not to eat fat.

Several of Qu's comrades join us. They are all in their twenties and have all been in the lamasery since their early teens. They say the government doesn't allow boys younger than sixteen to enter the lamasery anymore, but we have seen children as young as five running around in crimson robes. Qu says children can still be taken into the lamasery if an old living Buddha dies. They must have lost a lot of living Buddhas lately.

'What do you do every day?' I ask.

'We have duties from seven or eight in the morning until midday, then again from five until seven in the evening,' says Qu.

'How do you get food? Do you farm the land around the lamasery?'

'No, the local families support us.'

There is a tape player in one corner of the room. While I set up the tripod for a photo, Qu stows his Tibetan pop music cassettes out of view. He passes Andy a tape with a picture of one of Mao'ergai's living Buddhas on the cover.

'Put this on top of the tape player, will you?'

'Doesn't the living Buddha like music?' asks Andy. The lamas laugh. They're a humorous and playful bunch. They like to slap each other on the back, sometimes quite hard. The harder and more unexpected, the louder the laugh.

Andy says later he found it a familiar scene: the naughty young men overseen by older lamas and living Buddhas ready to scold them, the all-male environment, the arcane rules, discipline, timetables, repressed sexual energy. It's his old boarding school back in England, where he spent five miserable years without a girlfriend.

I grew up in thrall to a romantic, mystical image of Tibetan Buddhism. The longer we spend in Tibetan country, the more banal it becomes. Although Qu and his friends are all pleasant and apparently decent young men, I am increasingly falling out of sympathy with their way of life. Villages are poor. Temples are full of gold leaf. The lamas in Mao'ergai and elsewhere live in a fashion that smacks of medieval Europe. Every lamasery tells the same story. They were closed, sometimes razed during the Cultural Revolution, but now they are growing again. In the towns, lamas beg money from us to help build still more temples. No doubt Qu and friends are a step up the evolutionary ladder from good-for-nothings riding motorcycles, playing mahjong and drinking *bai jiu*, but it still feels like society's going backwards.

If Chinese people know nothing else about the Long March, they know about the Snow Mountains and the Swamps. No one ever asks me, 'Have you crossed the Five Ridges?' or 'Did you cross the Chishui four times?' But ever since we set out, people have pestered me to know if and when we will cross the Snow Mountains and the Swamps (or 'Grasslands', as they are often translated). Andy once joked that if we did nothing but cross the Snow Mountains and the Swamps, most people would accept we had completed the entire Long March.

Andy and I have heard conflicting reports. Some say the marshes are drained and Tibetan herders live all across them; others like Luo Kaifu purse their lips and warn that the bogs are still deadly. We don't debate our next move. We will put ourselves in the hands of a guide to take us from Mao'ergai to a place called Duolitai, where locals say there is food, lodgings and even a telephone. From Duolitai, a road runs north all the way to Banyou, where the Reds left the Swamps. Everyone in Mao'ergai agrees this is the way the Red Army's Right Column went.

We install our headquarters at the administrative centre of the Mao'ergai region, a one-street *xiang* called Shangbazhai that has no telephone and a highly unreliable electricity supply. Women and Long Marchers wash their clothes in a freezing stream at the end of the street. There are a handful of shops selling a remarkable range of goods: food, kitchenware, modern clothes, traditional Tibetan cloaks and dresses, schoolbooks, sweets, toys and Pepsi bottles filled with cheap petrol. The biggest shop doubles as our lodgings and is run by a former teacher named Dan Zhen. His living room is plastered with pictures of Communist Party leaders past and present, plus a selection of important living Buddhas.

'Basically, the land here is good,' says Dan. 'This town is remote, not poor. All we lack are decent communications to make life quite well off.'

Songpan County Town is 100 miles away down a dirt road – an all-day drive, for those that can afford it. It costs 50 yuan one way, which for many locals would be a full week's income or more. The post office promises to deliver letters to Beijing in twenty days. There's a Hui noodle shop opened this year by a mother and daughter from the county town, but we make our first food stop at Shangbazhai's one tiny restaurant, which is run by an efficient, no-nonsense Han woman.

People in Mao'ergai don't put themselves forward. No one speaks to us unless we address them first. In most towns, government leaders can hardly wait to introduce themselves and offer toasts. After we finish lunch, I ask the boss where I can find the mayor.

'He was eating at the table next to you,' she says. 'He just left.'

Mayor Zhang Yong is still on the street outside. I catch him up, introduce our Long March and explain our need for a knowledgeable local to lead us safely across the Swamps. Zhang is an undemonstrative, straightforward man, a Han from Heishui County Town who cannot speak a word of Tibetan. He listens gravely and immediately agrees to help. Since this area has no telephones, this is no small commitment. Zhang gets on his motorcycle and rides off in search of a suitable guide.

He returns after dusk with a forty-six-year-old Tibetan named Qiuga'r. He is the father of four grown-up children, a farmer and herder who owns sixty yak – a fortune of about 150,000 yuan at today's prices. Yes, he says, he knows the way to Duolitai, though he hasn't been over the Swamps for several years. We agree terms (150 yuan per day for Qiuga'r and two horses, in case you're ever

thinking of crossing the Swamps), shake hands and promise to be ready at sunrise.

The Swamps loom even larger than the Snow Mountains
in the horror stories of Long March veterans. In 1935,
they were nothing but empty wasteland. Some soldiers
were sucked down into the bog; many more starved to
death or collapsed from disease. Hundreds, perhaps
thousands of Red soldiers died in the trek north from
Mao'ergai. When the 1st Army Group was nearly
across, its commanders sent a message to the 3rd Army
Group, which was following close behind. They asked
that the 3rd bury any bodies they found and take a
count. Ten days later, they received a report that the 3rd
Army Group had found and buried 400 bodies.[3] Later,
the men and women of Zhang Guotao's Fourth Front
Army would be forced across the Swamps for a second
and third time. We met Fourth Front Army veteran Yang
Jin three weeks before beginning our own crossing. Yang
said that when his squad of fifteen men faced the
possibility of crossing the Swamps for a fourth time,
twelve of his comrades ran away. They weren't afraid of
bombs and bullets, but the Swamps were too much for
them.

'When we crossed . . . the Swamps, there was nothing
to eat,' said Yang. 'Our leader had his horse killed and we
even ate the skin and hooves. We ate bark, grass, branches
and leaves . . . We used our bayonets to chop them up
before we ate them. We certainly ate our leather belts. We
crossed the Swamps three times. During the second and
third crossings, we saw piles of bones of the dead.'

The nights in Shangbazhai are clear and freezing. The
roofs glisten with frost as we prepare to set out; the town
pool table is dusted with ice. Qiuga'r loads our gear on to
A'jia, an old white packhorse. We will travel light for the
first two days to Duolitai – Marchers on foot, our guide

astride a black horse named Guo Shi. Qiuga'r is wrapped
in a thick, green cloak, its sleeves long enough for two
arms. He wears a black-leather pork pie hat and his stern
face cracks easily into a metallic smile of the kind much-
prized by *National Geographic* photographers. His faith
in our walking ability is incomplete. 'Let's go!' he urges, as
we waste more time with preparations and photographs.
'Go!'

Within a mile, the sun strikes the valley and we begin to
shed layers of clothing. The fields are lit gold, dotted with
blue flowers and laced by brooks that tumble into the
Mao'ergai River. By midday, we are walking in T-shirts,
but every so often clouds obscure the sun and we wrap up
again as the temperature falls several degrees. The climate
here is capricious. In the afternoon, the thermometer hits
25°C; by midnight, it will be five below zero.

After nearly a year of being his own pack animal, Andy
feels guilty about overloading A'jia, whose bony hips jut
out.

'Don't you worry about this one. He's just old. He's
eighteen,' says Qiuga'r.

Neither A'jia nor Guo Shi wear shoes. Qiuga'r rides
along dirt paths and through fields as often as possible,
while we spend most of the first day on the gravel and dirt
road going east towards Songpan. Local lore has it that
the Reds turned north after crossing a mountain called
Lazishang, which we reach in mid-afternoon. From here,
we follow a small river that leads through boggy grassland
in a narrow valley, until the country opens out again near
sunset at a place called Guoxigou, where a handful of
herders have built shacks and enclosures for their animals.

'We should camp here,' says Qiuga'r. 'If we camp
where there are no people, the horses are not safe. There
are thieves.'

Qiuga'r makes sure the herders are happy to let us stay.
They are the first Tibetan people we have met with no

knowledge of Chinese at all. They are dark-skinned, with clear eyes and strong teeth. Tibetan teeth are especially noticeable after months of poor dentures in other parts of rural China. It's hard to talk above the noise of the wolfhounds, which are furious at the sight and smell of strangers. The dogs are leashed – for now.

The temperature plummets as the sun dips below the horizon. We eat as quickly as possible. Qiuga'r mixes a bowl of *tsampa*, the Tibetan staple, ground barley kneaded into a heavy and, to the uninitiated, barely digestible ball. He accepts my offer of a drop of Tabasco sauce to spice it up, claims to like it, but refuses to take any more. We stick to our usual diet of boiled rice and vegetables, filled out with dried tofu and spiced with curry powder and Tabasco. To our Tibetan friend, this is obviously the Western equivalent of yak meat and yak butter tea. Our cultures do not mix over dinner.

Memories of the Swamps are vivid in the oral testimonies collected by the '*My Long March*' project. Guizhou-born veteran Xia Jingcai said soldiers lived in fear of someone saying they looked fatter, because there were only poisonous wild vegetables to eat in the Swamps and those who ate them would swell up and die. Xia reckoned he owed his life to a horse. 'I felt so comfortable walking and holding that tail. Even today, the feeling I get from a car just can't be compared.'[4]

Our horses graze close by. Andy has grown attached to the cantankerous old A'jia, who has spent the entire day defying orders and trying to sneak a grass snack.

'He's got a mind of his own, doesn't he?' Andy says to Qiuga'r.

'Yes, he sure does. When he was only two, I was working with him and, because both my hands were busy, I bit the reins between my teeth. Suddenly A'jia bolted, and now . . .' Qiuga'r flashes his shiny metal grin. 'You see?'

As we prepare for sleep, I suddenly realize I am making a very big mistake. I am drinking coffee, which at 11,000 feet above sea level means I am going to need several visits to the toilet during the night – and the tent is now surrounded by growling wolfhounds released to patrol the area. They sniff all around the canvas, barking in anger and frustration at these alien objects. Guo Shi and A'jia whinny and beat their hooves. It's impossible to sleep, unthinkable to pop outside. I clutch my can of Mace and bless the beautiful Ayumi as I relieve myself into an empty bottle of orange-flavour Fifth Season.

We meet herders all through the valley north of Guoxigou. These are not the Swamps we read about, or which Long March veterans described. Deng Xiuying was thirteen when she and her six-year-old brother crossed with the Fourth Front Army, which their father had joined in 1932. 'Some people got stuck in the mire and just couldn't be saved and so we trod on their shoulders,' Deng told an interview for 'My Long March'.[5] She and her brother were later sold into slavery in a Tibetan area and lost contact. They found each other in 1963, after nearly thirty years apart.

Only occasionally do we happen on a swampy area that summons up those nightmare images. In these places, clumps of tufty grass protrude from shallow water – or at least, it looks shallow. The clumps are spongy and sway when you tread on them, but it's possible to walk from one to another and feel relatively secure. But if you miss and tread in the water, the ground slurps like a spoon scooping trifle and pulls at your foot. I test the edge of the swamp for research purposes, then circle around behind A'jia, who has a better feel for solid ground. As the Chinese idiom goes, 'The old horse knows the way.' The yaks also steer clear. Nothing enters the bog.

'Have the Swamps always been this way here?' I ask. 'Would there have been herders in 1935?'

'No,' says Qiuga'r. 'No one lived here then. But they were drained a long time ago and there have been herders ever since.'

Once over the hill from Guoxigou, we see no more people, though the landscape is unchanged. We cross three further valleys, and although no pass is more than 200 yards above the valley floor, the altitude makes progress exhausting. Without anyone to ask for help, Qiuga'r loses confidence in his knowledge of the terrain. Every hill looks the same and the valleys run in all directions. Rather than go direct to Duolitai, he opts for safety and strikes east towards the road that leads from Songpan County Town. I had imagined the Swamps as an endless flat plain, but we continue to go from valley to valley. Two hours after dark, we climb the highest rise yet, taking us to a breathless 12,000 feet. At the top, we find Duolitai at last. We eat egg-fried rice and sleep on the restaurant floor. Qiuga'r will set off home before sunrise. We are all too tired even to say goodbye.

Andy and I wake to the sight of a long-haired Tibetan motorcycle gang enjoying breakfast at the table next to our sleeping bags. The wild bunch model heavy, olive-green cloaks and accessorize with large knives on their belts – a special dispensation from the government in honour of Tibetan culture. Yang Xiao once told us how he visited a Tibetan town further west in Ganzi Prefecture, where the local police chief had recently banned the wearing of knives in response to a murder case. This measure provoked a riot of such proportions the army had to be called in to restore order.

The quality of daylight here is extraordinary. Colours are slightly washed out by its brilliance, emphasizing the chill in the thin air. In the dark the night before, I assumed we were at the pass over a mountain, but now I see we have reached a plateau that stretches north and west to distant horizons. Duolitai is a tent settlement around a mobile phone tower. It is strictly a summer location – everyone will decamp for lower altitudes in about a month. The herders will do the same. Although they have been drained and tamed, still nothing can live on the Swamps in winter.

Even here, this is not the oceanic plain of my imagination. Low hills line the horizon on all sides. Herders' tents are spaced regularly along the valley that follows the Banyou River north. Piles of rubbish mark the spot of recently vacated camps. Ten miles north of Duolitai, I smell a lunch stop. The litter tumbling past our feet also makes it quite easy to spot. A middle-aged Tibetan woman has set up temporary shop in a pair of tents by the roadside. One tent has a neat pile of several hundred empty beer bottles all up one side. Meanwhile, noodle packs and all other plastic and paper wrappings and containers are scattered to the four winds. Andy can't bear it. This is the most remote land he has ever seen; it is wild, beautiful and full of ghosts, and he can't take a step without treading in rubbish. He lectures the woman, 'Why don't you clear this place up? Can't you see how ugly this is?'

She looks blank. 'What do you want to buy?' she asks.

I can't be bothered anymore. I join a group of herders in the second tent. One is evidently a bit of a local clown. The others make jokes at his expense, and he plays along with them and invites more jokes. He is down on his luck and someone suggests I take him to England.

'What could he do there?' I ask.

'Do you have karaoke in England?' asks another of the crowd. 'He likes karaoke.'

'No, no karaoke,' I say. It's not true, of course, but I don't want to admit that England could ever have karaoke.

'Well, do you have prostitutes?'

'Of course. We have male ones, too – you could make some money like that.'

The crowd roars. The Swamps don't seem at all like a place of terror and death. They are full of life, laughter and sunshine. Tibetans whoop as they chase their herds of yak and horses. The long-haired nomads wave and call to us, but we avoid their camps. We sleep as far from their hungry hounds as we can.

Tibetans killed all the Reds they could. They cared nothing for Mao and Marxism; the soldiers were Han intruders and therefore unwelcome. 'In the Swamps of western Sichuan, we watched local bandits skin people alive,' recalled Deng Xiuying. 'There were four Red Army soldiers with four guns, but no bullets. Dozens of bandits bound the Reds to trees and used their knives, peeling their arms and legs . . . We hid in the grass scared out of our wits . . .'[6]

Years later, the Han returned to tame the land – and now the Tibetans have claimed it as their own. Today, they ride free on the unmarked graves of Red soldiers.

Late on the fourth day, the valleys gradually narrow and fill with bushy swamp. Large, aggressive mosquitoes emerge for the first time. We camp for the last time above the Banyou River; across the valley are the first homes we have seen since before Duolitai, simple wooden shacks next to animal enclosures. Six miles further on, at lunchtime on the fifth day in the Swamps, we reach the first permanent settlement, Baozuo Muchang, a jumble of temples, shacks and stockades, plus a couple of recent brick buildings for the school and government. There is a shop, whose owner asks if we can send him a video camera from England.

'I'll pay you back,' he promises.

The Red Army's Right Column left the Swamps at the village of Banyou, a further 6 miles north of Baozuo Muchang. At the time, Banyou was a deserted cluster of Tibetan tents and shacks. Today, it's one of the oddest sights of the Long March.

The village first appears on the horizon as a low expanse of short vertical lines. As we near, we see a shimmering armada of flagpoles and masts. Coloured sails are strung from mast to mast above houses constructed of dark mud, with curved roofs of rich turf, reminiscent of the *Teletubbies*' headquarters. Other buildings, however, are brand-new, red-brick structures. Towering prayer flags wave over neat bungalows.

A young man in a Tibetan cloak approaches. 'We'd better check,' says Andy. He addresses the youth, who doubtless thinks we look a lot odder than his home. 'Excuse me, where is this place?'

'Banyou,' says the young man.

'Did the Red Army once stay here?' I ask.

'The Red Army? Yes. They stayed here.'

We haven't washed for fifteen days. We look like tramps and smell like yaks. I'd like to report that at this triumphant moment in both of our lives, I make a memorable observation. Instead, I say, 'It's all downhill from here.'

Shaanxi

2004 GDP per head: 7,757 yuan ($937)
Population: 36,050,000
Ethnic minority population: 180,000 (0.5%)
Main minorities: Hui, Manchu, Tibetan,
Mongolian, Zhuang.
(China Census 2000, National Bureau of Statistics of China)

Days 347-384: 651 miles
27 September - 3 November 2003
Total: 3,911 miles

Shaanxi
陕西

Wuqi
County Town
吴旗县城

Tiebiancheng Zhen
铁边城镇

Zhangyaoxian Xiang
张崾岘乡

Luoboyuan
萝卜园

Hongde
洪德

Huanxian
County Town
环县县城

Xichuan
西川

何坪 Heping

Hedao 合道

Ningxia
宁夏

Sancha Zhen
三岔镇

孟塬乡 Mengyuan Xiang

牛湾村 Niuwan Cun

Pengyang County Town
彭阳县城

Liupanshan
六盘山

Qingshizui 青石嘴

Maozhuang Cun 毛庄村

Shenzi Xiang 什字乡

Gongyi Xiang 公易乡

Xichuan Cun 西川村

Shuangchengxian
双城岘

Sizichuan Xiang 寺子川乡

Tongwei County Town 通渭县城

Disanpu Xiang 第三铺乡

Bangluo Zhen 榜罗镇

Zhigou 直沟

Yuanyang Zhen 鸳鸯镇

Gansu
甘肃

新寺 Xinsi
草滩 Caotan

Wushan County Town
武山县城

蒲麻 Puma

间井 Jianjing

巴仁桥 Baren Qiao

Bali Xiang 八力乡

出隆村 Chulong Cun

Hadapu Zhen 哈达铺镇

腊子口 Lazikou

Minshan 岷山

Huayuan Xiang 花园乡

Dala Valley
Inspection Station 达拉沟检查站

Ruo'ergai
County Town
若尔盖县城

Dala Xiang 达拉乡

Qiuji Xiang 求吉乡

Baxi Xiang 巴西乡

Banyou 班佑

Sichuan
四川

Ningxia

2004 GDP per head:
7,880 yuan ($952)
Population: 5,615,500
Ethnic minority population:
1,939,000 (34.5%)
Main minority: 98.1% Hui
Other: Manchu, Dongxiang,
Mongolian.
(China Census 2000, National Bureau of Statistics of China)

Chapter 15

Wuqi

Soaked to the skin, Andy and I shiver by the stove in the inspection station at the mouth of the Dala valley. There has been no shelter in the valley since it started raining at dusk. One side of the road dropped straight into the river, the other rubbed against the mountainside. We've rarely looked so pathetic. At least I hope so – surely no one can fail to take pity on us in this state.

'What's the point of walking the Long March?' asks the middle-ranking of three inspection officials, whose job is to make sure illegal loggers can't drive their booty out of the valley. 'The paths aren't there anymore. What a waste of money.' He demands our documents and interrogates us on our movements and motives. Fortunately, he's too busy scoffing to notice that our visas have expired. Jia Ji will deliver new documents in a few days, and in the meantime I trust to the fact that people rarely look too closely once they realize our passports are in a foreign language. I nod and assure the official that, while perhaps there might be different points of view on the Long March, I consider his with the utmost respect and seriousness. Andy is silent.

We have actually been invited in by two local drivers who just stopped by for a smoke, drink and a chat. One is already passably drunk on cheap *bai jiu*. Another inspection official grows excited at the sound of an approaching vehicle. He rushes outside, only to return a few seconds later and shrug, 'It went through before I got there.'

It takes two hours of inane smiling and nodding before our good attitude and miserable condition are finally rewarded with a floor in the room next door. It's covered in rat shit and rats scurry around our sleeping bags. Welcome to Gansu, the second-poorest province in China.

Certain places have dominant colours that label them in my imagination. Guizhou, for example, is a deep, wet English green, while northern Sichuan is sky blue. Diebu County is grey. It's still Tibetan country, but the people are settled farmers, not roaming herders. They do not ride horses; they walk behind donkeys. Their homes are shacks made of wood and mud. The women and children sell apples by the roadside, but traffic remains rare. We walk east along the Bailong Jiang, the White Dragon River. Stony, semi-naked mountains tower on both sides, their peaks dusted with snow.

A couple work by the roadside. The man is holding a spade, but his real job seems to be supervising his wife, who is digging a deep hole in the ground. I stop to enquire about our destination.

'How far is it to Huayuan?'

'More than 20 *li*," says the man. (It turns out to be exactly 10.)

The woman pays no attention to us. She carries on digging. I ask the man, 'Why aren't you doing any work?'

He is affronted. 'I am working,' he says.

This is hardly the first superfluous man we've met. Almost every day, we pass groups of men and women at 'work', the women hard at it while the men enjoy a seemingly endless cigarette break. In towns, men are notable for loafing around, smoking, drinking and playing cards. Women take care of cooking, cleaning, child care and what little business there is. It makes no difference where we are, whether the people are Han or any other ethnic group. Men are the consumption side of the rural economy.

Andy and I continue on our way; Spade Man returns to supervising his wife.

Crossing the border from Sichuan into Gansu is easy, a simple stroll downstream into Diebu. The border between the Tibetan lands and the Han/Hui country to the north, however, is the great Minshan range that divides Diebu and Min counties. The only way over these mountains passes through the narrow gorge at Lazikou, where the last famous battle of the Long March began on the evening of 16 September 1935.

Mao was marching with a drastically reduced force. The suspicion and ill feeling between him and Zhang Guotao had burst into the open after the Right Column cleared the Swamps. Zhang had been dawdling for a fortnight, arguing for a move due north rather than east towards reunion with the Right Column. On 3 September, he telegraphed that the Left Column was unable to cross the flood waters of the Gequ River. He ordered the Right Column to halt and proposed the whole Red Army turn back south. Rightly or wrongly, Mao and his supporters interpreted this as a move to impose Zhang Guotao's will on Party and army. They didn't believe Zhang was telling the truth about the flooded river and insisted on continuing north. Zhang demanded that the Right Column obey his orders.

Soldiers loyal to Mao were outnumbered three- or four-to-one by the Fourth Front Army troops in the Right Column. Faced with a possible threat of superior force, Mao turned to a tried-and-trusted tactic. He ran away. His 1st Army Group was already across the Gansu border at Ejie. Mao, the Party leadership and Peng Dehuai's 3rd Army Group were in and around Baxi, 10 miles east of Right Column headquarters at Banyou. In the early hours of 10 September, the 3rd Army Group pulled out and started towards Ejie, two days' march away.

Later that morning when Zhang Guotao's right-hand

man, Right Column Political Commissar Chen Changhao, discovered this manoeuvre, he is said to have asked his military commander Xu Xiangqian, 'Should we fight them?'

Xu's famous reply translates roughly as, 'Can there be any reason for Reds to fight Reds?'

As Andy and I learned at Zhuokeji, Chen could have answered, 'Well, yes, actually . . .' As it was, he accepted Xu's point that comrades should not fight one another. Although Chen had men stationed along the escape route, Mao was allowed to flee with the remnants of his 1st and 3rd Army Groups (the 5th and 9th were with Zhang Guotao in the Left Column).

This episode worked out well for Xu Xiangqian, who enjoyed a long and successful career after the Revolution. He was named one of the Ten Marshals of the People's Republic of China in 1955 and later served as Minister for National Defence. Unlike old comrades such as Zhang Wentian and Peng Dehuai, Xu was allegedly protected by Mao during the Cultural Revolution. Whether or not that's true, he certainly emerged from that period unscathed.

Chen Changhao was not so fortunate. He was attacked during the Cultural Revolution as a 'running dog of Zhang Guotao' and is said to have killed himself with a drug overdose in 1967.

As Mao and his rump force approached Lazikou, there were probably no more than 10,000 troops left of the 86,000 which started the Long March from Yudu.

'Lazikou was simply superb as a strategic stronghold,' wrote Hu Pingyun, who was part of the company that was given the task of forcing the pass. The gorge is less than 20 yards wide at the point where the battle began, and its thickly wooded sides rise almost straight up to jagged heights at least 100 yards above the stream. Forces belonging to the Gansu warlord Lu Dazhang held the ground above the path.

According to Hu Pingyun, the battle began as soon as it was dark, around 6 p.m. The Reds charged several times, but were driven back by gunfire and grenades. The frontal assault was not called off until 2 a.m.[1]

The assault squad pulled back to rest while another group of soldiers was equipped and instructed to climb the gorge and find a way to attack from the enemy's rear. The frontal assault Party was reorganized and sent back into the fray for a fifth time. The tide turned towards dawn, when the sound of a Red Army bugle rose from behind the enemy positions. The company of climbers had evaded the defences and were now attacking from the rear. The Reds brought up reinforcements to support the frontal assault and the enemy's resistance broke. Lazikou's defenders fled to a second line of defence, which they also surrendered before dawn.[2] The path over the mountain of Minshan and into north-west China was open.

The gorge at Lazikou carries on for several miles with dozens of alternative emplacements available to defenders. Once again, it's incredible to think that local forces surrendered this seemingly invincible position. Once again, the only explanation I can think of is that they just didn't care enough. Unlike the Reds, the locals had nothing they believed was really worth fighting for.

Andy and I complete our climb over Minshan on 4 October, seventeen days later than the Red Army vanguard. The seasons are changing. Crossing the 10,000-foot pass, we trudge through snow for the first time since January. After crossing four Snow Mountains without a hint of the white stuff, I finally get a taste of what the Reds had to face. Once you lose your footing, it's a long slide back to where you started – especially if you're carrying heavy gear. The only signs of life on the icy north slope are poor shacks and shabby white Tibetan prayer flags. But towards evening, the air warms as the road levels out and the valley broadens. Suddenly it is full of people harvesting potatoes and drying fodder for the winter. They are Han. Further along the valley we meet white-capped Hui

Muslims as well. After seven weeks, the Tibetan lands are behind us. The snowy peaks of the Minshan range are also at our backs – the hills we look at now are low, rounded and terraced. The soil is dry, the landscape arid and the colour overwhelmingly brown.

Andy and I have been in poorer places: parts of Tongdao County in Hunan, all of Wangmo County in Guizhou Province, the borderlands between Guizhou and Sichuan provinces. But we have never walked through such an interminable stretch of poverty as this. The main mode of transport is an ox cart, its wooden wheels not even bound with iron. Houses are made of mud. The air hangs heavy with the smell of cheap coal. Electricity is an unreliable luxury. Without the abundant streams that run through Sichuan, there are no local hydroelectric stations. With no water and no power, there is scant opportunity for industry. After sunset, we arrive in dark towns. In Puma, there has been no electricity for ten days and there's no way of knowing when it will return.

Despite these drawbacks, at first we both feel more at ease in Gansu than we have done for many months past. The people are especially reticent, which is relaxing in itself, and the harsh climate has encouraged them to think more about home comforts. The most important of these is the *kang*, a king-size brick bed that is either warmed by electric blankets or – in the traditional manner – heated right through by a slow-burning coal fire. Although it has no mattress, the *kang* gives me the best nights I've known for almost twelve months. As we march, I'm delighted to see no more rice paddies. Wheat is the staple crop here, noodles the staple dish, and we can buy bread more digestible to our own northern stomachs. Even Andy has a healthy appetite.

But we have grown too complacent, too soon. The trials of the Long March do not end at Lazikou.

In the town of Hadapu, the Reds' first stop after

crossing Minshan, they found copies of the *Shaanxi Daily* newspaper which told them there was a soviet base led by a Communist named Liu Zhidan in northern Shaanxi Province. The uncertainty was finally over. The Long March was coming to an end. We didn't expect that, instead of taking it easy and enjoying their success, the Reds would sprint off faster and further than ever before. From the border of Gansu to the end, we will walk 620 miles in 35 days, with one day's rest.

The lie of the land here is the most difficult we have ever tried to read. All our experience suddenly counts for nothing. In the empty spaces of Sichuan, it was often relatively easy to find the path, because there was one and one only. A compass is pointless in Gansu. There are just too many circular paths to choose and making sense of local advice is extremely difficult. The dialects are the thickest since Hunan.

At times, I look down and realize we are walking over the ceilings of caverns. There is no knowing how thick or stable these footpaths are, nor how deep are the caverns. The footpaths are precipitous and frightening because they are pocked with holes. The path could collapse at any moment. We follow one that has a crack running all the way down its centre, obviously ready to fall away from the hillside. Halfway down, I see the opposite hill has already collapsed, covering the valley floor – and our path – in mud.

I test the mud with my hiking stick. It seems to have set. I take one step, then another, and then on the third step my right foot breaks through the surface. As I try to pull out my foot, the second foot breaks through as well. I have no idea how deep this stuff is and I'm already sinking fast. Andy stretches out from a point just off the mud and pulls off my rucksack. He hands me his walking stick. I jam both sticks into the mud. They sink up to their handles. I'm not too clear about this memory, but for the first time on the Long March, I think I'm about to start panicking.

I get a grip and stop trying to pull my right leg straight out, because it feels like my groin could rupture at any moment. Instead, I discover there is just enough give in the mud to allow a little sideways jiggle, and somehow that jiggle allows me to draw my foot upwards slightly. I jiggle more enthusiastically and my right foot emerges from the ooze. I plant it one step back and sink into the mud again, but now I know what to do. A minute's more jiggling and Andy can help pull me free. Terrified and exhausted, but free.

As we retrace the cracked path back up the way we came, my foot plunges through the surface of the dry clay. It's only a two-foot drop and I'm physically unharmed, but I walk the footpaths from now on in constant fear.

Andy, stronger by the day, reaches for the traditional morale booster.

'Let's have a cup of coffee.'

I pick up the boiled-water thermos. It's empty. I call to the young woman who runs the restaurant, 'Do you have any boiled water?'

The boss is sat chatting with an older lady, perhaps a relative. She points to the empty bottle and stops listening in the second it takes me to tell her there's nothing in it. I pretend to check and then walk across with the empty thermos to ask again.

'There's no boiled water,' says the relative.

I repeat her words in what I hope she will perceive as an incredulous tone.

'There's none,' she assures me.

'Well, could you boil some, then, please?' I ask.

They ignore me. I ask again and the relative finally tells the boss lady she ought to boil some water. The morale booster has backfired. I slump back to the table and my blackening mood spews forth, sweeping Andy up with it.

'Why do I have to spell things out 10 fucking times?' I rant. 'I'm the only customer stood in the middle of a fucking restaurant holding an empty fucking thermos, and

I have to practically fucking beg the boss to get off her arse and put the fucking kettle on.'

'Yeah,' says Andy. 'For fuck's sake, how long have we been dealing with this shit? Lazy fuckwits just say *"mei shi"* and hope you'll fuck off.'

At this enlightening moment, one of the children squeezed into the room coughs on Andy. Children seem to cough on Uncle Andy a lot.

'Fucking hell! Why can't they put their hands over their mouths when they cough?'

'They only put their hands over their mouths when they smile or laugh.'

'When they're not spitting!'

The same thought strikes both of us at about the same time.

'Do you hear what we sound like?' I ask.

'Racists?' suggests Andy.

How did that happen? We were both brought up to believe that travel broadens the mind. The Long March was supposed to help us understand Chinese people and show them something good about us. Instead, it's turned me into a ranting bigot.

The boss puts a thermos on the table. 'Here's your boiled water,' she says, smiling pleasantly.

While I become ever more dull and disagreeable, the country grows increasingly interesting as we cross a low range into the Ningxia Hui Autonomous Region, where men wear white skull caps and large brown sunglasses, fields are sown with potatoes and three-wheeled tractor/trailers account for 95 per cent of traffic, carrying the men and potatoes to market. Calls to prayer drift across the valleys. The Muslim communities of Ningxia have a vibrancy that recalls – indeed surpasses – the Christian congregations we met in northern Yunnan. New or restored mosques are a feature of almost every village.

To our relief, no one mentions Iraq. In fact, hardly

anyone says anything at all. We spend half an hour in the local government compound in Gongyi Xiang, studying the route ahead from a surprisingly detailed memorial stone. White-capped government workers go about their business without talking to us. Only if we greet them first do they nod gravely and return the salutation.

The finest sight is the green onion dome of the Xinglong Zhen mosque, which we can see from the hillside 2 miles away. Directly opposite the mosque stands a concrete obelisk commemorating the Long March. The memorial is only seven years old, but it's already dilapidated. Locals pay it scant respect – the concrete apron at the back of the obelisk is covered in human turds.

Thanks to his Long March health problems, Andy is now obsessed with bowel movements. We have read the Red Army soldiers were similarly concerned with Chairman Mao's toilet troubles. The Chairman had spastic bowel syndrome and the longer he went without going, so to speak, the worse his mood became. A successful squat allegedly brought cheers from the troops: 'The Chairman's bowels have moved!'[3] Andy has adopted this phrase to celebrate his own performances of duty. (Curiously, the bowel movements of the Great Helmsman were the only thing censored from the Hong Kong edition of this book.)

Some days before we reached Xinglong, Andy felt a sudden urge. Noticing a low, mud wall in the field to our right, he dashed off to do his duty in private. To the left of the road, the ground fell gently away in broad terraces that led down to the village of Siluoping. I passed a few minutes taking photos of the valley and the ruined fortress that sits on the hill opposite, above Siluoping. We have seen similar structures frequently since leaving the Tibetan country. From high ground, I have counted as many as five at one time, dotted around the hilltops. In former times, villagers retreated to these thick-walled enclosures for protection against roving bandits.

I hailed a peasant who was harvesting potatoes just below the road. Guo Yuanyuan confirmed we were on the Red Army trail, but he had something more important to tell about local history. When Andy returned, I greeted him with the gleeful news.

'You know you just shit on the Great Wall?'

I didn't expect to meet the Great Wall of China on our journey. The main section runs north of the Long March route, but here was a southern spur of Mao's favourite emperor Qin Shihuang's original rammed-earth structure. Once Guo had opened my eyes, I could see the line of the wall stretching from horizon to horizon, though it was no more than 4 feet high at any point. It looked so fragile it was remarkable to think it had endured for 2,200 years. But for Andy's bowels and Guo Yuanyuan's potato harvest, it wouldn't be in this book. Who would imagine a Great Wall that is only a pile of clay shorter than a man?

The last great mountain range of the Long March rises out of the plain east of Zhangyi Xiang, where we lunch and take advice on where to cross. The main pass over Liupanshan, where Mao crossed and where the memorial stands, is 20 miles to the south at Dashuigou, or Liupangou, as some locals call it. But some say there is a pass taken by the Reds only about 3 miles away, directly above the Han village of Maozhuang.

The villagers describe the path over the mountain and tell us, yes, Red soldiers did cross that way. About an hour after setting out, however, I insist we turn around. I have already fallen once on the icy hillside and I don't believe Andy's theory that it will be 'OK if we just get over this bit'. Our own Long March rules stipulate the coward must be respected at all times, and so we work our way back down and head south along the valley, looking for an alternative pass.

We find it at Gangou above the village of Weijiashan, where we stop for an instant-noodle lunch and are be-friended by Zhang Tiancheng.

'There is a pass,' says Zhang, 'Some small units of the Red Army went over here, but it's very hard and the ground is very slippery and dangerous.'

After our first attempt, we're not inclined to dismiss this warning. But the main pass is still 12 miles south and would mean a full day's extra march. We're determined to try. Zhang walks out of the village with us.

'I'm afraid you won't find the way,' he says. 'I will come with you.'

'It's too far,' says Andy, but he doesn't argue too hard. Back in the city, it might seem unreasonable to take a sixty-three-year-old man up one of the highest peaks of the Long March trail (we measure the pass over Gangou at 8,960 feet), but peasants have different standards. Zhang could probably carry our backpacks and cameras too. Without him, we might well be forced back down to spend the night in Weijiashan.

The path disappears time after time as we work our way exclusively along the left side of the gully – the opposite side faces north and is covered in ice. It is surely only a matter of days before this pass, too, will be completely closed.

With Zhang's help we are at the top in little over an hour and a half. Our last guide of the Long March points out the line of the footpath into the plain. From here, it really is all downhill. There will be no more snow and ice.

'I respect your spirit very much,' says Zhang. 'Give me a call when you find a place to stay tonight. Let me know you're OK.'

What can we say? Compared to this man, who risks his own safety to protect ours for no reasons other than simple kindness and fellow feeling, who are we to talk about spirit?

Re-entering Gansu north of Pengyang, navigation becomes more difficult than ever. We have entered the loess country of the Yellow River basin. Loess is a fine, wind-blown dust that looks dry and dead, but is actually very fertile if you have any water to irrigate it. When the Red Army reached this area, Otto Braun noted that, 'cave dwellings more frequently replaced houses.'[4] In minor villages, at least, little has changed in that respect. Although the hills are fairly gentle, narrow gorges slice through the loess. The gorge walls are mostly too steep and unstable even for peasants to trust, so footpaths are little shorter than the roads, winding in great half-loops that have us walking in the wrong direction for two thirds of the day. We used to dread the words '*fan shan*', 'cross the mountain', when asking directions. Now, our hearts sink at the sound of '*guo gou*', 'go through the gorge'.

The landscape has also confused the cartographers. Our maps have never been more useless. We lunch in Yaoji Xiang, which on the map is about 2 miles from Liuyuan Xiang. Liuyuan is actually 9 miles distant. We reach it at sunset and then get hopelessly lost searching for our final destination, Mengyuan Xiang, in the dark. We're in Niu-wan Cun, from where dirt roads run in all directions. We seek clarification from a group of peasants heading home late from the fields. They point back across the gorge to the road we left twenty minutes before.

'But that's the wrong direction,' I object.

'No, go back over the gorge and take the big road,' insist the peasants. I don't believe them. I find a second opinion.

'Go back over the gorge and take the big road.'

It doesn't make any sense. We ask a third group, sat around an open fire enjoying the clear night sky. They point us back over the gorge to the 'big road'.

It's impossible to go against three separate, identical opinions – especially in the dark. We recross the gorge, climb to what might, with a bit of imagination, be termed a 'big road', and head for a dim light-bulb outside a cave home. Two teenagers, a boy and a girl, are sweeping the courtyard.

'I'm scared to ask,' I say to Andy. 'You do it.'

'No, you do it.'

'Excuse me,' I say, 'Could you tell us which way we should go for Mengyuan?' The boy points back the way we came.

'Cross the gorge that way,' he says.

'You mean via Niuwan?'

'Yes.'

The children must think English people are very highly strung. Their simple directions are met with a pyrotechnic display of British swearing. By the time we calm down, their father, Wang Zhixian, has emerged. I ask him if he'd mind us pitching our tent in his courtyard.

'Never mind a tent,' he says. 'Come inside and have a cup of tea.'

Wang gives us a cave all to ourselves. His son brushes dust off the *kang* and prepares blankets, while his wife brings us a thermos of boiled water. Then they leave us alone to cook our own dinner and rest.

I have never stayed in a cave before. It's not at all the way I imagined. For a start, it's warm and comfortable, far better than a wooden south-China peasant house. Our cave and the main cave where Wang and family live are about 4 yards high and wide, and 15 yards deep. Wang says each took him about a fortnight to dig. Water comes from a well a few steps down the hill, but there is electricity and even a satellite TV dish.

More than nine months and 2,500 miles ago, Andy asked First Front Army veteran Wang Daojin what he thought was meant by 'Long March spirit'. Wang said, 'Hard struggle, selfless dedication, steadfast faith.' I think I find these qualities best embodied in a Communist Party member who lost his job as a cadre in Liuyuan Xiang because he flouted planned birth rules. Wang now has four children and he has lived in this cave and farmed 3.3 acres of land since the late 1980s. The two children we meet are both in lower middle school; their elder siblings attend upper middle school in the county town. Wang hopes they will all go to university. He is the eldest of eleven brothers and sisters. One of those brothers and two sisters have graduated from university – all financially assisted by their big brother's extraordinary dedication to his family.

'How did it feel to lose your job and have to come back to Niuwan to be a peasant?' I ask.

'It was hard, of course,' says Wang. That's all he has to say on the matter. And he says it with a smile.

The Long March of the Red First Front Army ended on 19 October 1935, when the tattered survivors of the 86,000 who had left Yudu one year earlier reached the Shaanxi Soviet base area at Wuqi Zhen. There is no precise official estimate of the number who arrived at the end of the Long March. 'A few thousand' was the best the authorities could say at the museum in Wuqi. Zhang Guotao wrote that 'comrades' in Shaanxi told him the figure was fewer than 4,000.[5]

The Shaanxi Soviet was the creation of Liu Zhidan, a member of the Communist Party since 1925 and a former student at Chiang Kai-shek's Whampoa Military Academy. He was from Bao'an in northern Shaanxi, an area that suffered a terrible famine in 1929. Liu formed his first armed revolutionary detachment in 1931; by 1934, he had established a base around Bao'an comprising all or parts of twenty counties.[6] In September 1935, his forces were reinforced by the Red 25th Army Group. This was originally part of Zhang Guotao's Fourth Front Army, but had been left behind and isolated when the Fourth retreated from its base in summer 1932. The 25th Army's march to the north-west was an epic in itself, but remains little known and under-researched. What is known, however, is that their arrival had dire consequences for Liu Zhidan and his men. Rumours took hold that Liu was a Guomindang agent and his army was riddled with traitors. Hundreds were arrested in the purge that followed. Liu himself was tortured, while many others were executed. The First Front Army arrived just in time to put a stop to the purge and save Liu Zhidan's life.

Liu didn't survive much longer. He was killed in action in April 1936. According to a conspiracy theory recently revived by Jung Chang and Jon Halliday, he was actually murdered on Mao's orders because Mao feared Liu might challenge him for control of the Shaanxi Soviet.[7]

Four days after arrival, Mao Zedong told a cadres meeting in Wuqi, 'The Central Red Army has completed a one-year long-distance march.' He calculated they had marched on at least 267 days: 'Rest days did not exceed 65; battles did not exceed 35 days.' Mao declared they had marched across 11 provinces. They had walked 25,000 *li*.[8]

The Long March was over. The legend had already begun.

But the war and uncertainty went on. Twelve months after Mao and his men, the troops of the Second and Fourth Front Armies also reached the Shaanxi base, completing the gathering of all the main Communist forces in north-west China. In the meantime, Chiang Kai-shek was preparing what he called the 'last five minutes' of his war to wipe out the Reds.[9] This time, the Communists were saved by what became known as the 'Xi'an Incident'.

On 12 December 1936, Chiang Kai-shek was detained in Xi'an, the capital of Shaanxi. His captor was Zhang Xue-liang, the former warlord of Manchuria whose troops were now stationed in Shaanxi. Zhang was a Communist sympathizer who had been trying to convince Chiang to fight the Japanese instead of the Reds. Fearing Chiang would shortly remove him from command because of his lacklustre anti-Communist efforts, he now tried to force his compliance. If that failed, Zhang knew he had the backing of the Communists and assumed that meant the Soviet Union would also support him if he overthrew Chiang. The Chinese Communists were thrilled. Zhu De immediately declared Chiang should be killed. They all reckoned without Stalin.

By this stage, Stalin no longer cared about the Chinese civil war. His primary concern was that Japan should devote its resources to fighting in China, rather than attacking the Soviet Union, and he believed only Chiang Kai-shek could organize effective Chinese resistance against the Japanese army. The Soviet reaction to the 'Xi'an Incident' was immediately negative. Zhang Xueliang discovered he had been deluded to believe that Stalin would back him over Chiang. When the Chinese Communists received instructions from Moscow, they were incredulous. Moscow declared the 'Xi'an Incident' was a Japanese plot to obstruct Chinese unity and sabotage the anti-Japanese movement. The Chinese Communists were ordered to resolve the incident peacefully.

The Communist Party of China was subject to the rigid discipline of the international Communist movement. They also knew they had to keep the Soviet Union happy if they hoped to receive financial and military aid in their fight against Chiang Kai-shek. Without Communist support, Zhang Xueliang was a broken reed. Chiang Kai-shek was released on condition he declare a 'united front' with the Communists. Mao was not happy about the united front. He wanted the Soviet Union to back him and to hell with Chiang Kai-shek. Chiang wasn't pleased, either, but the Japanese threat persuaded him to put off his reckoning with the Reds.

The 'Anti-Japanese War' began in earnest in summer 1937. The Communists largely confined themselves to guerrilla operations. The only significant exception was the so-called 'Hundred Regiments Battle' of August 1940, launched on the initiative of Peng Dehuai. Mao later criticized Peng severely for exposing the strength of the Reds to the Japanese. A subsequent Japanese campaign against the Communist base area was known as the 'Three Alls' – kill all, burn all, destroy all. By the time that was over, the population of the Shaanxi base was down from 40 million to an estimated 25 million.[10] In 1941, the 'united front' became a virtual dead letter after the Guomindang attacked the Communist New Fourth Army. This battle appears to have been the result of an egregious manoeuvre by Mao, who deliberately set the New Fourth Army up. This not only broke the united front, but had the bonus of getting rid of the New Fourth Army's political commissar, Xiang Ying, who was murdered and robbed soon after he escaped the battlefield. Xiang had opposed Mao on several occasions over the previous ten years. Otto Braun said Xiang had warned him before the Long March against 'underestimating the seriousness of Mao's partisan struggle against the Party leadership'.[11]

With the united front finished and the Japanese too dangerous to provoke, the Communists pulled in their horns and concentrated on building up their forces for an eventual resumption of civil war. Mao focused on consolidating his personal power. He was now unchallenged as leader of the Communist Party. Having seen off Zhang Guotao on the Long March, he put down his last serious rival in 1938. Wang Ming had been Party leader in the early 1930s, before he handed over to Bo Gu and went to Moscow as Chinese representative to the Comintern. He was the head of the Moscow-trained faction of Party leaders and had important supporters in the Kremlin. When he returned to China in November 1937, he believed he could take over the Party once again. What he failed to appreciate was that the most important man in Moscow had made up his mind about Mao. Stalin curtailed Wang's challenge in September 1938, when he issued instructions via the Comintern that, 'in order to resolve the problem of unifying the 'Party leadership, the CCP [Chinese Communist Party] leadership should have Mao Zedong as its centre.'[12]

That wasn't enough for Mao. In autumn 1941, he launched what became known as the 'Yan'an Rectification Campaign'. This quickly developed into an attack on all the Chinese Communists who had studied in the Soviet Union, headed by Wang Ming, together with just about anybody else who had ever disagreed with Mao. While others bowed to the assault and abased themselves with self-criticism, Wang Ming stood up to Mao and tried to fight back, but he almost immediately fell ill – poisoned, he claimed (with some justification, as he suffered another mystery illness the following year). Although his health eventually recovered, his political career did not. Wang ended his days in exile in the Soviet Union. By the time the Rectification Campaign was over, wrote Philip Short in his 1999 biography of the Chairman, 'Mao would no longer be the first among equals. He would be the one man who decided all – a demiurge, set on a pedestal, towering above his nominal colleagues, beyond institutional control.'[13]

After Japan surrendered in 1945, the Communists and Guomindang almost immediately resumed full-scale civil war. But while ten years earlier Mao had been in charge of just a few thousand raggedy men, now he commanded an army several hundred thousand strong. By the time Chiang Kai-shek was chased across the water to Taiwan in 1949, the Red Army, renamed the People's Liberation Army, numbered in the millions. On 1 October 1949, Mao mounted the Tian'anmen Square rostrum and declared the war was won. 'The Chinese people have stood up,' he said. The Communist Party now ruled the People's Republic of China.

As we approach Wuqi, our struggle is almost over, our dream about to be fulfilled. Andy stops to ask a group of Hui peasants how far it is to the border of Shaanxi Province. 'You'll be there in the time it takes to smoke a cigarette,' says one man.

It would be nice if our Long March could end like that – an easy stroll and a relaxing smoke. It's a glorious evening, the yellow earth now glowing orange in the setting sun. The fields are empty and fallow. There are about 60 miles to go, just three more days of these lonely roads before we are pitched back into 'normal' life. These are moments that deserve to be savoured.

Instead the real end of our Long March is a dash to total chaos. We take a break about half a mile from the bridge over the Luohe River, from where the main road runs through the centre of Wuqi County Town. Jia Ji has told us this bridge is our official finish line. The town is several shades of dusty brown, darkening as the sun sets. It's 5.30 p.m. and we're gathering quite a crowd – adults on their way home from work, children heading home after school. At the back of this crowd, a greasy-haired character from Wuqi Television is bobbing up and down and yelling at us. He has lost his cool.

'You must move on,' he squeals. 'The leaders are waiting!'

Andy feigns deafness. I give him a smile and a wave. A few people in the crowd wave back. We're all having a lot of fun. The crowd is growing so large it's starting to block the street. We move up a flight of stone steps to make room for more people and let them see us properly.

The TV man cries, 'There are too many people on the bridge! The traffic is blocked! The leaders! The leaders!'

We're waiting for Jia Ji to tell us she's ready. Every step of the way, she has encouraged us, protected us, organized us and fed the cats. We owe this moment to her, more than anyone. We didn't walk 4,000 miles to spoil Jia Ji's party by being early.

'The leaders!'

'We'll be with you in a minute,' I call.

'*Mei shi*!' shouts Andy.

Some people will say anything to force you to co-operate. Of course the real reason the TV man is pushing us is that he is desperate to kow-tow to his leaders. He keeps shouting, 'Too many people!' 'Traffic blocked!'

Rubbish. We like to think we're popular, but frankly, we know we're not *that* popular. The mobile rings. Jia Ji says, 'Where are you? Come on, everyone's waiting.' It only takes a couple of minutes to come within sight of the bridge.

'Oh, my God,' says Andy.

There must be 500 people on and around the bridge. Most of them appear to be children. We have often joked with Jia Ji that we would like to arrive to a heroes' welcome with cheering crowds. Jia Ji has taken us literally. She has called up the local school to announce our arrival and suggest the kids come along to watch. The traffic is completely blocked.

Three policemen hold open a narrow corridor. A red welcome banner is stretched across the end, but I can't see what it says because it has been turned around to face the photographers and television cameras. Jia Ji and the Mayor of Wuqi, Kong Qiuli, are on the other side of the banner, holding bouquets and the banner our friends gave us when we set out from Yudu, 384 days and 4,000 miles ago. The crowd starts to applaud. Children are reaching out to shake our hands. Jia Ji and the Mayor are waiting. We glance at each other. Neither of us has shaved for a fortnight and we haven't washed for five days.

I've seen real celebrities deal with this situation on TV. The Queen never seems to have any trouble, but I guess she gets more than three Bobbies. The moment we start to shake hands, the crowd surges forward and engulfs us. Children squeal with excitement. Even the policemen are smiling, although they are being tossed around by the mob along with us. Up ahead, Andy's girlfriend Jiao Pei is swallowed up by the crowd as she walks backwards trying to video the scene. The cameraman from Reuters stops filming and starts trying to save his tripod from collapsing in the stampede. The press of the crowd carries us up to the Mayor, who just has time to lay our friends' banner around my neck before she, too, is lost in the crush. Andy clings to his bouquet and I hug Jia Ji as the Long March is swept across the finish line by a tide of laughing schoolchildren. We will never again be happier, hairier or smellier.

Epilogue

How Long is a Long March?

I remember walking a dirt road in the dark, being interviewed by two journalists: Richard Spencer for the *Daily Telegraph* and Oliver August for the *Times*. They have spent half a day in a taxi looking for us. We crossed the border into Shaanxi at sunset, and now there's less than three days to Wuqi.

I can't recall who asks, 'What have you learned during this year on the road?' I evade the question with an amusing statistic. 'I've learned the "25,000-*li* Long March" isn't actually 25,000 *li*,' I say. 'It's probably between 12,000 and 13,000 *li*. And I always thought Chairman Mao was only 30 per cent wrong.'

Everybody laughs. 'So it's not such a long march, then,' says Spencer. August makes the joke headline. 'Yeah, "Long March not so long".'

I knew from the start the Long March wasn't 25,000 *li*. The *li* has changed over the centuries, but in the 1930s it was understood to equal half a kilometre (550 yards). By Mao's own maths, then, every single one of the 267 days the Reds were on the march they walked an average of 46.5 kilometres, or 29 miles. I knew that was impossible. I didn't believe even the vanguard units could maintain such a pace, let alone the convalescent units, baggage carriers, cooks and all. Besides, one look at the map gave the lie to Mao's calculation. Where the Reds' daily departure and destination points could be identified, the distance between them was usually around 19 to 32 kilometres (12 to 20 miles).

When Andy and I set out, I guessed we faced around 18,000 *li*, or 9,000 kilometres (5,625 miles). As we walk into Shaanxi, we've just completed 12,000 *li* (3,750 miles). I'm glad I was wrong. Even though it was only 12,000 *li*, half what Mao promised, it has taken us fifteen days longer than it took the Red Army to reach this point. I reach the end of the Long March trail with my respect for the Reds' accomplishment not just intact, but increased. The fact Mao got his sums wrong doesn't diminish the Long March.

I'm sure the Chairman had better things to do than count how far he walked every day. Accuracy of measurement didn't matter; the Long March was an epic of courage, sacrifice and endurance no matter if it was 10,000 or 100,000 *li*. Mao chose 25,000 as the symbol of the army's struggle and triumph. But because Mao said it, the figure passed into legend, and most people came to accept that legend as fact.

And because we're so accustomed to this knowledge, which we've discussed with journalists many times before, Andy and I totally overlook the fact that Spencer and August aren't just joking.

The 'Long March not so long' gag goes global. It makes the Yahoo Top 5 news stories. The next time I log on to the internet, I find nearly 100 variations on this theme from newspapers all over the world. A *Hindustan Times* editorial combines it with an ironic attack on George W. Bush and the missing weapons of mass destruction in Iraq. 'What next?' asks the *Times*, 'The not-so-great Wall of China?'

The Chinese press takes a different approach. A friend at *China Daily* tells me the features editor rejected our story on the grounds that it's 'too controversial' to say the

Long March isn't 25,000 *li*. The Chinese government's Xinhua news agency reports our accomplishment, but doesn't mention the distance. Only two reports include the details: one is a full-page feature in the Shanghai *Xinmin Evening News*; the other is the one we write ourselves for *Beijing Youth Daily*, which glosses the measurement with a footnote explaining how 'experts confirm' the Long March is really 25,000 *li*.

Bureaucrats bend over backwards to insist we must be wrong. Officials at the Wuqi memorial make the hilarious suggestion that we didn't have to walk so far because we used the new main roads. Another 'expert' explains that the 25,000 *li* refers to the marches of the First, Second and Fourth Front armies all added together. The problem with this ingenious effort is that Chairman Mao referred to the 25,000 *li* in October 1935, a year before the Second and Fourth armies completed their journeys to the north-west.

The fact that the 25,000 *li* belong to propaganda rather than historical fact is not completely suppressed in China. Most of the above discussion appeared in the Chinese edition of this book, although the publisher's first instinct was to cut it out. At the press launch, the publisher specifically told journalists not to dwell on the issue of the Long March's length. But while our conclusions are in the public domain, they are not discussed. Any mention of the length is cut out of press or television interviews.

In summer 2005, an editor at *Chinese National Geography* [sic] was preparing a special feature on the Long March. She asked me to write an article explaining why I believed it was not 25,000 *li*, and approached Luo Kaifu to write a rebuttal. Since retracing the Long March in 1984–5, Luo has risen to a position of some influence. He initially agreed to co-operate. I wrote my article and another historian from the Military Academy of Sciences also wrote a rebuttal. The day before the magazine went to press, Luo Kaifu read my piece. He immediately withdrew his co-operation, the whole feature was canned and the editor in question was given a severe rebuke. I heard she was 'unclear' about the reasons. 'As you know,' another editor told me, 'the Chinese media is a minefield.'

I found the sensitivity about Maomei more predictable. Journalists were simply nervous about anything that touched on Mao's private life. The main reason the Chinese press avoided this story was because they lacked precedent. While preparing the Chinese edition, the editor told me she had been approached by a journalist from one of China's most popular magazines, wanting to know if Xiong Huazhi's story would be included. If it appeared in our book, then he would feel safe to pursue it himself. Once again, the publisher's instinct was to cut it out. Ultimately, a severely curtailed version appeared and journalists again were advised not to write about it.

I still think about Maomei more than anything else. I feel now, even more than I felt at the time, that if Xiong Huazhi really is the lost daughter of Mao Zedong and He Zizhen, then hers would be one of the most remarkable stories of this or any other year. I have always been intrigued by family sagas, by secrets and the whims of fate. I imagine the scene in 1935: a distraught He Zizhen handing over her newborn baby, never to see her again. I have stood in the village where that happened. I may have shared a cup of tea and sticky rice cakes with that child, grown old without ever knowing her own history. The possibility captivates and moves me.

Xiong Huazhi's time is short and she may never know the truth. Andy and I sent her some photographs after we finished the Long March, and her son-in-law, Xiong Minghu, wrote back to say she had recently been visited by a former bodyguard to He Long, commander of the Second Front Army. This man told her Li Min, Mao and He's only known surviving child, was aware of Xiong's story, as were the central government authorities. Recently, Andy and I met Li Min's son, Kong Jining, who is preparing a documentary on He Zizhen's life. He is also aware of Xiong Huazhi. I hope his own research will convince him that there is a serious possibility that Xiong is his aunt, and that this knowledge will persuade Li Min to consent to a DNA test. I hope this will happen – sooner rather than later. As Xiong said to Andy and me, it's a simple thing.

The publication in 2005 of Jung Chang and Jon Halliday's biographical attack on Chairman Mao, *Mao: The Unknown Story*, has made it fashionable to denigrate the Long March. Reviewers have parroted Chang and Halliday's charge that the Long March is part-fiction and Maoist propaganda. The march wasn't even that hard, readers learn. Mao and other leaders 'lounged in litters like landlords', while Chiang Kai-shek not only deliberately let them go, but even helped them along the way. 'The Long March,' Roy Hattersley wrote in the *Observer*, 'is a fraud.'

What rubbish. The Long March is nothing of the kind.

The Long March is not a fraud to Yang Jin, who broke down in tears as he described his final battle, when he charged across the dead bodies of his fallen comrades. It is not a fraud to Zhang Chaoman, who was strung up and tortured for helping the Reds cross the River of Golden Sands. It is not a fraud to my friend Alec Shen's grandfather, who marched as a teenage Red soldier. He was so tired that he fell asleep over his rifle during one skirmish. He was awoken in the morning by the bugle call and nudged the comrade lying to his left: 'Come on, wake up, we have to go.' His comrade was dead.

On 19 November 1995, senior veterans gathered at the Great Hall of the People in Beijing for a 60th anniversary commemoration of the Long March. After several speeches in praise of Chairman Mao, General Xiao Ke, former commander of the 6th Army Group, suddenly stood up and spoke impromptu: 'The real Long March [was achieved through] the efforts of every single Red Army soldier. We should not, as we did in the past, make a cult of personality'.[1]

It has always been obvious that Mao and his followers twisted the tale of the Long March for their own ends. Mao's role was mythologized to the point where, as Xiao Ke implied, it seemed he had single-handedly saved the Red Army and defeated Chiang Kai-shek. This is nonsense, but it's equally nonsense to throw the baby out with the bathwater. It's absurd to suggest that the Long March is bogus because it was somehow less difficult than it ought to have been. Did the Reds lose around 90 per cent of their forces because Chiang Kai-shek helped them along? Whatever use Mao made of it for personal glory and propaganda, the Long March still stands as one of the most epic and important stories of the twentieth century. Once Mao's role is reduced to its proper proportions, it's easy to see why many young Chinese people still find it an inspiring tale.

Two days before Wuqi, Andy and I were interviewed on the road by a Reuters TV crew. The producer, Elke Rohmer, asked me, 'Would you do it all again?'

'No, definitely not,' I said.

'Why?'

'Because when we set out, I didn't know what the road ahead would be like. I could afford to be optimistic. Now I know exactly what it's like and how difficult it is. I couldn't make myself go through that, knowing what was ahead. It's too tough.'

I believed that when I said it. But now, after more than a year back in the big city, I'm not so sure. All the old complexities and uncertainties of 'normal' life are back. I miss the simplicity of life on the road. Our concerns were so basic – food, shelter and movement – and there was (almost) always a reassuring sense of forward motion. But most of all, I miss the comradeship. It sounds outdated and maybe 'communistic', but I can't think of another word to describe the quality of relationships on the Long March.

For Andy and me, it wasn't just a matter of friendship; it was about support, encouragement and loyalty. We were also helped by hundreds of people, friends and strangers alike. In my imagination, they all became comrades of the road, whether they let us share their homes for an evening or just wrote us an email. I felt we had all become part of a common endeavour.

Perhaps that was as close as I came to feeling what Red Army soldiers felt on the Long March. It's a feeling that washes away the irritations, hardships and fears of the journey. It's magical and I miss it. If Elke asked me again now, would I do it all again, I might give a different answer. I might say: if it meant recapturing that feeling, then yes. Yes, I would.

Endnotes

Introduction

1 Philip Short, *Mao: A Life*, Hodder & Stoughton, London, 1999, p 222.
2 For scurrilous detail on Mao's sex life, see in particular Zhisui Li, *The Private Life of Chairman Mao*, Arrow Books, London, 1996.

Chapter 1: First Steps

1 Hong Kong Trade Development Council; *China Daily*, 16 November 2004.
2 R.A. Bosshardt, *The Restraining Hand: Captivity for Christ in China*, Hodder and Stoughton, London, 1936, p 64.
3 The *Xinhua News Agency* reported a figure of 358 million for end-May 2005 (report filed 21 June 2005).
4 罗开富，《红军长征追踪》（上册），经济日报出版社，2001, p 25.

Chapter 2: A Minority of Two

1 Jonathan Fenby, *Generalissimo Chiang Kai-shek and the China He Lost*, The Free Press, London, 2003, p 68.
2 *Ibid* p 62.
3 *Ibid* p 148.
4 Short, *op cit* pp 187–8.
5 *Ibid* p 203.
6 Harrison Salisbury, *The Long March, The Untold Story*, Harper & Row, 1985, pp 62–3.

7 *Ibid*, p 205.
8 罗开富, *op cit* p 32.
9 Louisa Schein, *Minority Rules: The Miao and the Feminine in China's Cultural Politics*, Duke UP, Durham & London, 2000, p 72.
10 *Ibid* p 68.
11 《中国民族概论》, 宋蜀华陈克进著, 中央民族大学出版社, Beijing, 2001, pp 260–3.
12 Schein, *op cit* p 110.
13 *Ibid* p 84.

Chapter 3: The Xiang River

1 Harold Isaacs, 'The Peasants' War in China', *New International*, Vol.2 No.1, January 1935, pp 25–7.
2 Salisbury, *op cit* p 101.
3 李镜, 《新写长征图文档案》, 2002, p 133.
4 *Ibid*.
5 《北京青年报》2004年10月13日第B1版.
6 Liu Bocheng, *Recalling the Long March*, Foreign Languages Press, 1978, p 7.
7 《长征大事典》, 贵州人民出版社, 1996, pp 1917–9.

Chapter 4: The Tongdao Incident

1 Liu Bocheng, *op cit* p 7.
2 Otto Braun, *A Comintern Agent in China 1932–39*, University of Queensland Press, St Lucia, 1982, p 91.
3 Agnes Smedley, *The Great Road*, Monthly Review Press, New York, 1956, p 315.
4 Salisbury, *op cit* p 302.

Chapter 5: Zunyi

1 Braun, *op cit* pp 94–5.
2 *Ibid* p 71.
3 I'm particularly indebted to Dr Frederick Litten for his comments about the Zunyi Meeting in 'The Myth of the Turning Point: Towards a New Understanding of the Long March', in *Bochuner Jahrbuch zur Ostasienforschung*, Band 25, 2001, S.3–44.

4 Salisbury, *op cit* p 122; Braun, *op cit* p 98.
5 Braun, *op cit* pp 101–2.
6 Salisbury, *op cit* p 122.
7 Braun, *op cit* p 104.
8 *Ibid.*
9 Salisbury, *op cit* p 123.
10 Frederick S. Litten, 'Otto Braun's Curriculum Vitae – Translation and Commentary' in *Twentieth-Century China*, Vol.23, nr.1, 1997 pp 31–61.
11 As cited in an unpublished reference work compiled by the Wuqi County Government.
12 Although Zhou did say this, I discovered later that he borrowed the quip from the English historian A.J.P. Taylor.
13 I take a picture that is later censored from a photo album about our Long March published in Beijing by China Intercontinental Press.
14 Salisbury, *op cit* p 129.
15 Salisbury, *op cit* p 148–9.
16 William Lindesay, *Marching with Mao*, Hodder and Stoughton, 1993, p 109.
17 《我的长征—寻访健在老红军》（下册）, 解放军文艺出版社, Beijing, 2004 p 497.
18 《北京青年报》2004年10月13日第B1版.
19 《我的长征—寻访健在老红军》（下册）, 解放军文艺出版社, Beijing, 2004, p 674.

Chapter 6: The Lost Daughter of Chairman Mao

1 Braun, *op cit* p 115.
2 Richard Evans, *Deng Xiaoping and the Making of Modern China*, Hamish Hamilton, London, 1993, p 146.
3 See in particular Jasper Becker, *Hungry Ghosts: Mao's Secret Famine* (The Free Press, New York, 1997). At least 20 million people died in the famine of 1959–61. This figure was given by Party Secretary Hu Yaobang in 1980, based on contemporary documents compiled for the Party leadership (Short, *op cit* p 505). Jung Chang and Jon Halliday recently estimated 'close to 38 million' based on Chinese demographic statistics (Jung Chang and Jon Halliday, *Mao: The Unknown Story*, Jonathan Cape, London, 2005, pp 456–7), but this is a sensationalist piece of arithmetic. 'Close to 38 million' is the population shortfall in 1961

based on a projection from the 1958–9 population increase (or in 1960 based on the 1957–8 increase, by Chang and Halliday's calculation). Citing that as the death toll takes no account of the sharp drop in the birth rate during the famine. See *China Statistical Yearbook 1984*, also 《曲折发展的岁月》, 河南人民出版社, 1996, p 272, which estimates 'approximately 40 million' missing people owing to death and lowered birth rates.

4 Jürgen Domes, *Peng Te-huai: The Man and the Image*, Stanford University Press, 1985, pp 120–6.

5 Helen Praeger Young, *Choosing Revolution: Chinese Women Soldiers on the Long March*, University of Illinois Press, Urbana and Chicago, 2001, p 202.

6 *Ibid* pp 202–3.

7 Salisbury, *op cit* p 151. Many Chinese histories cite Baisha as the birthplace of Mao and He's child.

8 Braun, *op cit* p 110.

9 All units barring one, which was to stay behind and oversee the formation of partisan brigades and the establishment of the border-region base area.

10 扎西会议史科选编, 威信文化体育局, 2002, pp 12–5.

11 Salisbury, *op cit* p 156.

12 Braun, *op cit* p 111.

13 Short, *op cit* p 631.

14 *Ibid* p 628.

Chapter 7: The Four Crossings of the Chishui

1 《中国工农红军第一方面军长征史事日志》, 贵州人民出版社., Guiyang, 1999, p 123.

2 *Ibid* pp 142–3.

3 Salisbury, *op cit* p 161.

Chapter 8: Dark Country

1 Interview with Wang Daojin, Zunyi, 13 January 2003.

2 World Report on Road Traffic Injury Prevention, World Health Organization, 2004.

Chapter 9: SARS

1 Braun, *op cit* p 113.
2 *Ibid* p 114.

Chapter 10: End of the Road, Part 1

1 Salisbury, *op cit* pp 176–8.
2 S.B. Sutton, *In China's Border Provinces: The Turbulent Career of Joseph Rock, Botanist-Explorer*, New York, 1974 pp 246–8. Cited in Salisbury, *op cit* p 376.
3 Salisbury, *op cit* p 187.
4 Details from Jiaopingdu Long March Memorial Hall.
5 Lindesay, *op cit* pp 98–9.

Chapter 11: Blood Brothers

1 See Stevan Harrell (ed.), *Perspectives on the Yi of Southwest China*, University of California Press, Berkeley & Los Angeles, 2001.
2 Evans, *op cit* p 182.
3 J.A.G. Roberts, *The Complete History of China*, Sutton Publishing, Stroud, 2003, p 445.
4 Short, *op cit* p 540.
5 Roberts, *op cit* p 450.
6 Chang and Halliday, *op cit* p 535.
7 Short, *op cit* p 544.
8 As testified by Li Chunting, whose father Li Tingzan saw the naked squad return to headquarters. Interviewed in Beijing, 17 July 2005.
9 Xiao Hua, 'Crossing the Greater Liangshan Mountains', in *Recalling the Long March*, Foreign Languages Press, Beijing, 1978, pp 72–7.
10 Information from Anshunchang memorial, also Jonathan Spence, *God's Chinese Son*, Flamingo, London, 1996.
11 See, for example, Yang Chengwu, 'Lightning Attack on the Luting Bridge', in *The Long March: Eyewitness Accounts*, Foreign Languages Press, Beijing, 1963, pp 96–109.

Chapter 12: Luding Bridge

1 Smedley, *op cit* p 321.
2 Lindesay, *op cit* p 113.
3 Accounts differ as to whether the bridge was entirely bare, or whether half the bridge on the enemy side was still intact. I'm inclined towards the latter version, as it conforms to the Guomindang's own contemporary report and makes the Reds' success easier to comprehend.
4 Yang Chengwu, *op cit* pp 106–7.
5 Chen Changfeng, *On the Long March With Chairman Mao*, Foreign Languages Press, Beijing, 1986, p 48.
6 Chang and Halliday, *op cit* pp 159–60.
7 *Ibid* p 158.
8 Braun, *op cit* p 38.
9 《长征大事典》, 贵州人民出版社, 1996, p 2161. I have not been able to consult the original document, so I keep an open mind about its reliability.
10 Joseph Stilwell, 'The Present Trend of the Chinese Communist Party and the Formation of the Red Armies', 29 January, 1936. US Military Intelligence Reports: China, 1911–1941, UPA: Frederick/MD, ca. 1983, from the National Archives: Record Group 165, Military Intelligence Division Files: China, Reel XII, frames 241–52 (p 5, frame 245). My thanks to Frederick Litten for providing this information.
11 Joseph Stilwell, *The Stilwell Papers*, Foreign Languages Press, Beijing, 2003, p 106.

Chapter 13: The Snow Mountains

1 Chen Changfeng, *op cit* pp 52–5.
2 Salisbury, *op cit* pp 236–7.
3 Zhang Guotao, *op cit* pp 366, 372.
4 We interviewed Yang Jin in Chengdu in September 2003.
5 Zhang Guotao, *op cit* pp 378.
6 *Ibid* p 400.
7 Salisbury, *op cit* p 254.
8 Edgar Snow, *Red Star Over China*, Grove Press, New York, 1968, p 203.

Chapter 14: The Swamps

1 《我的长征—寻访健在老红军》（下册），解放军文艺出版社，Beijing, 2004, p 414.
2 This was First Army Group Political Commissar Nie Rongzhen's suspicion. Salisbury, *op cit* p 260. It also seems like plain common sense.
3 Salisbury, *op cit* p 271.
4 《我的长征—寻访健在老红军》（上册），解放军文艺出版社，Beijing, 2004, p 280.
5 *Ibid* p 39.
6 *Ibid* p 39.

Chapter 15: Wuqi

1 Hu Pingyun, 'How We Captured the Pass at Latsekou', in *The Long March: Eyewitness Accounts*, Foreign Languages Press, Beijing, 1963, pp 117–23.
2 Lieutenant-General Chang Jen-chu, 'Red Flag Over Latsekou', in *Stories of the Long March*, Foreign Languages Press, Beijing, 1960, pp 132–3.
3 Salisbury, *op cit* p 121.
4 Braun, *op cit* p 143.
5 Zhang Guotao, *op cit* p 445.
6 Salisbury, *op cit* pp 290–1.
7 Chang and Halliday, *op cit* pp 179–80.
8 Details of Mao's speech are from an internal publication of the Wuqi County Government.
9 Fenby, *op cit* p 3.
10 *Ibid* p 366.
11 Braun, *op cit* p 87.
12 Short, *op cit* p 366.
13 *Ibid* p 379.

Plate Section

Huang Zhen, *Sketches on the Long March*, Foreign Languages Press, Beijing, 1982.

Epilogue

1 As recorded at the time by another participant in the meeting. Personal interview, Beijing, May 2005.

Index

Mr China by Tim Clissold

The incredible story of a Wall Street banker who went to China with four hundred million dollars and learned the hard way that China doesn't play by Western rules

In the early nineties, China finally opened for business and Wall Street wanted to get in on the act. When the investment bankers arrived from New York with their Harvard MBAs, pinstripes and tasselled loafers, ready to negotiate with the Old Cadres, the stage was set for collision between Wall Street's billions and the world's oldest culture. *Mr China* is an extraordinary, amusing and eye-opening account of the arcane world of traditional Chinese business.

'Shocking, funny and culturally sympathetic tale of the perils of doing business in Asia's wild west.' The *Economist*, Books of the Year

Chasing Che by Patrick Symmes

A freewheeling adventure through the wide open spaces of South America on the trail of Che Guevara

In 1952, 23-year-old Ernesto Guevara and a friend left their native Argentina to motorcycle the back roads of South America. Eight months later, the freewheeling youth had evolved into the man known as Che. His account of the trip, *The Motorcycle Diaries*, would become a classic and a Hollywood film. Nearly half a century later, Patrick Symmes sets off on his BMW R80 G/S to find the people and places encountered by Che. Masterfully detailed and as insightful as it is entertaining, *Chasing Che* transfixes us with the glory of the open road, where man and machine traverse the unknown in search of the spirit's keenest desires.

'An exhilarating blend of travel, reportage and history.' *Outside*

Children of Kali by Kevin Rushby

Through India in search of bandits, the thug cult and the British Raj

They murdered more than a million Indian travellers without spilling a drop of blood. They were inspired by religious fanaticism, yet came from many faiths. Their weapon was the handkerchief, their sacrament sugar and their goddess Kali. They were the thugs, the greatest criminal gang in history and one supposedly exterminated by the British in the 1830s. Part history and part personal record, *Children of Kali* reveals how British India demonized millions as hereditary criminals, setting off a witch-hunt whose effects are still felt today. It is a book about the misunderstandings of what is alien and exotic, and few things have been more misunderstood than the nature of Kali herself.

'Rushby is at his best evoking the sheer joy of travel.' *Literary Review*

A Brief History of the Dynasties of China by Bamber Gascoigne

A vibrant portrait of Imperial China

The names of the great Chinese dynasties are familiar to us, yet who can actually place a Tang horse or a Ming vase in its social or cultural context? Although China's great empire lasted for longer than any other, no country has suffered such an imbalance between the fame of its art and the obscurity of its history. By focusing on the key characters of the eight major dynasties, Bamber Gascoigne brings to life 3,500 years of Chinese civilization. His expert account opens the door to a world that was for so long inaccessible to the West.

'A highly readable and evocative account of Chinese history.' *New Statesman*

A *Brief History of the Boxer Rebellion* by Diana Preston

The dramatic story of China's war on foreigners, 1900

Fuelled by hatred of foreigners and all they stood for, the ferocious uprising of Chinese peasants and ensuing siege of Peking in the summer of 1900 sent shockwaves around the world. Diana Preston brings thundering to life this 55-day confrontation between the 'Boxers', so-called for their martial-arts skills, and the Westerners – such as the young Herbert Hoover – they terrorized.

'Fascinating . . . penned with an obvious addiction to the delicious little details of history: whimsical, outrageous and macabre.' *Washington Post*

Order form overleaf

No. of copies	Title	Price	Total
	Mr China Tom Clissold	£8.99	
	Chasing Che Patrick Symmes	£7.99	
	Children of Kali Kevin Rushby	£7.99	
	A Brief History of the Dynasties of China Bamber Gascoigne	£7.99	
	A Brief History of the Boxer Rebellion Diana Preston	£7.99	
	Grand Total		£

Name: _____

Address: _____

_____ Postcode: _____

Daytime Tel. No. / Email: _____
(in case of query)

Three ways to pay:
1. **For express service telephone the TBS order line on 01206 255 800 and quote 'LM1'. Order lines are open Monday – Friday 8:30a.m. – 5:30p.m.**
2. I enclose a cheque made payable to **TBS** Ltd for £ _____
3. Please charge my ☐ Visa ☐ Mastercard ☐ Amex ☐ Switch (switch issue no. ___) £ _____

Card number: _____

Expiry date: _____ Signature: _____

(your signature is essential when paying by credit card)

Please return forms (*no stamp required*) to, Constable & Robinson Ltd, FREEPOST NAT6619, 3 The Lanchesters, 162 Fulham Palace Road, London W6 9BR. All books subject to availability.

Enquiries to readers@constablerobinson.com.
www.constablerobinson.com

Constable & Robinson (directly or via its agents) may mail or phone you about promotions or products. Tick box if you do not want these from us ☐ or our subsidiaries ☐.